Social Origins of Distress and Disease

Social Origins of Distress and Disease

DEPRESSION, NEURASTHENIA,
AND PAIN IN MODERN CHINA

Arthur Kleinman, M.D.

Yale University Press
New Haven and London

Designed by Nancy Ovedovitz and set in Times Roman type.
Printed in the United States of America by BookCrafters, Inc.,
Chelsea, Michigan.

Library of Congress Cataloging-in-Publication Data

Kleinman, Arthur.
Social origins of distress and disease.
Bibliography: p.
Includes index.
1. Somatoform disorders—China. 2. Depression, Mental—
Somatization—China. 3. Neurasthenia—Somatization—China.
4. Social medicine—China. 5. Pain—Psychological aspects.
I. Title.
[DNLM: 1. Depression—psychology. 2. Neurasthenia—
psychology. 3. Pain—psychology. 4. Sociology, Medical—
China. WM 171 K64s]
RC552.H8K54 1986   616   85-29597
ISBN 0-300-03541-1 (alk. paper)

The paper in this book meets the guidelines for permanence and
durability of the Committee on Production Guidelines for Book
Longevity of the Council on Library Resources.

10   9   8   7   6   5   4   3   2   1

To the patients in the Psychiatry and Internal Medicine Clinics at the Second Affiliated Hospital, Hunan Medical College, who participated in the studies reported in these chapters.

They cannot represent themselves; they must be represented.

Karl Marx, *The Eighteenth Brumaire of Louis Bonaparte*

. . . we see the lives of others through lenses of our own grinding and . . . they look back on ours through ones of their own.

Clifford Geertz, "Anti Anti-Relativism"

Medicine is a social science, and politics nothing but medicine on a grand scale.

Rudolph Virchow

Contents

Preface

The origins of this book go back to 1969, when I initiated a series of anthropological and psychiatric field-research studies of illness and care in
Chinese society. Over the next decade I spent a total of three years on Taiwan
working on this project, and also accumulated experience in clinical research
and practice with Chinese-Americans. I was thus prepared, on my first visit
to the People's Republic of China in 1978, to transfer these research interests
to the mainland. By 1980 I was already conducting research at the Hunan
Medical College (the former Yale-in-China Medical School), which has long
been one of China's leading schools of medicine, especially in psychiatry.
At the time this book was written, I had completed three clinical studies at
the Hunan Medical College—the first to be conducted by an American or
Western psychiatrist in China since the establishment of the communist state
in 1949.

Social Origins of Distress and Disease reports on what I have observed
and learned. It opens a rather unusual and revealing window on the lived
experience of individual Chinese that adds, in a small though perhaps special
way, to our growing understanding of Chinese society. But this book is also
about another subject: affect and affective disorder. I have studied depression
and neurasthenia in China as much to come to a better general understanding
of how culture relates to emotions, mental illness, and human distress generally as to learn in particular about the experience of illness among Chinese.
I wanted also to understand how distress and suffering are made meaningful—
interpreted—by laymen and health professionals in China, and how those
interpretations compare and contrast with Western, especially American,
meanings. Finally, I wished to better understand the social origins of distress
in order to learn how these structural sources and their demoralizing consequences can be more effectively remedied.

A number of questions are packed into this slim volume. To arrive at a
more discriminating understanding of the illness experience of patients in
China, and thereby to penetrate to a level of personal and social life that is

ix

often hidden from observers of Chinese culture, it is necessary to begin with an overview of three closely interrelated subjects: neurasthenia (one of the most common medical and lay diagnoses in China), depression (one of the most prevalent diagnoses of mental illness worldwide but not widely diagnosed in China), and somatization (the expression of personal and social distress in a language of bodily complaints and through a pathway of medical help-seeking). The first three chapters introduce each of these subjects and discuss their historical background and current significance in China, in North America, and cross-culturally; chapters 4 and 5 report the findings from studies of these illness experiences among patients at the Hunan Medical College. Chapter 6 is a casebook from the Hunan research files; it presents the stories of thirteen patients, grouped to illustrate somatization as illness experience and its social sources. Special emphasis is given to the description of psychological casualties of the Cultural Revolution. Chapter 7 offers an interpretation, based on these and related findings, of how clinical problems in China are organized and expressed through personal experience and social life—what illness means—and assesses the role of culture in the experience and understanding of emotion.

This research endeavor would not have been feasible without the help of many individuals and institutions. I wish to acknowledge the financial support I received for my research in China from the Committee on Scholarly Communication with the People's Republic of China of the National Academy of Sciences, the Social Science Research Council, the Rockefeller Foundation, and the Milton Fund, Harvard University. In China, my research greatly benefited from the help of colleagues at the Hunan Medical College, to whom I am extremely grateful: Wang Peng-chen, former President; Ling Ming-yu, former Dean and founding Director, Department of Psychiatry; Young Derson, Vice President and Professor of Psychiatry; Shen Qijie, Professor and Director, Center for Research in Psychiatry; and Drs. Zheng Yanping and Huang Nangda, members of that department. I also wish to thank Drs. Miao Jinsheng and Dai Tze-shu, formerly postgraduate Fellows at the Hunan Medical College, now at the Zhejiang Provincial Psychiatric Hospital and the Hangzhou Psychiatric Hospital, respectively, as well as Drs. Shi Zuorong and Chen Xuechin, Department of Medicine, Second Affiliated Hospital, Hunan Medical College.
None of these individuals is in my way responsible for the ideas in this book, several of which are sharply divergent from those of my Chinese colleagues. I am grateful to two Harvard Medical students, Jennifer Haas for

helping to collect the data on primary care patients, and Jim Kim for his assistance with the data analysis. I also wish to thank my colleagues at Harvard and the University of Washington, Professors Chang Kwang-Chih, Tu Wei-Ming, Byron Good, Mary Jo Good, Paul Cleary, Alan Brandt, Nur Yalman, Stanley Tambiah, Sally Falk Moore, David Maybury-Lewis, Jack Carr, Noel Chrisman, Charles Keyes, and Wayne Katon, for their responses to earlier reports of this project. Professors David Mechanic, Issy Pilowsky, and Lin Tsung-Yi offered advice and encouragement at critical points in the book's gestation. Special thanks go to Professors Leon Eisenberg and Ezra Vogel, who read the original manuscript and raised critical questions that led to its revision. Inveterate and unamended faults are my own.

I cannot hope to give adequate acknowledgment for all the help I have received from my wife, colleague, and comrade-in-arms, Joan Kleinman. Sinologist, field-research assistant, editor, and critic, she deserves to be co-author but is unwilling to be so named, since, she demures, "it is not my field."

I wish to thank the D. Reidel Publishing Company and the University of California Press, respectively, for their permission to reprint materials that first appeared in an article in volume 6, issue 2 (1982) of the journal *Culture, Medicine and Psychiatry* (portions of which appear in chapters 1, 4, 6, and 7) and in the introduction and penultimate chapter in the book *Culture and Depression* (portions of which now appear in chapters 2, 3, 5, and 7). Materials contained in chapters 4–7 were the subject of the Hume Lecture, Yale University; a talk on the ninety-fifth anniversary of the birth of Norman Bethune at Bethune College, York University; and lectures and seminars given at the Department of Psychiatry at the New York Hospital, McLean Hospital, the Cambridge Hospital, the University of Washington Medical School, the Department of Social Medicine at Harvard Medical School, the Peabody Museum and the Fairbank Center for East Asian Studies at Harvard University, Michigan State University, the University of Houston, Rice University, Duke University, the Department of Anthropology at the University of North Carolina at Chapel Hill, Rutgers University, the University of British Columbia, the University of Adelaide in South Australia (the Flory Lecture), the WHO Workshop on Psychosocial Aspects of Primary Care at the Shanghai Psychiatric Institute, and the Canadian Association for Medical Anthropology. I am grateful to the faculty and students who listened to these presentations and raised the hard questions that led me to rethink many of the ideas developed in this book.

Carol Casella-Jaillet patiently transferred hundreds of sheets of handwritten scrawl to the word processor and graciously put up with multiple revisions at which even the machine balked. At the Yale University Press, Ellen Graham graciously and sagely shepherded the volume through the editorial and production phases; Michael Joyce's red pen made the prose sparer, the argument sharper.

Finally, I wish to thank my Chinese patients, to whom this volume is dedicated, for teaching me so very much about the complex and contradictory realities in China, in psychiatry, and not least of all, in my own thinking.

A.K.

Prologue

Reductionist explanation attempts to derive the properties of wholes from intrinsic properties of parts, properties that exist apart from and before the parts are assembled into complex structures. It is characteristic of reductionism that it assigns relative weights to different partial causes and attempts to assess the importance of each cause by holding all others constant while varying a single factor. Dialectical explanations, on the contrary, do not abstract properties of parts in isolation from their associations in wholes but see the properties of parts as arising out of their associations. That is, according to the dialectical view, the properties of parts and wholes codetermine each other. The properties of human beings do not exist in isolation but arise as a consequence of social life, yet the nature of that social life is a consequence of our being human. . . . It follows, then, that dialectical explanation contrasts with cultural or dualistic modes of explanation that separate the world into different types of phenomena—culture and biology, mind and body—which are to be explained in quite different and nonoverlapping ways.

Lewontin, Rose, and Kamen (1984:11)

PROBLEM FRAMEWORK

In the following chapters depression is viewed as a disease characterized by psychobiological dysfunctions which appear to be universal, but which is best regarded as a relationship between a person and society. Depressive illness not only reveals the relationship a person establishes with society; it also illumines the influence of society on individuals. This social influence extends to the person's cognitions, emotions, even physiology. Analyzing the relationship of depression (or any disorder) to society offers a glimpse of a sociosomatic reticulum (a symbolic bridge) that ties individuals to each other and to the local systems within which they live. Depression is thus a

1

social affect and disorder: the origins of depression are meanings and relations in the social world, and these in turn are its consequences. The social world is affective; it is embodied in the individual and his or her disorders.[1]

A dialectical relationship exists between symptoms and society. The relationship is strongly influenced by macrosocial forces—economic, political, and institutional arrangements—but the sociosomatic connection is mediated by the meanings and legitimacies that symptoms hold for particular people in particular local systems of power. Symptoms in the lives of patients whom I studied in China are interpreted through the meanings and legitimacies that depression, pain, weakness, and other key complaints hold for them, their families, their relationships in the work unit, and their medical system. Since the individuals I studied interpreted their symptoms as neurasthenia, the relationship between neurasthenia and depression is examined and compared in China and the West. This examination illustrates how culture shapes the strategic interpretation and negotiated experience of *illness*.[2] Understanding of how social factors produce the connection between neurasthenia-depression and pain as the cause of *disease*[3] parallels the interpretation of its cultural meaning. This interpretation provides a particular instance of a general cultural process by which cultures project their socially constructed categories onto nature and thereafter regard them as natural in order to validate their social norms as "natural" (Taussig 1980a:3–4). The neurasthenia-depression-pain connection takes us into a central though poorly understood sector of Chinese psychiatry and society, and does the same for Western psychiatry and culture.

This connection, which expresses the dialectic between symptom and society, agency and structure, is referred to hereafter as *somatization*. For the purposes of simplifying and unifying a complex, contested term, somatization is defined as the normative expression of personal and social distress in an idiom of bodily complaints and medical help-seeking. To make sense of somatization requires interdisciplinary collaboration between anthropology and psychiatry. If the cross-cultural psychiatric investigation of depression, neurasthenia, and pain is to determine their social sources and cultural variation, it must draw on the theory and methodology of anthropology to interpret somatization. And if anthropological analyses are to account for the psychobiological processes central to the dialectic between social world and physiology embodied in somatization, anthropology must also begin with an interactive (culture ↔ nature) framework. This volume, like other of my writings, seeks to build such an anthropological psychiatry and psychiatric anthropology.

DEVELOPMENT OF A RESEARCH PROGRAM

This interdisciplinary approach to the study of culture and illness in Chinese society has been worked out over the past fifteen years. The studies described in the following chapters were conducted at the Hunan Medical College, where in 1980 I spent five months in the department of psychiatry interviewing one hundred individuals diagnosed as cases of neurasthenia who were then outpatients in the department. Why neurasthenia and why China?

Neurasthenia is a diagnosis invented in North America and widely used earlier in this century throughout the West; it is no longer officially sanctioned in the United States and has fallen into disfavor in Western Europe. Nevertheless, it remains the most common psychiatric outpatient diagnosis for neurotic disorders in China. In contrast, depressive disorder is the most frequent psychiatric outpatient diagnosis in the West and is becoming one of the commonest primary care diagnoses in the United States; at the time of our study, it was rarely diagnosed in China. Were our Chinese psychiatric colleagues calling neurasthenia what American and Western European psychiatrists called depression? The earlier research I had conducted in Taiwan (Kleinman 1980), as well as interviews in a number of outpatient clinics throughout China in 1978 (Kleinman and Mechanic 1979; Mechanic and Kleinman 1979), indicated that this might be happening. Were the prevalence (at least the treated prevalence, because we were not allowed to conduct community-based epidemiological research in China), symptomatology, and course of depression in China and the United States significantly different? Were the sources of vulnerability and the precipitating factors the same? And did depression have the same consequences for the sick person and the family in the two societies? If so, what could such findings inform us about the universal and culture-particular aspects of depression? These were some of the questions that guided the original research (Kleinman 1982).

Another question beckoned. What might be seen in each society by opening a window on neurasthenia and depression in China and North America? I was interested in peering through this window at everyday life in China and observing its problems and the indigenous ways they are interpreted and dealt with.

Divergent historical patterns in the development of medical categories of depression in China and the West were an intriguing cultural background to our research. Depression (glossed as melancholia) was recognized in ancient Greece and has held a culturally significant place in the West ever since. In contrast, when we began our study, a noted Chinese psychiatrist concluded

that classical Chinese medicine did not develop a detailed clinical categorization of a syndrome with a family resemblance to depression until fairly
late in its historical transformation: namely, in the Ming Dynasty (Tseng
1974). In modern times, furthermore, indigenous Chinese categories of what
Westerners call depressive disorder have not been widely used. Chinese
psychiatrists, who employ a largely biological approach to mental disorder,
did not regularly use the term when we began our research. It is used even
more rarely by Chinese patients and families. The current practice of traditional Chinese medicine emphasizes materialist somatopsychic models
much more than the earlier psychosomatic ones that characterized the indigenous Chinese medical tradition over the millennia. Hence the social and
psychological aspects of disease (including depression) are not assigned much
importance in China's health care system.

The chief results of our 1980 study are reviewed in chapter 4. In 1983 I
returned to the Hunan Medical College to initiate two additional studies,
which were conducted between April and August. In the first, my wife and
I followed up a subsample of our 1980 subjects who had been diagnosed as
suffering from both major depressive disorder and chronic pain syndrome.
In this three-year follow-up, we examined how course of illness and treatment
outcome related to social problems in the workplace, family, and community.
In 1980 we identified these problems as major sources of patient distress.
The second study, conducted by a Chinese-speaking Harvard medical student
working under our supervision and together with our Chinese colleagues,
looked at the same questions among chronic pain patients attending a primary
care clinic at the Hunan Medical College. These studies provided prevalence
rates of depression in psychiatric and primary care settings. The studies also
evaluated the ties between depression, pain, and problems in patients' life
circumstances and the broader social system. Chapter 5 presents the findings
from each of these studies. In chapter 6, I also describe selected cases, from
which the statistical findings are derived, whose vivid stories of their illness
experiences illustrate the major themes developed in the book. Chapter 7
discusses the significance of the findings for the theoretical questions we
have raised.

Our colleagues in China have debated our findings and especially our
interpretations, have initiated their own projects, and in so doing have begun
to rethink the place of neurasthenia and depression in their own society (see
Xu 1984, n.d.). Our anthropological handling of the concept of somatization
has attracted much interest and criticism. I was invited by the editors of
China's *Referential Journal of Psychiatry* to contribute a review article

(Kleinman 1984), which has stimulated a further series of exchanges (Xu 1984; Zhong 1985). The questions of social causality and consequences of depression and somatization I have raised have not been the reason for the critical attention my work has received. Psychiatrists in China are openly perplexed about how to resolve the neurasthenia-depression controversy and have found it more prudent to follow clinical and biological research paths instead of social ones which are particularly sensitive in the People's Republic and are only now being authorized. China's psychiatrists are cautiously initiating studies of stress and social support (Zheng and Young 1983; Xu 1983) that should indicate how generalizable the data from our small samples at a single institution are and, in so doing, provide more reliable information about the place of depression and somatization in Chinese society. Our contribution in no way comprises a final answer to this controversy; what we have done is to intensify interest in the competing hypotheses and to insist they be tested in a broader social frame.

Comparing our China studies with studies on depression and somatization conducted in North America and the United Kingdom (Brown and Harris 1978; or those reviewed in Katon et al. 1982, 1984), including our current clinical research on patients with chronic pain syndrome in Boston, many of whom are also suffering depressive disorders, convinces me that the general points from our cross-cultural research are as relevant for the West as they are for China.

Generalizing from patient samples to the world's most populous society is a dangerous undertaking, especially when the focus is pathology, not normality. But generalizing is justified because so little is known about the experience of serious problems in everyday Chinese life. The Chinese let Westerners see so little of the structural tensions their society faces that the study of neurasthenia is particularly revealing. Examination of changes in the living standards and health conditions of the majority of the Chinese people since the Communist victory in 1949 must, on balance, come down on the side of progress, sometimes enormous progress. Greatly improved mortality (infant mortality rate: from 200 to 20–30 per thousand births), morbidity, and life expectancy (35 to 68 years) rates, control of epidemic disease (venereal disease, cholera, tuberculosis, opium addiction, and so forth), elimination of child slavery, destitution, and widespread starvation, better housing, and a functioning rural and urban health care system are impressive accomplishments (see chapters in Kleinman et al. 1975; Wegman et al. 1973). A comparison of the social chaos, economic and political breakdown, deaths from wars, forced migration, and famine in the thirty-five years prior to 1949 with the thirty-five years since 1949 confirms this assessment. In the mental health field, for example, fewer than sixty psychiatrists were practicing in all of China before 1949, and less than 1,000 psychiatric beds were available for a population of 500 million. At present there are 3,000 psychiatrists and more than 60,000 psychiatric beds. Anyone reading Lamson's (1935) account of the horrific social pathology in China in the 1930s must be deeply impressed by the transformation of social life. But the same transformation has created great problems, which also need to be understood.

THE CHINESE SETTING

Background

In 1953, four years after the Communist victory on the mainland and in the anti-American years of the Korean War, the name of the Yale-in-China Medical College, or as it was known in China, Hsiang-Ya, was changed to Hunan Medical College. Since the 1920s the complex of schools organized under the Yale-in-China name had included junior and senior middle schools, whose best graduates went on to train in medicine under the supervision of American and Chinese physicians. By 1949 many of the Chinese faculty had worked their way up from middle school to medical school and had received advanced training, sometimes at Hsiang-Ya or other of China's leading teaching hospitals (Peking Union Medical College, West China Christian Union Medical College) and occasionally in the United States. Most were fluent in English, some were Christians, all had some ties with the United States—characteristics for which they would be persecuted, first during the Anti-Rightist Campaign and later during the Cultural Revolution.

In the 1930s Dr. Ling Ming-yu, a Hunanese graduate of Hsiang-Ya and scion of a scholarly family, went north to the Peking Union Medical College (PUMC) to study neuropsychiatry with Dr. R. C. Lyman, an American professor at PUMC and one of the first trained psychiatrists to teach neuropsychiatry in China. Traditional Chinese medicine recognized no psychiatric specialty, though the major psychoses and hysteria had been diagnosed and treated since the early period of the classical Chinese medicine texts. In 1897 Dr. Kerr, a missionary physician in Canton, overcame major difficulties and established the first psychiatric hospital in China. The first set of formal lectures on psychiatry from a biomedical perspective were delivered in Tung Wah Hospital in Hong Kong in 1905.

Dr. A. H. Woods, a neurologist, became the founding director of the division of neurology and psychiatry at Peking Union Medical College and the first professor of neurology and psychiatry at a Chinese medical school in 1919. He initiated courses in both subjects in 1922, but it is uncertain if he trained even a small number of Chinese in these fields (Wong 1950). In 1932 he was succeeded by Lyman, who arrived in China in 1931 and left in 1937. During his short term Lyman attracted and trained many of the first generation of native leaders of Chinese psychiatry, who in turn trained a large number of China's current senior academic psychiatrists,[4] including Dr. T. H. Suh, who later went to work in Shanghai, and Dr. Y. K. Hsu, who remained at PUMC. Dr. Y. L. Cheng, Lyman's associate, later went to Chengdu to develop psychiatry at the West China Christian Union Medical College (now Sichuan Medical College). Cheng's students included Dr. C. Y. Wu, who practiced in Beijing, Dr. K. T. Tao, who developed Nanjing into a major psychiatric center (before it was crippled by the anti-rightist labels affixed to key staff during the Anti-Rightist Campaign and Cultural Revolution),[5] and Dr. C. Y. Lin, who also went to teach in Chengdu (Ling 1984).

Lyman taught an eclectic psychiatry ranging from neurological to psychoanalytic perspectives. He possessed a strong interest in sociology and social work and encouraged both at PUMC (Lyman 1939). Lyman recognized the important contribution social problems and cultural factors made to mental illness. Following in the biosocial interactionist tradition promulgated by Adolph Meyer, the great psychiatrist at Johns Hopkins who created an American school of psychiatry based on a pragmatic, eclectic model of psychopathology that linked life history to neurobiological and environmental determinants of behavior, Lyman (1941) supported research and teaching on the neurological, personality, and sociocultural influences on mental illness within a broadly integrative psychosomatic framework for diagnosis and therapy. This framework contained many of the components and their relationships that are currently expressed by the biopsychosocial model in medicine (Engel 1977), although the terminology Lyman used was not explicitly systems theory. In the department of psychiatry Lyman ran at PUMC Bingham Dai practiced a psychodynamic approach to personality problems, Francis Hsu worked at medical social work, L. C. Chou and Y. C. Lu conducted a sociological study of mental patients, and other researchers conducted psychometric, neuropsychiatric, and clinical studies, including investigations of major psychotic disorders and drug addiction. Even by world standards of the time this was both a remarkable group of young scholars and a notable program.

Professor Ling Ming-yu returned to Hsiang-Ya from Lyman's tutelage at PUMC in 1934, and quickly developed a clinical unit of neurology and psychiatry. The Anti-Japanese War and the invasion of Hunan by Japanese troops forced the staff of the Hsiang-Ya Medical College, including Dr. Ling, to move first to Guizhou for six and a half years, and then to Chongqing from the winter of 1944 to August 1945. When the school moved back to Changsha, the buildings erected in 1920 had been burned to the ground by the Nationalists' scorched earth policy and by the Japanese. During these years of turmoil, migration, and rebuilding it was difficult to develop a teaching unit, but the neurology and psychiatry unit had survived and was poised for a period of rapid growth, as were China's other leading psychiatric centers in Beijing, Shanghai, Nanjing, and Chengdu.

Another early center for psychiatric work was in Shanghai. There Dr. Fanny Halpern of the University of Vienna had taken up a teaching post in 1933; she later set up a department of neuropsychiatry at St. John's University. In 1935 she helped organize a Committee on Psychiatry of the Chinese Medical Association and initiated a series of lectures on mental hygiene. Professor Xia Zhenyi, who is presently professor of psychiatry at the Shanghai First Medical College, directs academic work at the Shanghai Psychiatric Institute, and is one of the major figures in Chinese psychiatry, is a former student of Dr. Halpern. During this period the Japanese ran several medical schools in Manchuria and taught neuropsychiatry organized along the descriptive biological lines that had originated in Germany and been carried to Japan by expatriate medical academics.

In 1940 Dr. Y. K. Huang, another Hunanese student of Lyman's, moved from PUMC to join Dr. Ling. The clinical neuropsychiatric service they ran had been a part of general medicine, but in 1948 it became an autonomous service with three beds and a limited space for outpatients. After 1949 the department of neuropsychiatry at Hsiang-Ya rapidly expanded to twenty-five beds and contained a much larger outpatient clinic. There were more trainees in this period (including one of China's current psychiatric luminaries, Dr. Young Derson), as well as postgraduate research students from various parts of China. By 1953, when the title of the college was changed to the Hunan Medical College, Professor Ling had become dean. In 1958, when the Hunan Medical College opened up a new teaching hospital (the Second Affiliated Hospital) in the eastern part of Changsha, a psychiatric inpatient unit of sixty beds was established, along with a separate outpatient clinic, laboratories, and doctors' offices. The department formally split into separate departments of psychiatry and neurology in 1964; the former is located at the Second Affiliated Hospital, the latter at the First. The conceptual orientation of the department of psychiatry was eclectic, but the introduction of Russian neuropsychiatry in the 1950s[6] and the Communists' anathematization of psychoanalysis pushed it in an increasingly biological direction.

During the Cultural Revolution Dr. Ling and his psychiatric colleagues in Changsha, like psychiatrists and psychologists throughout China, were officially stigmatized and attacked. Of the six senior members of the department of psychiatry two were put under such great pressure that they committed suicide, one was sent to a rural county hospital in the mountainous border region between Hunan and Sichuan, where he practiced general medicine for a decade but was not allowed to continue study or practice in psychiatry (he is now in the United States), and three (including Dr. Ling) remained in Changsha, where they were severely criticized. Professor Ling was demoted to the ranks of the lowest-level physician, did not practice psychiatry or teach, was subject to intensive self-criticism and struggle sessions, and as the former head of an American-connected school unjustly suffered from the foreign association by being regarded as little better than a spy. A paper Professor Ling had written in the 1950s, which outlined a program to modernize psychiatry as a profession in China, was used as evidence of his alleged falling away from the Maoist ideology. Ironically the paper has since become something of a blueprint for the present-day revitalization of psychiatry at the Hunan Medical College.

During these years, Dr. Young, Professor Ling's former student and successor, received equally harsh treatment from the Red Guards because of his defense of the core psychiatric position that mental illness is an illness, and not wrong political thinking as the Maoists held. The current director of the psychiatry department's Center for Psychiatric Research, Dr. Shen Qijie, tried to keep the clinical services of the department afloat (all teaching and research had ceased) while under constant pressure from the revolutionary committee that had taken over the Second Affiliated Hospital. He was the target of an all-hospital struggle session because a nurse, whom he had correctly diagnosed as suffering from schizophrenia, had become a member of the revolutionary committee and accused him of wronging her for counterrevolutionary reasons. The situation of China's fledgling professions of psychiatry and psychology during these destructive years was similar everywhere.

During the 1960s, the Hunan Medical College was downgraded from one of China's national medical schools to a provincial school, thus reducing its budget and staff and further demoralizing the faculty and students. At the end of the Cultural Revolution the college was restored to its former position; it was also made one of China's five major training centers in psychiatry, responsible for postgraduate training for a group of provinces whose population exceeds 250 million. But because Hunan Province's leading cadres were ultra-leftists until recently, and because the foreign currency available to fund modernization projects in the province's institutions is limited, rehabilitation of the Hunan Medical College has proceeded at a slower pace than at its sister institutions in Beijing and Shanghai.

Present Situation

The Hunan Medical College's department of psychiatry is housed at the Second Affiliated Hospital, which is the work unit *(danwei)* for its members. The department occupies a very old and small outpatient clinic and an equally rudimentary inpatient building to the side of the hospital. Both seem primitive compared to the relatively new and large buildings housing the other departments' clinics and wards. This structural emblem of marginality is completed by a high wall separating the psychiatry department's inpatient unit from the rest of the hospital. At the time of our research the laboratory facilities in the psychiatry department were short of modern equipment, but the leaders of the department were planning an expansion to a new, six-story building that would house a Center for Psychiatric Research, and substantially enlarged and modernized wards, clinics, and teaching facilities. The move is expected to be completed in the summer of 1986.

In 1980 the department consisted of a semiretired and invalided senior professor, Ling Ming-yu, two associate professors, Young Derson and Shen Qijie, who effectively directed the department on a daily basis, and another associate professor, Gong Yaoxian, one of the few medical psychologists in China, who directed a division of psychological testing. In addition there were six senior lecturers and lecturers, including one, Dr. Zuo Chengye, who was virtually the full-time editor of the psychiatric section *(Referential Journal of Psychiatry)* of the journal *Foreign Medicine*. Four postgraduate fellows were finishing M.A.-level theses based on clinical research conducted in the hospital, and another eight or ten visiting physicians from other psychiatric units were obtaining advanced training. No new postgraduate trainees in psychiatry had been accepted for some years, but in 1983 several interns began their postgraduate psychiatry training in the department, and senior medical students again began to rotate through the inpatient psychiatry ward. From 1979 to 1985 at least seven members of the department's faculty visited the United States on study tours of up to one year, and an equal number of American psychiatric researchers worked at the Hunan Medical College.

The Second Affiliated Hospital, though one of the two teaching hospitals of the Hunan Medical College, functions as an autonomous work unit (danwei). In 1980 there were about 750 inpatient beds, but the hospital was in the process of increasing its size to more than 800 beds. Of the 1240 members of the staff, 33 were professors and associate professors, 195 lecturers and visiting physicians, 150 resident physicians, 335 nurses, 133 technicians, 110 administrative cadres, and 316 workers divided into 22 clinical and technical departments. The families of more than half live in the danwei, which in almost all respects is similar to the Second Affiliated Hospital of Hubei Provincial Medical College described by Henderson and Cohen (1984) in their definitive account of the Chinese hospital. Most of the members of the department of psychiatry live in the danwei.

The clinical facilities of the department include a 60-bed inpatient unit and an outpatient clinic that sees between 100 and 150 patients each day, six days each week. The outpatient registration of ten cents means that the clinic is accessible to virtually all who reside near or in the city. As the main referral center for Hunan Province (whose population is more than 55,000,000), many patients come from distant towns and communes in the countryside. Because of its renown in psychiatry, the department even attracts patients from neighboring provinces. Workers, peasants, professionals, and cadres—all of China's social classes—mix freely in the clinic and on the ward.

But the Second Affiliated Hospital does contain a special medical ward for high-ranking urban and provincial cadres; it is much more spacious, better furnished, provides higher-quality food, and has its own medical staff. On this special unit many of the patients are older cadres with neurasthenia. They stay for several months at a time, often together with their families, enjoying a leisurely rehabilitation program of rest, well-prepared meals, mild exercise, and special medical treatment in an attractive garden setting that looks suspiciously like an exclusive resort for China's new elite class. In effect, the unit provides a modern variant of the Victorian rest cure for neurasthenia enjoyed by the rich in nineteenth-century Europe and America. Although in 1983 my wife and I lived on this unit, we were not permitted to include its high-level patients in our studies—one of the few restrictions placed on our research activities in 1980 and 1983.

In 1980 my wife, two children, and I lived in a staff apartment in a faculty housing building on the campus of the Second Affiliated Hospital about one hundred feet from the main hospital building. Three years later my wife and I occupied an inpatient room in the special ward for cadres. Each day we went either to the inpatient or outpatient psychiatric units to conduct interviews with patients. All interviews were conducted in rooms set aside for research to assure privacy and so as not to interfere with busy clinical units. We also spent part of our time observing in various units, and I frequently participated in clinical rounds and consultations. We developed friendships with a number of staff members, and in the fashion of ethnographers spent our free time in informal talks and activities as participant-observers in the lived reality of the hospital work unit. Since 1980 several members of the department of psychiatry have worked with me in the United States, where we have furthered our collaborative ties.

Nineteen-eighty was a very special time to be in China. This was the short-lived period immediately after the Cultural Revolution and the fall of the Gang of Four when ordinary Chinese were encouraged by the Chinese government to speak out about the "bitterness" of their experiences over the preceding decade and a genuine outpouring of written accounts formed a literature of "the wounded" (cf. Barme and Lee 1979; Link 1983; Thurston 1984–85, 1985).

Most of our patients were very open with us, in large part because of the political climate. Once a clinical account began, medical and psychiatric details gave way to an often lengthy, always intense recounting of a life history. We began to realize that however much we thought of these narratives as part of our research project, for many of the patients and their families they carried another significance altogether. We were enlisted as witnesses to hear the words that came tumbling forth, recounting tragedies and crises. For us they took on shape as clinical accounts, but for our patients and our Chinese colleagues they had a life of their own as oral histories of personal and cultural wounds, of a time to be mourned. Once a story got going, like Coleridge's *Rime of the Ancient Mariner* or the tales of survivors of extreme and traumatic life experiences anywhere, we were not expected to ask questions or intevene, but to participate in the account by intensely listening as a life story unfolded toward its shared but nonetheless rending dénouement of pain and loss.

After the narration was completed, we—patient, family members, researchers—would return to the mundane research task of filling out clinical rating sheets and questionnaire forms. But each of us was aware that we had experienced a rare catharsis.[7] In 1983 the accounts of new patients would become briefer and thinner. Yet since we had already learned so much in the earlier interviews, those patients whom we first encountered in 1980 continued their life tales as before. This volume has benefited greatly from these personal narratives. Although I have principally drawn on them to amplify the research study of neurasthenia in Chinese society, the reader of chapter 6 will encounter materials that depict the Cultural Revolution (and other disruptive periods in modern China's continuing societal transformation) as personal and social trauma. These cases, it seems to me, at times cast a moral effect beyond the bounds of our analytic framework and attest to the poignant particularity of human suffering that transforms social changes into individual existential defeats and desperation. I am honored to have shared in these life stories, stories that have affected me deeply, and I hope that by reporting them in the technical categories of anthropology and psychiatry and thereby recasting human subjects as objects of professional inquiry I have not entirely lost for the reader the moral meanings with which they were movingly entrusted to me and asked to be retold.

One
★
Neurasthenia

Fact . . . is experience. . . . Facts are never merely observed, remembered
or combined; they are always made. . . . Fact is what we are obliged to
think, not because it corresponds with some outside world or existence, but
because it is required for the coherence of the world of experience. . . . All
facts imply a theory. . . .

Oakeshott (1933:42–43)

One of the most remarkable powers of the human mind—less often
commented on than its power to proliferate senses—is its power to exclude,
or suppress, feasible meaning . . . [but] such an agreement is not permanent
nor inclusive: signification may be controlled and focused within a like-
minded group but the excluded or left-over meanings of words remain
potential. They can be brought to the surface and put to use by those
outside the accord or professional "contract," as well as by those future
readers for whom new historical sequences have intervened.

Beer (1984:1255)

HISTORICAL BACKGROUND IN THE WEST

A striking difference in the epidemiology of psychiatric disorders in China
and the West is the very high prevalence in the former and low prevalence
in the latter of neurasthenia.[1] In the psychiatric outpatient clinic of the Hunan
Medical College neurasthenia is the most common diagnosis given to neurotic
patients; whereas in the clinics at Harvard and the University of Washington,
where I have taught, I have not once seen this diagnosis applied. Neurasthenia
is an equally popular diagnosis in psychiatric and medical clinics throughout
China, and just about as unpopular in similar clinics in the United States
and Britain. It is widely diagnosed in other Chinese cultural settings that
differ markedly from China in political economy and social structure: that
is, Hong Kong and Taiwan. In the West, and more specifically, the United

14

States, where it originated, neurasthenia tends to be regarded as old-fashioned, an anachronistic carry-over from earlier times (circa 1880–1930) when it was a popular diagnosis in lay as well as professional medical circles.

Physicians in the United States, Great Britain, other Western societies, and Japan diagnose depression, anxiety states, hysteria, and stress-related psychophysiological reactions where several generations ago they would have diagnosed neurasthenia. Indeed, it has been suggested that neurasthenia may be currently employed in Chinese settings in the same way it was earlier in the West: as a more respectable somatic mantle to cover mental illnesses and psychological and social problems that otherwise raise embarrassing issues of moral culpability and social stigma (Kleinman 1980:119–78). The term *neurasthenia* was apparently introduced to China by Western physicians and medical missionaries and by Japanese health professionals in the late nineteenth and early twentieth centuries, but this fascinating example of cultural diffusion has never been a subject of historical inquiry.

The American neurologist who popularized the term beginning in 1868, George M. Beard (1880), regarded neurasthenia (or nervous exhaustion as he also called it) as a family of disease problems long recognized by laymen and medical professionals in the West under such terms as "general debility," "nervous prostration," "nervous debility," "nervous asthenia," "spinal weakness," and the like.[2] The Greek-based word *neurasthenia* literally meant "lack of nerve strength." Beard defined neurasthenia as "a chronic, functional disease of the nervous system,"

> the basis of which is impoverishment of nervous force, waste of nerve-tissue in excess of repair; hence the lack of inhibitory or controlling power—physical and mental—the feebleness and instability of nerve action, and the excessive sensitiveness and irritability, local and general, direct and reflex. The fatigue and pain that temporarily follow excessive toil, or worry, or deprivation of food or rest, are symptoms of acute neurasthenia, from which the chronic form differs only in permanence and degree. . . . The vague and multitudinous symptoms that accompany neurasthenia are largely the result of reflex irritation that takes place, not only through the ordinary motor and sensory nerves, but through the sympathetic system and vaso-motor nerves. (p. 115)

Beard described neurasthenia as a functional disease of the nervous system without structural organic changes but distinct from mental illness (insanity).[3] The early New York neurologist was emphatic that "Nervousness is a physical not a mental state, and its phenomena do not come from emotional excess or excitability" (1881:17). Through this claim he established the disorder as the subject of his newly developing medical specialty (cf. Sicherman 1977; Rosenberg 1962).

Intriguingly, Beard called neurasthenia the "American disease," and said it was much more common in the United States (especially the Northeast) than in Europe. He also asserted it was greatly increased in prevalence owing to the "pressures" of modern civilization. He held neurasthenia to be routinely misdiagnosed as either hysteria or hypochondriasis, or organic (heart, gastrointestinal, gynecological, spinal) pathology. Beard's clinical impression was that neurasthenia was commoner in women, though also common in men, that its greatest prevalence occurred in young adulthood and early middle life, that members of the educated and wealthier class, especially physicians, were at greatest risk to develop neurasthenic symptoms, that those symptoms were "real" not imaginary, that neurasthenia led to over-utilization of physicians' services, that it was often associated with drug addiction and alcoholism, and that its chronic course waxed and waned but would respond to appropriate treatment. Therapy was a multi-sided approach involving diet, hygiene, massage, medication, electric stimulation, and appropriate use of rest, work, and change of work.

Though it sometimes was inherited, "shocks" of bereavement, domestic troubles, and worry owing to financial and work difficulties contributed to its development. Among its many and variegated symptoms, Beard regarded the following as most typical: headache, pain of various kinds, pressure and heaviness in the head, noises in the ears, lack of concentration, irritability, hopelessness, morbid fears (general anxiety and specific phobias, including fear of disease and of work), dizziness, insomnia, poor appetite, dyspepsia, sweating, tremors, dysesthesia, exhaustion, temporary paralysis, sudden failure of sensory functions, palpitations, involuntary emissions, impotence, and so forth (Beard 1880:15–85).

Drinka (1984:191) has captured Beard's description of the prototypical neurasthenic Victorian male in the evolutionary (that is, social Darwinist) and electrical metaphors that were leading cultural preoccupations of his age and that dominated Beard's pathophysiology and therapy:

> A person with a nervous tendency is driven to think, to work to strive for success. He presses himself and his life force to the limit, straining his circuits. Like an overloaded battery, or like Prometheus exhausted from reaching too high for the fire of the gods, the sufferer's electrical system crashes down, spewing sparks and symptoms and giving rise to neurasthenia.

Beard's even more successful rival Weir Mitchell emphasized the plight of Victorian women that led them into neurasthenic lifestyles, and advanced a complementary image of women suffering from exhausted nerves caused by unhappy love affairs, loss of social position and wealth, " 'the daily fret and worrisomeness of lives which, passing out of maidenhood, lack those distinct purposes and aims which, in the lives of men, are like the steadying influences of a flying wheel in the machine' " (Drinka 1984:201). Hence neurasthenia could be caused either by too much or too little nerve force, as the result of too much or too little serious work on the sensitive nervous system of usually upper-class patients.

Gilbert Ballet, professor in the faculty of medicine in Paris, in the third edition of his widely read *Neurasthenia* (Ballet 1908) disputed Beard's contention that it was an American disease, but agreed that its symptoms had been reported by medical writers throughout history. Nonetheless it had become more common in the nineteenth century owing to the "pressures" of society. He saw degeneracy as a heredity vulnerability (which most European physicians emphasized) and excessive brain work and poor education as social ones. But unlike hysteria, hypochondriasis, anxiety neurosis, and melancholia, which were mental disorders, Ballet insisted, "Neurasthenia whatever be its etiology consists in a state of nervous exhaustion; now nervous exhaustion is something real, which can be appreciated and even measured" (Ballet 1908:120). Still in Ballet's influential view: "The depressing emotions, that is to say, vexation, anxiety, disappointments, remorse, thwarted affection, in a word all states of sorrow and disquiet—these are the usual causes of nervous exhaustion" (p. 25).

Ballet shrewdly commented on the problem of amplification of somatic complaints and suppression of psychological troubles that neurasthenia posed for the clinician:

> Some [neurasthenics] describe minutely with unwearying insistence symptoms of a secondary order, and hardly mention those of real importance. Others speak abundantly of their headache and their muscular weakness, but deliberately conceal their emotionalism, their childish fears, their states of anxiety, and the powerlessness of their intellectual faculties, all symptoms which it would offend their self esteem to confess. (p. 42)

This experienced clinician called headache, backache, weakness (neuromuscular asthenia), insomnia, and dyspepsia the primary symptoms, to which he added cerebral depression—weakness of personality, will, memory, and moral character leading to hypochondriacal complaints. The cause of this mental debility was organic weakness in the nervous system, whether due to pressures, traumas, or excessive masturbation, just as it was the cause of primary symptoms and a wide range of secondary somatic symptoms, of which vertigo, dysesthesia, and palpitations were foremost. Ballet's somatopsychic dualism captures the feeling of the most distinguished medical men of his day who had contributed to the voluminous neurasthenia literature, for example, Galton, Charcot, Krafft-Ebing, Meynert, Freud, Dejerine, and Weir Mitchell, most of whom agreed with him that though the cause was organic the treatment should principally consist of psychological and social therapies. The impressively large *Handbuch der Neurasthenie* (1893), edited by Franz Carl Muller, a German physician, contained an almost exhaustive bibliography and stamped the disorder with the high status seal of German medical science.

Sicherman (1977), writing about the place of neurasthenia in the late nineteenth century, describes how Beard and other early contributors to the literature drew not only from the dominant scientific metaphors of their day but also from the nonmedical self-images of Victorian society to explain the problem: "the overloaded electric circuit and the overdrawn bank account." Nervous energy was viewed as limited, and contemporary society was thought to place "inordinate demands on that supply." In an age preoccupied with the capitalist marketplace, supply and demand were ready explanatory models.

Research of a scientifically suspect kind conducted in France and Germany allegedly demonstrated a physiological lesion in neurasthenia. But the research seems to have measured nonspecific autonomic nervous system arousal and confused this general state of strain in the individual with a hypothesized specific abnormality in the nervous system that has never been documented in a century of research studies (Drinka 1984:214–16). In keeping with the cultural values that informed their medical theories, European authors emphasized hereditary degeneracy and took a much less optimistic view of the treatment of neurasthenia than did their American colleagues. Both European and American physicians, working in an era of limited technical knowledge, not surprisingly misdiagnosed infections and endocrinological disorders as neurasthenia, but these made up a relatively small number of cases.[4]

After the turn of the century, neurasthenia began to be replaced in the West by disease terms that both tapped the increasing medical and popular interest in psychological causation, such as hysteria and hypochondriasis, and those that attempted to specify a more precise organic pathology, such as "neurocirculatory asthenia." Among the multitudes who were given the illness label of neurasthenia were William James and Sigmund Freud. In his adolescence and young adulthood Beard himself suffered from symptoms that, had the term been in existence, would have fit its founder (Sicherman 1977), and doubtless contributed to its creation. With the increasing interest in sexual sources of mental disorder, Beard entertained several sexual sources of neurasthenia and Freud (along with many others) attributed its cause more specifically to masturbation vitally weakening the body's nervous force. Weir Mitchell, the most popular Amerian physician of the Gilded Age, who developed a rest cure for his upper-middle-class neurasthenic female patients, regarded the moral aspects of neurasthenia as determinative. This is what William James thought when he went through his experience of the dark night of the soul in search of his self-identity and career direction, and was diagnosed and treated for neurasthenia. For Mitchell and James, and for many other Americans for whom the Calvinist tradition was a palpable part of their upbringing, neurasthenia was a weakness in will power, the somatic embodiment of conflict in morality and religion.

Howard Feinstein, in his *Becoming William James* (1984), canvasses the cultural origins and interprets the chief social functions of neurasthenia for William, Henry, and Alice James and their contemporaries:

> In mid-nineteenth-century New England it [neurasthenic invalidism] coalesced from a romantic and puritanical matrix into a durable social role. Salvation through work, condemnation of idleness, suspicion of pleasure, and a belief that suffering leads to grace flowed from the puritan source. Insistence on self-expression, a high valuation of leisure, and the admiration of delicacy and acute sensibility issued from the romantic. In such vigorous crosscurrents, illness had considerable utility. It provided social definition, sanctioned pleasure, prescribed leisure for health, protected from premature responsibility, forced others to care, and expressed inadmissible feelings while protecting vital personal ties. (1984:213)

Indeed, Durkheim, writing in the 1890s, went even further, though perhaps intending irony: "Now today neurasthenia is rather considered a mark of distinction than a weakness. In our refined societies, enamored of things intellectual, nervous members constitute almost a nobility" (Durkheim 1952:181).

In this transitional age between traditional and more modern society, neurasthenia was one of the medical labels that began to replace religious descriptors for what today would be called "stress." Society was becoming more secular and bureaucratic, and the helping professions were gaining ascendancy in defining personal problems (Lasch 1979), a development Rieff (1966) has termed the "triumph of the therapeutic." With time, more psychological interpretations of distress and idioms of complaining would begin to replace the somatic complaints of neurasthenia in American and European society (though a somatic idiom of distress has remained popular in the West up to present).

By the turn of the century, "traumatic neurasthenia" was being described

among railroad workers and miners as a rough working-class equivalent of
fatigue and invalidism of upper-class neurasthenic sensitivity (Figlio 1982).
Chatel and Peel (1971) report that the French medical literature was especially
interested in the industrial and occupational sources of neurasthenia. During
the contemporary period of western colonial expansion in Africa and Asia,
"tropical neurasthenia" was described as a work problem of European co-
lonials. The racialist views of the time paternalistically viewed neurasthenia
and mental illnesses as nonexistent among indigenous populations, whose
"primitive" living conditions and thought processes were regarded as free
of worry and psychic conflict, which were attributed to the sensitivities in-
culcated by Western civilization. For example, in 1871 Dr. John Dudgeon's
report on Peking's health problems for the Imperial Maritime Custom's yearly
Medical Reports noted that nerves and mental illness were not problems
among the Chinese, who, in the absence of the pressures of Western life,
had "no worry."

Drinka (1984:230) is one of the few contemporary chroniclers of neurasthenia in the West to draw attention to problems in the doctor-patient relationship. Neurasthenic patients were often difficult to cure, symptoms persisted, and both parties were aware of the illness's social function of
sanctioning withdrawal from and manipulation of social relationships without
conferring blame on the patient, although neither could address the issue
openly. Physicians took a paternalistic approach that mirrored the male/fe-
male, parent/child, and employer/worker relations of the times. The doctor
was a moral policeman who guided patients through respectable, upper-class
Victorian ways of coping with sex, sleep, friendship, food, tobacco, alcohol,
work, and the excitements of modernity (Drinka 1984:235), telling them how
to behave so as to avoid or reduce the risk of neurasthenia. Drinka (1984:236)
points to the Victorians' strict double standard of "respectable" manhood
and womanhood, the high value placed on choosing a safe career and marrying wisely, and the responsibility to preserve the family fortune and good
name as examples of the social sources of personal and group distress among
the upper classes. But no student of the period has yet systematically analyzed
the social origins of neurasthenia across class, gender, and society.

CONTEMPORARY SITUATION IN THE WEST

In the 1940s and 50s, American psychiatrists began to debate whether neurasthenia was a unified and useful disease category. The multitude of diverse
symptoms and its indiscriminant use led more critically minded physicians

to view neurasthenia as a wastebasket containing many different kinds of disorders. For example, Chrzanowski (1971), commenting on Chatel and Peele's (1971) review of the status of neurasthenia in psychiatry, said what many academic psychiatrists were arguing; namely that neurasthenia had become a "mythical diagnosis which stands in the way of psychiatric progress." Fearing that the Chatel and Peele review would be the basis for restoration of the category, he debunked it as "a meaningless concept." Although neurasthenia is no longer listed as a disease entity in the latest (1980) Diagnostic and Statistical Manual (DSM-III) of the American Psychiatric Association, it was listed as neurasthenia neurosis in prior editions. In the Ninth Revision of the World Health Organization's International Classification of Disease (ICD-9), neurasthenia is defined as:

> A neurotic disorder characterized by fatigue, irritability, headache, depression, insomnia, difficulty in concentration, and lack of capacity for enjoyment (anhedonia). It may follow or accompany an infection or exhaustion, or arise from continued emotional stress. (DSM-III 1980:425–26)

There is substantial pressure on WHO by academic psychiatrists from the West to remove neurasthenia from the forthcoming ICD-10.

Except for pointing out that this diagnosis was rarely used in the recent past, the authors of DSM-III enigmatically refer readers who search the index for the term *neurasthenia* to read about dysthymic disorder (neurotic depression) without explaining why. DSM-I, published in 1952, did not include it in the section on "Disorders of Psychogenic Origin or Without Clearly Defined Physical Cause or Structural Change in the Brain," but referred to it as psychophysiologic nervous system reaction, while DSM-II, published in 1968, labeled it neurasthenic neurosis and stated:

> This condition is characterized by complaints of chronic weakness, easy fatigability, and sometimes exhaustion. Unlike hysterical neurosis the patient's complaints are genuinely distressing to him and there is no evidence of secondary gain. It differs from Anxiety neurosis (q.v.) in the nature of the predominant complaint. It differs from Depressive neurosis (q.v.) in the moderateness of the depression and in the chronicity of its course.

This definition marked the official transition from somatopsychic to psychosomatic conceptualization of neurasthenia, just as DSM-III marks the transition from the "American Disease" to "not a disease in America."

The assertion that social gain is absent is amazing in light of neurasthenia's history, and represents a disturbing desocializing of psychiatric disorders that in the dominant psychoanalytic language of the time were viewed only as biological *or* psychological problems. The European-based ICD-9 had to gain approval from WHO's non-Western members, including China's health representatives, and ambiguously implies both psychogenic and organic etiology, thus maintaining the original definition of the term. This vague status was apparently meant to bridge biomedicine's Cartesian dualism with a polysemous medical term that implied psychophysical integration and bio-psychosocial holism, even if it stood for organicity first. (A similar function is filled by the concept of "stress" in contemporary biomedicine.) The historical transformation of neurasthenia from a somatic to psychosomatic to psychic state, and its ultimate dismissal as a pseudo-disease, reflects a major cultural change over the past one hundred years. Neurasthenia's role in popular culture was superseded when psychosomatic and psychological constructs became acceptable means for interpreting problems in everyday living, and euphemisms, indirection, or liminal ambiguity were no longer required.

NEURASTHENIA IN THE CHINESE CONTEXT

In standard Chinese, neurasthenia is rendered as *shenjing shuairuo,* literally neurological *(shenjing)* weakness *(shuairuo).* In Taiwan and Hong Kong as well as in China, this term is widely recognized and applied by laymen, for whom it appears to connote an ailment with vague, protean signs and symptoms believed to be due to weakness of the nervous system, the brain, and the body generally. Its characteristics are bodily weakness, fatigue, tiredness, headaches, dizziness, and a range of gastrointestinal and other complaints. From 1978 to 1983 psychiatrists in China routinely told me that neurasthenia is a disorder of brain function involving asthenia of cerebral cortical activity. In this view, the psychological symptoms of neurasthenia have the same origin as somatic symptoms in the putative organic pathology held to underlie neurasthenia. This explanation is quite similar in form to the somatopsychic orientation (bodily changes cause changes in mind and emotion) of traditional Chinese medicine as it is currently practiced.

Chinese textbooks (for example, the authoritative and widely used textbook of *Internal Medicine* edited by the Shanghai First Medical College and the Zhongshan Medical College [vol. 2, 1980:1034–36], and the textbook of *Chinese-English Terminology of Traditional Chinese Medicine* published by the Hunan Science and Technology Press [1983:144, 210–19] point out that neurasthenia is currently conceived in traditional Chinese medicine as a decrease in vital energy *(qi)* caused by harmful factors both exogenous (for example, toxic chemicals or other factors in physical and social environment) and endogenous to the patient's bodily constitution. These factors are held to produce changes in the functioning of the five internal organ systems (*wuzang:* heart, liver, spleen, lungs, kidneys), cause a deficiency of vital energy *(qi),* and lower bodily resistance. Although patients suffering chronic diseases are thought to be particularly susceptible to these pathological changes, healthy persons can also be affected. The current perspective in traditional Chinese medicine differentiates a number of types of neurasthenia, including:

1. Liver-kidney *yin* deficiency, in which the chief symptoms are dizziness, distended feeling in the head, blurred vision, tinnitus, fever, bitter taste, insomnia, spermatorrhea, and a pulse that is either "stringy, faint and rapid or faint and weak."
2. Heart-kidney disharmony due to pathogenic abnormalities in the physiological relationship of the heart *yang* and kidney *yin,* whose main symptoms are insomnia, dysphoria, palpitations, frequent dreams, spermatorrhea, and so forth.
3. Heart and spleen weakness in which amnesia, insomnia, frequent dreams, reduced appetite, loose stools, fatigue, weakness, and faint and weak pulse are said to predominate.
4. Neurasthenia owing to depression of vital energy *(qi)* in the liver, which is characterized by emotional symptoms associated with chest discomfort, hypochondriacal pain, depression, anxiety, irritability, anorexia, abdominal distension, menstrual irregularities, and a variety of other complaints.

This classification integrates traditional Chinese medical theory with biomedical theory in a synthesis dominated by the somatopsychic orientation of both. Chinese psychiatrists and other physicians generally have little to say about this aspect of their work, but it is this kind of conceptual integration which makes the Chinese psychiatric understanding of neurasthenia and other disorders unique.

This somatopsychic view of neurasthenia also squares with the biological orientation of current Chinese psychiatry and is consistent with the materialist views of Russian neuropsychiatry (in particular the Pavlovian physiological theory of conditioned reflexes and differentiated inhibitions) which were greatly influential in China in the 1950s, when many of the leading psychiatrists in China today were completing their training.[5] In Taiwan, where the influence of American psychiatric theory is strong, the term *neurasthenia* is current among general practitioners. Psychiatrists tend to translate it into other diagnostic categories, especially the neuroses and personality disorders associated with hypochondriasis, yet they too are still willing to speak about "neurasthenia" with patients and—to a lesser extent—colleagues.

Foundations of Psychiatry, the first volume of the important
sive *Psychiatry* published by five of China's major depart-
itry at the Hunan Science and Technology Press in 1981,
graphs of its 640 pages to neurasthenia, the commonest of
ic diagnoses, whereas depression, the least common of di-
a total of six pages in two different sections. Can this be
∣ of uncertainty about the scientific status of this popular
cultural and professional term? In this textbook neurasthenia is discussed
in one paragraph, under the heading Illnesses of Neurological Function
(Neurological Illnesses), and in another under Personality Disorders, where
neurasthenic personality is covered in one long sentence. Echoing Beard's
definition of neurasthenia as well as a concern to distinguish it from psychosis,
illnesses of neurological function are said to be:

> those that cannot be confirmed to have any organic basis. The patient has fairly
> good insight, and normally does not confuse subjective pathological experience
> and fantasy with external facts. Although their behavior can be greatly influ-
> enced, they still inwardly keep within the limits tolerated by society, and their
> personality also remains intact. (*Foundations of Psychiatry* 1981:268)

The definition of neurasthenia in the *Foundations of Psychiatry* volume is
rather similar to that of the ICD-9, except for the strong emphasis on abnormal
neurological functioning and failure to mention anhedonia (joylessness):

> Neurasthenia is a type of functional illness usually accompanied by loss of
> vegetative neurological function which includes fatigue, irascibleness, unstable
> and depressed mood, difficulty in concentrating attention, a definite decrease
> in recent memory, and sleep with many dreams or loss of sleep. It can develop
> after infection or exhaustion, or be set off after prolonged neurological stim-
> ulation. It does not include mental diseases with the symptoms mentioned
> above that result from physical disease. (*Foundations of Psychiatry* 1981:268–
> 69)

Life stress as a precipitant is notably missing, but my conversations with
the authors indicate that they are now prepared to accept it as another provoking agent.

As I have already noted, it is not certain how the concept of neurasthenia
entered China. Both Western medical missionaries and Japanese medical
authorities seem to have contributed to its translation and popularization.
Neurasthenia had been introduced into Japan from German medicine (Suzuki
in press). But once part of Japanese medical culture, it took on a life of its
own. Hence, even though a somatopsychic interpretation of neurasthenia
as neurological exhaustion seems to have fit well with both biomedical and
traditional medical systems in Japan (Lock 1980, n.d.), Shoma Morita, one

of the early and most original Japanese psychiatrists, published a treatise on neurasthenia *(shinkeisuijaku)* in 1922, which he reconceptualized as *shinkeishitsu,* or a particular type of obsessional neurosis. He gave a decidedly psychological interpretation to the patient suffering from neurasthenia:

> A person with a particularly strong need to live a full life, perfectionist tendencies, and extreme self-consciousness. . . . This person encounters some unpleasant event that focuses attention on a particular problem; blushing, headaches, and constipation are typical samples. He becomes quite concerned about the problem, and he becomes increasingly conscious of its effects on his life. He becomes caught in a spiral of attention and sensitivity which produces a sort of obsessive self-consciousness. (Reynolds 1976:9–10)

For the period prior to World War I, I could find no reference in the *China Medical Journal,* or in its medical missionary and imperial customs predecessors, to neurasthenia, though all the issues of these journals are not available. In 1915 Alfred Reed reviewed "Nervous Diseases in China" without mentioning neurasthenia (or depression). J. L. McCartney, writing in the *China Medical Journal* in 1926 on "Neuropsychiatry in China," also fails to mention neurasthenia, but his paper is concerned with a predisposition to mental weakness that sounds very similar. McCartney, in his book *Oriental Nerves,* cited a series of psychosocial causes of mental illness and nerves identified by physicians practicing in China whose views he had surveyed. These included business anxiety, bereavement, lack of achievement, disappointment in love, domestic troubles, excessive study, loss of property, troubles growing out of the chaotic political and military situation during the mid-1920s, loneliness, sexual maladjustment, and problems resulting from cultural change—many of which had been cited as factors contributing to neurasthenia in the Western medical literature. McCartney's two-part review sympathetically canvassed the psychodynamic formulation of neurosis, the somatic masking of psychiatric disorders including depression, and discussed the symbolic meanings of symptoms, indicating that the readers of the *China Medical Journal*—missionary physicians, expatriate Western medical educators and public health personnel, and the few thousand Chinese who had trained in Western medicine—had access to an increasingly sophisticated psychological discourse. McCartney (1926) regarded the Chinese as a "nervous people" given to "oriental nerves" because of the great social changes of the time and their "want of self-control." The stage was set for the transfer of neurasthenia to a Chinese context.

The first reference in the *China Medical Journal* to neurasthenia that I could locate is a brief abstract in its Current Medical Literature section in 1923, citing a review of neurasthenia in a Belgian medical journal by F.

Dauwe. The abstract emphasized the symptoms of headache and dyspepsia—complaints with special salience in Chinese culture—owing to nervous overwork, and pointed out that neurasthenia is a mental condition resulting from the physical state of the patient, a product of exhaustion, not the imagination. This brief blurb warned against introspection and egotism and ended with a cryptic phrase: "Almost all these patients love the stress which exhausts them and cannot withdraw from it because it is their means of livelihood" (*China Medical Journal* 1923:523).

Herbert Day Lamson, an American sociologist who taught at the University of Shanghai in the 1930s and surveyed the state of mental illness in China in a chapter of *Social Pathology in China* (1935:421), reviewed a study by A. H. Woods on the incidence of "nervous disease" in hospitals in Peking; the study examined 429 treated cases of neurasthenia. The diagnosis was given to cases who experienced: (1) chronic and pronounced diminution in energy that was not due to syphilis or other medical disorders; (2) oversensitivity to sensory stimuli that produce mild pain, headaches, nausea, dyspepsia; (3) striking fatiguability. Students constituted a large number of these cases, many morbidly introspective, whom Woods describes (somewhat patronizingly) as "not greatly interested in practical affairs or in applying to actual problems the principles learned in their schools. They have had little relief through creative outlets for the seething swamp of ideas generated in their brains. We have excluded from this category cases of syphilitic neurasthenia, those following sexual over-indulgence, and drug intoxication, and those acquired neurasthenias which resulted from over-work." Woods went on to explain the sources of his patients' neurasthenia and their psychosomatic effects: "Among the Chinese, fear of disapproval, 'loss of face', loss of affections, anxiety as to business, lawsuits, are some of the conditions which individuals find it particularly hard to face. Illness often follows apparently as a result of metabolic sequelae to the emotional disturbance, often as an unconscious dramatic way out of the predicament which will provide a plausible explanation for failures and admit of retaining of some degree of self-respect" (Lamson 1935:422). Psychological and social aspects of neurasthenia, then, were well known in the 1920s and 1930s in China, at least among some expatriate Western practitioners and researchers.

The earliest article on neurasthenia in Chinese that I have been able to find is a paper published in the 1930s in the *Tong Ji yixue jikan*, a journal printed in Shanghai. This article, "Neurasthenia", by Song Mingtong (1936), is worthy of detailed inspection, since it further shows how this disorder was regarded in China, circa 1930, at least by some Chinese practitioners of biomedicine. Song begins his review by calling neurasthenia "a widespread social illness" affecting many in China, particularly the young. Although acknowledging it is an hereditary nervous disorder, Song notes that even people who are healthy, "who live in the vile conditions of the present day," are easily affected, regardless of whether the chief contributing problems are in the family, work, or at a national level in the society. Song laments the fact that many of the young have become "parasites" on society because of this disorder. Because there is no evidence of a specific physical lesion, pharmacological treatment is ineffective. Of psychiatric treatment, he says it is too new a science to be sure of its results. Moreover, diagnosing neurasthenia, Song admits, is a large problem because it is readily confused with other disorders.

Song regards this "neurological reaction" as a problem a person has for an entire life, and he indicates that it often affects the entire family. He lists as the main symptoms phobias, sleep disturbance, clammy, moist hands, and fingernail biting. Song notes that these symptoms are often found among "only sons" who are pampered from childhood and therefore lack the ability to adapt to the pressures of the environment. But sometimes environmental pressures can be severe enough to affect even healthy persons. Overwork and overstimulation persisting over a period of time are common causes of neurasthenia, especially for people in the city who originally lived in the countryside, and especially if they are engaged in mental work. Furthermore, recovery from infectious disease, chronic poisoning, and other internal factors may be important in the etiology of neurasthenia. Chronic medical disorders— like gastric and duodenal ulcers, biliary disease, and gynecological diseases— in which the symptoms may be slight, may contribute to a person becoming neurasthenic. Among the predisposing conditions is unbearable loss.

Song, writing as if he had had extensive clinical experience with the diagnosis and treatment of neurasthenia, notes that in spite of the patient's wearyingly detailed repetition of minor complaints the practitioner requires a detailed history and must not lose the patient's faith. Diagnosis may be based on what the patient doesn't say as much as on what he does. In the clinical interview the practitioner can observe the patient's perception, attention, and memory deteriorate as he becomes tired and reveals an "embittered spirit." Patients focus on bodily complaints and believe they have particular organic problems (for example, heart or intestinal problems), even though there is little evidence of organic malfunctioning and more evidence of psychiatric difficulties. The latter include the embittered emotion already noted as well as confusion, fear of death, fainting spells, sleep disturbance, appetite disturbance, frightening dreams, mental dullness, hopelessness, and a sense of inefficacy. Physical examination because of complaints of cloudy vision and ringing in the ears reveals no organ pathology. Song mentions that some neurasthenic patients are excessively sensitive to particular inner sensations like bowel functioning. Because of their fear of illness, they take drugs, including opium and alcohol.

Song points up the conviction neurasthenics have that they cannot resolve their difficulties (both great and minor) because of lack of energy and a tendency to magnify problems. He also notes compulsive thoughts, including helpless fears of doing or saying the wrong thing in social situations. Song describes a range of physiological manifestations from changes in blood pressure to rapid pulse rate. He writes of a change in sexual urge that is common, as well as impotence, early morning emissions, abnormal sexual urges, and irregular menses. Song goes on to show how difficult prognosis and treatment are, especially for patients who are chronic cases. He does not believe that chronic cases can be completely cured; even those that improve may recur under appropriately provoking circumstances. Song closes by describing how work is affected by neurasthenic patients who feel depressed or angry, and remarks that those who attend the neurasthenic are made uncomfortable by his behavior. At any time in his life, the person with this proclivity to become neurasthenic can either develop the disorder or more serious neurological disease.

Thus, the very first report in Chinese that we have located in the medical literature presents a discriminating and subtle picture of neurasthenia that emphasizes its putative biological basis but also includes a fairly broad review of contributing factors and consequences of a psychological (most notably, depressive) and social (including family, work, political) character. The review also suggests that neurasthenic patients are problem patients for the practitioner because they frequently either fail to improve or experience recurrences of their complaints, are difficult to diagnose and treat, suffer from emotional problems, and have difficulties in their relations with significant others.

In the 1938 edition of the *Cihai (Sea of Words)*, the authoritative Chinese dictionary published in Shanghai and reprinted in Taiwan in 1969, it is of great interest that neurasthenia, which is viewed as a chronic disorder without an effective medical treatment, is described as having the following symptoms: headaches, dizziness, insomnia, depression, memory loss, appetite loss, lack of energy. This list emphasizes the symptoms of clinical depression, including mood, appetite, sleep, and energy disturbances, although neurasthenia is defined in keeping with Beard's original description, as a disorder of the nervous system. The 1965 Hong Kong edition of the *Cihai Xinpian (The Sea of Words, New Edition)*, like most Chinese writings on neurasthenia, does not mention depression, but emphasizes a wide range of somatic complaints in addition to anxiety. Following Beard, it argues for the importance of a program of work and rest. The modern Chinese literature has thus shown awareness of various psychological and social dimensions of neurasthenia for some time.

In their 1969 review of *Psychological Research in Communist China: 1949–1966*, Robert and Ai-li Chin place great emphasis on the contribution of Pavlovian neurophysiology to the model of neurasthenia reported by psychologists in modern China, "according to which unfavorable external conditions can bring about tension in the higher nervous system in excess of its capacity thus causing a weakening in the functioning capacity of the brain tissues and a lack of balance or confusion in nervous activity" (p. 70). They cite a survey of neurasthenia in Peking in 1959 in which females constituted twice as many cases as males, 87 percent were " mind workers," 13 percent laborers (pp. 74–75). But other studies showed hardly any sexual difference and reported similar rates among peasants and laborers. The Chins cite the work of Wang Ching-ho and Li Hsin-t'ien (1960) in the *Chinese Journal of Psychology*, which compared the etiology of neurasthenia (for example, work, study, daily life problems) among populations of students, workers, and military personnel. Whereas the ultimate causal factor, following Lenin, is always taken to be the person's "recognition process" of the concrete situation, contributing causes included work responsibility beyond the limits of self-perceived ability, or overconcern about work responsibility, difficult, unfamiliar, and high-pressure work, loss of interest in work, excessive self-demands regarding studying (together with heavy load of studies), life tragedies (including unhappy marriage, bereavement, financial difficulties, problems with co-workers, and so forth), and impatient, anxious, oversensitive, and dogmatic personalities. Rational components of the self (cognitive recognition of concrete situation and moral will) were seen as more significant than emotions in the etiology of neurasthenia.

The Chins show the writings of the psychologist Li Hsin-t'ien (which ended with the advent of the Cultural Revolution) to be especially sensitive to psychosocial factors. Li recognized the waxing and waning course of the problem, the effect of work and study problems on amplifying patients' physical complaints, and the tendency for symptoms to change fairly frequently.

The Chins (1969:100) summarize the leading psychological theory of neurasthenia prior to the Cultural Revolution, when the work of China's entire psychological profession ended, only to start up again in the past few years with a rather different set of interests. Based on dialectical materialism's view of the person, psychological activity is regarded to be entirely the "reflection" of objective reality, the concrete conditions of social life. This reality is in constant change, which in turn produces material changes in the person that are held to be the basis for functional changes in psychological processes. Mental disorders result when the balance of excitation/inhibition of the nervous system is upset, or when the nervous system is rendered unsuitable for working at capacity owing to excessive environmental pressures, somatic disease, or incorrect attitudes and thoughts. Conditions of work, study,[6] and living are external influences on the person. Because of differing conditions of social life, individuals differ in their recognition process. This carries over to influence attitudes or emotions regarding work and study. Pessimistic, depressed attitudes can produce decreased brain-tissue activity and cell work.

Using this theory, China's medical psychologists concluded, apparently without recognizing the epidemiological irony, that neurasthenia is widespread and difficult to cure in capitalist countries, where the objective reality of social life is conducive to this disorder. They claimed that under socialism neurasthenia had decreased and was easier to treat. By the time of the Great Leap Forward, and again during the Cultural Revolution, neurasthenia had clearly become an embarrassment to this type of analysis and ripe for political intervention.

In the 1950s and 1960s the *Chinese Medical Journal* carried several articles devoted to neurasthenia, indicating that psychiatrists also were interested in neurasthenia, that it was a frequent psychiatric diagnosis, and that at least one major therapeutic mass campaign (the rapid combined treatment system) had been initiated on a national level to control it. The 1950s campaign (Rapid Combined Treatment of Neurasthenia 1959), undertaken during the Great Leap Forward, applied physical labor, talk therapy (both group and individual), drugs, and mass political techniques to treat a condition held to have social and personal as well as organic sources (cf. C. P. Lin 1958; references cited in T. Y. Lin, in press).

During the political campaign against neurasthenia large numbers of cases were identified. Whereas earlier their behaviors might have been labeled as moral or ideological deviance, the diagnosis of neurasthenia gave afflicted individuals a socially acceptable name for their problems. Although high rates of successful treatment were claimed, the findings have not been substantiated by follow-up studies or by repetition of the original studies. In private Chinese psychiatrists have reported skepticism about the longer-term effects. It was in the short-term political interest of cases labeled neurasthenic to improve, in order to avoid labor reform and struggle in their "small groups." It is thus uncertain what percentage of those who claimed to be successfully treated actually were. But the fact that an entire national political campaign was organized around neurasthenia suggests the key society-wide significance this problem has taken on in the People's Republic.[7] The literature of this period is remarkable for the failure to take into account individual differences in the course and treatment of neurasthenia. Individualism was seen as a capitalist phenomenon, whereas in the Cultural Revolution class factors and political motivation were seen as crucial to understanding the cause and treatment of neurasthenia. Regrettably, since all research and writing in psychology and psychiatry ceased during the Cultural Revolution, it is not known what impact this sociopolitical change had on the diagnosis and treatment of neurasthenia. However, given the current prevalence of neurasthenia in the People's Republic and the continued sense of inadequacy in its treatment, it is unlikely that the impact was extensive or persistent.

Xu Youxin (1956), writing in the very first volume of the *Chinese Journal of Neurology and Psychiatry,* attempted to find cultural authorization for illness similar to neurasthenia in early Chinese medical texts of the Six Dynasties and Sui and T'ang Dynasties, and concluded that the symptoms of conditions resembling neurasthenia could be found in discussion of Wind Disorders, a category which covers a range of psychiatric disease. He suggests that though the term was introduced from the West, the problem it maps was long recognized by Chinese physicians, who categorized it in other ways.

More recently, Xu Youxin and Zhong Youbin (1983), leading psychiatric theoreticians in Beijing, draft a taxonomy of neurosis that subsumes neurasthenia. Xu and Zhong differentiate four type of neuroses: neurasthenia, anxiety, depression, and hypochondriasis. The diagnosis of each disorder is based on four criteria: symptomatology, duration, severity, and exclusion of other disorders. The authors note that "the diagnosis of certain types of neurosis is also determined by the preponderant emotional state or mood, which must persist for a certain length of time. A patient with neurasthenia, for example, may present depressive mood at times, but the mood is by no means predominant in the clinical picture and its span is less than half of the duration of the illness."

Xu elsewhere has put aside his earlier attempt to place neurasthenia in the Chinese medical tradition. Instead, in a 1982 article in a leading Chinese psychiatric journal, Xu traces the history of neurosis in the West and places neurasthenia within that context. Hysteria, in contrast, he argues is not a neurosis. Nonetheless he makes perfectly clear that neurosis, though of foreign origin, is a clinically useful diagnostic category in China. Xu regards neurosis as a disturbance of energy manifesting a "protracted psychological conflict" that creates pain for the patient, but not of a verifiable physiological kind.

The diagnostic criteria Xu and Zhong (1983) establish for neurasthenia need to be described in full since they are by far the most elaborate diagnostic criteria that have been published in the Chinese medical literature over the past few years. Whereas many of their psychiatric colleagues in China are increasingly uncomfortable with neurasthenia as a scientific psychiatric category, partly in response to the widespread skepticism Western researchers have for neurasthenia, Xu and Zhong (1983) reaffirm their view that it is an important and valid category. Their diagnostic criteria for neurasthenia state that patients must experience at least three of the following groups of symptoms:

1. Emotional disturbance (worry, nervousness, easily aroused).
2. Mental excitement owing to work, studies, conversation, movies, TV, or other entertainment, or activities perceived as painful or unpleasurable by the patient.
3. Feeling the brain fatiguing easily or its functioning being diminished (including poor concentration, poor memory, difficulty forgetting troublesome thoughts, ineffective and confused thinking, feeling of unclarity).
4. Nervous pain associated with muscle tension, taut feeling in head, feelings of swelling or pressure in the brain, pain in neck muscles or back muscles or limbs.
5. Sleep disturbance (difficulty falling asleeep, sleeping too lightly, easily awakened, frequent unsettling dreams).

These symptoms must be of at least three months duration and must influence effectiveness at work, studying, and conducting daily household chores. The following disorders must be excluded before the diagnosis of neurasthenia can be made: anxiety neurosis, depressive neurosis, hypochondriasis, compulsive neurosis, phobic neurosis, hysteria, psychosis, and neurasthenia secondary to brain injury or a medical illness.

Xu and Zhong offer an explanation of the emotional problem in neurasthenia. Worry is due to unrealized hopes or problems resulting from conscious, conflicting desires. "Patients with a long history of illness," the authors contend, "either intentionally, semi-intentionally, or semi-unintentionally shift the object of their irritation from large life events to daily trivial matters." "Worry," they go on to say, "always contains some grievance or an attitude of discontent with reality. . . . The patient knows clearly that he is worried and that the bitterness has no way of resolving itself."

In an especially revealing characterization of Chinese patients with neurasthenia, Xu and Zhong advert:

> The patient thinks his life is a kind of burden, that work or study is oppressive to him. He always thinks he has too much to do, or that he cannot do it well. He often looks pressed about his job, feeling his responsibilities and obligations as necessary, and is scarcely happy or pleased with his work. Because of this he does not dare to relax, and when he has the opportunity to take leisure time, he cannot relax. He is embittered because he cannot "let go." Many times he sees that he has "done too much" or he "cannot unwind," etc. Even when he knows what is the cause of his tension, it is hard for him to change.

Xu and Zhong distinguish the psychological processes of neurasthenia from those of hypochondriacal neurosis. They say of the latter: "[the patient] has the tendency to blame the illness for his personal failure and misfortune, even to the point of making it the center of his life, gradually forcing a special style of getting along with people." This is the fullest description of the neurasthenic's psychological state in Chinese. It emphasizes symptoms which in Western psychiatry are associated with depression, anxiety, and personality disorders.

In a provocatively titled recent contribution, Zhong Youbin (1983) addresses the question, "Has Neurasthenia Disappeared?" Zhong, who concurs that Russian neuropsychiatry had an overly strong influence on Chinese psychiatry in the 1950s and 1960s, attributes the central prominence of neurasthenia in the Chinese diagnostic system to the importation of a tripartite Russian classification of neurosis in which neurasthenia figured importantly along with hysteria and obsessive compulsive neurosis. Zhong, in striking contrast to Xu, calls neurasthenia a "wastebasket" diagnosis because so many distinctive psychiatric problems receive this ubiquitous label. He notes that in recent years Chinese psychiatrists have begun to move away from Russian nosology and to replace it with Western views of depression and anxiety. But he cautions about dropping this diagnostic category, even though it may not be the same as Beard's original description, since it is clinically useful. Zhong concludes that it is too early to say if neurasthenia in China is changing or disappearing as an illness.

Nonetheless, this surprising paper illustrates the disquiet many Chinese psychiatrists feel about neurasthenia. Part of the difficulty is the great sensitivity China's psychiatrists (like its professionals, intellectuals, and modernizers generally throughout this century) have to the importation of new categories from the West that call into question traditional formulations and approaches to current problems and give the sense that the Chinese categories are neither up to date nor good enough. The great irony, of course, is that in defending neurasthenia as part of their efforts to build a uniquely Chinese psychiatry that combines biomedicine with indigenous approaches, China's psychiatrists are arguing on behalf of a fully sinicized import from an earlier age. A traditional Chinese response to foreign influence, syncretism, can be seen in recent attempts to combine neurasthenia with current psychiatric nomenclature so as to create such pragmatic hybrids as "neurasthenic depression."

A new direction in the Chinese medical literature appears in Xu Yun's (1983) remarkable exploration of social pathology in China and its influence on organic diseases, psychosomatic disorders, depression, and somatic preoccupation. Xu reviews research around the world that indicates the close relationship of disease to social factors. He describes the role of political and legal problems, family troubles, occupational difficulties, and economic factors on disease causation, and indicates that social problems exert their effect on the individual's personality and self-esteem as much as on his bodily processes. This is the first detailed exploration of the social sources of neurosis and medical disorders in the Chinese medical literature that I have come across. Indeed, the vast majority of papers—even those by psychiatrists and psychologists—are silent on the topic. Xu's paper indicates that it is now legitimate for Chinese health professionals to study how social problems in China contribute to ill health. In this light, it is important that the *Foundations of Psychiatry* text, under the section "Causes of Psychiatric Illness," has three pages devoted to "Unfavourable Social Environment" that cover social separation, marriage and family, urban/rural and cultural factors.

Xu Yun cites research conducted in China indicating that individuals whose jobs block their creative needs can develop psychiatric and psychosomatic disease, as well as somatic preoccupation with low back pain, arthritis, and other health problems. He also notes that overly strenuous work can make the individual ill, producing anxiety, low morale, depression, and interference with bodily awareness. Routinization of industrial work contributes to these problems. If society cannot reward workers appropriately with increased income or job advancement, then problems arise in human relations, productivity, and for the individual's self-esteem and self-worth, which can lead to suicide and mental illness. The importance of psychological tolerance in communicating the individual's ideas is stressed. Though much in the paper is legitimated by reviewing Western authors, Xu reasons that this work applies to China too, and he outlines a broad range of social research questions that could be applied to disease generally, including neurasthenia. This review is a powerful reminder of the limits of research that emphasizes psychological and biological factors but fails to consider the social context of neurasthenia.

The Japanese syndrome of *shinkeishitsu,* which interpreted neurasthenia as neurosis, together with the American missionary physicians' notion of "neurasthenia" brought to China a multi-sided concept that combined both organic and psychological concerns from the outset. Chapters 3 and 7 show how neurasthenia in the Chinese setting has been interpreted in terms of the leading explanatory models of traditional Chinese medicine and biomedicine, both of which condense physical and psychological causal attributions, with a definite predilection for somatopsychic (from body to psyche) predominance. In this respect, neurasthenia in China carries meaning similar to that given it at its inception in the West.

Did the collective behaviors and experiences subsumed by neurasthenia as an illness category decline in the West and greatly increase in China? Or is it a matter of change in the usage of the category? In the absence of epidemiological studies in the general population, it is impossible to provide a definitive answer. The chapters that follow rephrase these questions and provide a new way of configuring their answers. Is there something about rapid and disruptive societal transitions—both the long-duration transition of social structures toward modernity and short-duration political and economic transformation—that either place individuals at greater risk for the life problems and bodily dysfunctions mapped by neurasthenia, or that simply encourage the use of this idiom of distress? Does the breakdown of tightly organized systems of social control intensify personal troubles, "exhaust" the collectivity, require new coping styles (medical and mental rather than religious and moral)? Does the movement from more traditional sources of social control and group meaning to more loosely knit, fluid, modern institutions and ideologies create problems for particular categories of persons?

Two

★

Depression

A purely disembodied human emotion is a nonentity.
William James, *The Principles of Psychology*

BACKGROUND

The comparative epidemiology of depression in Chinese and Western societies is the reverse of neurasthenia; and for that reason to understand neurasthenia we must first review depression. Here high rates of the disorder are reported for the West, and extremely low rates for China. For example, Boyd and Weissman (1981), reviewing a large number of English language reports which they interpret using the recent Research Diagnostic Criteria (RDC) for depression, note that 9 to 20 percent of the population are diagnosed as depressed in community surveys. The point prevalence of clinical depression (not including manic-depressive disorder) in industrialized Western countries in studies employing newer diagnostic techniques is 3.2 cases per 100 males and 4.0 to 9.3 per 100 females. (Interestingly, the highest rates currently reported are for Africa (14.3 for men and 22.6 for women), where twenty-five years ago very low rates were reported, a point I shall return to below.) Boyd and Weissman also note that where the Schedule for Affective Disorders and Schizophrenia (SADS) and RDC are used, the lifetime prevalence of major depressive disorder is 8 to 12 percent for men and 20 to 26 percent for women.[1] For comparison, the lifetime prevalence of manic-depressive disorder they cite as less than 1 percent. Hence depressive disorder—a syndrome of dysphoria (mood disturbance), cognitive dysfunction, and disturbances of sleep, appetite, energy, psychomotor activity, all leading to social impairment and personal distress—is one of the commonest disorders in the West.[2]

Depressive disorder rates in China are either unreported or extremely low. The psychiatry outpatient clinic at the Hunan Medical College saw 361 patients during a one-week period during the summer of 1980, 30 percent of whom were diagnosed as neurasthenic and 1 percent of whom were diagnosed as depressed (see tables 1 and 2, in the appendix). Relatively similar figures have been reported to me from other psychiatric clinics in China, where neurasthenia accounts for a third to half of all outpatient diagnoses, while minimal numbers are recorded for depression. When we conducted our studies in China in 1980 and 1983, no study had been reported, either a community or clinic-based survey, that used RDC to determine the prevalence (untreated or treated) of depression. Indeed recent epidemiological reports of psychiatric disorders in China still frequently do not refer to depression, and where they do, present data either for manic-depressive disorder (for which only low rates are reported) or for involutional psychosis (Lin and Kleinman 1981).[3] Within the last two years, partially as a response to the research we report in chapters 4 and 5 and to a greater extent because of international criticism and professional pressure, Chinese psychiatrists have begun to diagnose more depression, but neurasthenia is still diagnosed much more frequently and the rates of depression that are diagnosed are low (Xu 1984, n.d.: Zhong 1985).

Causal factors of a number of kinds have been hypothesized as responsible for depressive disorders. While a body of evidence implicating abnormalities of neurotransmitters in the central nervous system and family history of depression in first-degree relatives suggests a genetic predisposition, the simplistic bioamine hypothesis that has been the dominant biological schema of depressive etiology (namely, that in depression there is a decrease in key bioamine neurotransmitters in the brain) is being called into question. The biology of depression appears to be complex. What is known is that depressed patients demonstrate disregulation of REM (rapid eye movement) sleep and other biorhythms, including thyroid and cortisal hormone secretion, indicating limbic system and neuroendocrine axis abnormalities as well as autonomic nervous system arousal. The still dominant psychoanalytic hypothesis that depression is caused by anger turned inward against the self as a defense against loss of a particular kind has never received empirical confirmation. There is research evidence for the contribution of stressful life events and impaired social support, but the more interesting and important work has centered around interdisciplinary frameworks relating psychological, social, and biological variables that influence individual responses to loss.

Brown and Harris (1978) present data in support of a hypothesis that:

hopelessness is the key factor in the genesis of clinical depression and loss is probably the most likely cause of profound hopelessness. But it is not just loss of a particular "object" that has to be dealt with so much as its implications for our ability to find satisfactory alternatives. (p. 234)

The immediate response to loss of an important source of positive value is likely to be a sense of hopelessness, accompanied by a gamut of feelings, ranging from despair, depression, and shame to anger. Feelings of hopelessness will not always be restricted to the provoking incident—large or small. It may lead to thoughts about the hopelessness of one's life in general. It is such generalization of hopelessness that we believe forms the core of a depressive disorder. (p. 235)

These authors demonstrate that vulnerability factors (working-class background, marriage, presence of small children in the home, lack of employment outside the home, absence of a confiding intimate relationship, loss of a maternal figure in childhood, optimistic or pessimistic personality factors) predispose *women* to depression by lowering self-esteem so that provoking agents like loss or threat of loss or long-term difficulty yield specific hopelessness that is then generalized into depression.[4]

Brown and Harris also indicate that in the absence of provoking agents susceptibility factors such as those Beck (1971) describes as negative cognitive schemata about self (worthless and ineffective), others (undependable and untrustworthy), and the environment (frustrating) make individuals susceptible to depression. A large literature on social learning agrees with this formulation of the social origins of depression (see Carr and Vitaliano in press; Carson and Adams 1981; Lewinsohn 1974; Coyne 1976; Bandura 1977; Seligman 1975).

Although Brown and Harris do not explain how these vulnerability, provoking, and susceptibility factors relate to the biological changes characteristically found in clinical depression, an extensive psychiatric literature points toward psychophysiological alterations both in the etiology and the effects of depression (Depue 1979; Klerman 1981). That biological, psychological, *and* social process are interrelated in depression has become, at least for some clinical researchers and epidemiologists, an accepted truth (Akiskal and McKinney 1973; Whybrow, Akiskal, McKinney 1984), but it is not known how this relationship is organized and sustained. Nonetheless, the evidence is compelling that, in addition to biological change and psychological experience, social relations and meanings are implicated in the onset, process, and consequences of depressive illness. The crude Cartesian dichotomy between reactive (psychosocial) and endogenous (biological) depression, which persists despite the fact that psychiatrists are aware of its inadequacy, as well as that of mind/body dualism more generally, is scientifically untenable. So far no significant cross-cultural research on the psychological and social factors and their psychodynamic and sociosomatic correlates has been conducted; we simply do not know how they apply to Chinese depressives. What we do know about depression in the West, however, indicates what we need to learn to derive a more discriminating understanding of neurasthenia and depression in China.

HISTORICAL BACKGROUND OF DEPRESSION IN THE WEST

Beginning with Hippocrates, melancholia (depression) was viewed as organically based in an excess of black bile (Simon 1978:229),[5] a view that was passed down well into modern times by Galen's influential writings (Jackson 1969). While the humoral theory eventually gave way to chemical and mechanical causal attributions, the somatopsychic or physiological psychology orientation continued to dominate the medical literature and lay views (Jackson 1980). By the seventeenth and eighteenth centuries the long-held association of hypochondriasis (morbid fear that one is ill in the absence of pathological evidence of disease) with melancholia was beginning to break apart; Willis, followed by Sydenham, both eminent physicians of the period, categorized melancholia as an independent disorder. But medical men had clearly associated depression with the hypochondriacal amplification of physical complaints and continued to relate such somatic exaggeration to melancholy as an affect, if not melancholia as a disease. Hypochondriacal melancholy was attributed to problems involving the spleen and later to "pathological vapors." Current biological views of depression and somatic preoccupation are thus underpinned by a long Western medical tradition of viewing mental problems as organically based, a tradition that related both of these syndromes, and neurasthenia as well, to somatic pathology.

Fischer-Homberger (1983:46–48) notes that before Beard defined and popularized neurasthenia, hypochondriasis carried the more general meaning of somatic amplification, particularly of gastrointestinal complaints, which covered much of the meaning neurasthenia later assumed. After the 1880s hypochondriasis acquired a more narrow definition, so that it came to stand for only one kind of neurasthenia, nosophobia (fear of illness). Unlike neurasthenia, however, since the mid-eighteenth century hypochondriasis had been viewed as the effect of the imagination on the body. In the nineteenth century imagination became a pejorative term, and hypochondriasis—but not neurasthenia—was classified as a "maladie imaginaire." The relationship between neurasthenia, depression, and hypochondriasis remains central even now; indeed I argue that to understand any of these problems we must grasp how all three interrelate.

The West possesses an alternative explanation of depression, however, which also has a long history. Jackson (1978) shows that *acedia* was a Western religious concept that overlapped melancholia, and that the history of acedia and melancholia was closely linked to changes in Christianity and medicine. Each took on different meanings at different times and altered the meanings of the other. In medieval religious texts acedia came to signify an interior quality like sorrow, while in the popular idiom it continued to radiate earlier meanings of a moral nature (sloth). At one time acedia conveyed an internal state, at another time an external behavior. Eventually it lost its coherence as a distinct condition, while melancholia came to signify both the disease and the affect. Beginning in the sixteenth century, as Western society became more secular and less religious, acedia, like the other cardinal sins, gave way to the four temperaments and the humoral theory of behavior. Jackson shows that both acedia and melancholia mapped symptoms of great historical continuity, as well as changing styles of symptom perception, expression, and labeling. He demonstrates especially melancholia's changing association with distinctive explanatory idioms over time: somatic, psychological, religious, and moral. The historical antecedents of "depression" disclose divergent meanings, the remnants of which provide "depression" with its ambiguous symbolic significance in contemporary lay and professional usage: feeling state/disease, physical/psychological etiology, or moral/medical problem. (Neurasthenia shares this polysemy.) Jackson's historical account reveals that religious, illness and behavioral categories are rooted in the changing arrangements of the social structure. What has happened to categories and idioms is the outcome of the long-term transitions from ancient to medieval to modern epochs and the more rapid transformations of church, medical profession, and institutions of learning within each period. As in the discourse on acedia and melancholia, so in the discourse on depression the same error of entification (or misplaced concreteness) is reflected in the asocial, ahistorical professional tendency to reify names as things. But Jackson's analysis also indicates that behind the flux and flow of social reality some forms of human misery show a perduring somatic grain. This somatic quality constrains experience as much as the mutable categories that model it and the social arrangements that cause misery and shape the categories themselves. This dialectic is as central to neurasthenia as it is to depression.

Only in the West in very recent times, beginning in the Victorian period and accelerating after Freud, have psychological and psychosomatic views of these disorders become popular in both medical and lay circles. The recognition that biological, psychological, and social features of depression (and neurasthenia) need to be integrated in clinical research is just beginning to be widely shared. Among practicing psychiatrists around the world, appreciation of the contribution of social and cultural factors in depression is still poor. A large gap looms between what researchers know and what clinicians actually do.

DEPRESSION IN CHINESE CULTURE

Classical Chinese medicine early on recognized major psychotic disorders and hysteria and developed a unique, interactionist, psychosomatic perspective on disease and emotion generally. Sadness and grief were listed as two of the seven cardinal emotions in the earliest medical text, *Huangdi neijing, su wen* section (written more than two thousand years ago), and were therefore of at least theoretical interest to traditional practitioners. Yet Tseng (1974) contends it was late in the historical transformation of Chinese medicine, in the Ming Dynasty, that anything approaching the categorization of the phenomenon labeled by the Western clinical concept of depression seems to have been fully elaborated. And though there are earlier sources that mention depression, it never became as culturally important to Chinese medical commentators as it did to medical authors in the West.

In Ch'eng Chih-fan and Chang Ch'i-shan's (1962) review of ideas of mental illness in the Chinese medical classics, little if any mention is made of depression. Xu Youxin (1956), reaching to find some early historical precedents for the condition in the Chinese tradition, noted that *Treatise on the Causes and Symptoms of Disease,* written by Chao Yuanfang and others in early seventh century A.D., gives a recognizable description of depression. For example, there is a "prolonged crying syndrome" (*kujuhou*) in which the person's crying is said to be so intense and full of grief that the emotion affects the functioning of the internal organs. When *qi* (vital energy) becomes deficient, a pathological *qi* (*xieqi*) enters the abdomen and leads to a heavy, sinking feeling in the limbs. Thereafter the afflicted person cannot restrain his mournfulness and his grief (Juan 24). Xu takes this passage to indicate a clinical recognition of depression, its psychogenic source, and its clinical manifestation. It also would seem to exemplify a thoroughgoing psychosomatic and somatopsychic model of pathology.

But *Qing Yue's Medical Text* (1710), first published in the Ming Dynasty around 1624, is the earliest text we could find that technically defines depression as a detailed clinical category and elaborates it conceptually as an autonomous taxon. The author, Zhang Jiebin, affixed the term *yu* to this category, and today this term remains central to the designation of depression as a psychiatric disease. With considerable analytic sophistication Zhang Jiebin divided depression into three subtypes: (1) depression resulting from excessive anger *(nuyu)*, (2) depression resulting from excessive thinking *(siyu)*, (3) depression resulting from excessive worry *(youyu.)* The clinical signs and symptoms of the last sound much like those described for severe cases of depression in the West: a mournful or grieving mood (dysphoria), loss of interest (anhedonia), alarmed feelings (anxiety and agitation), loss of appetite, fatigue (loss of energy), lack of spirit or ambition, failure to respond to things that stimulated the person in the past. *Qing Yue's Medical Text* mentions the characteristic breathing changes in depressive disorder, and even describes what Beck (1971) has termed the negative cognitive schemata of self-inefficacy and perception of the world as frustrating: namely "whatever the depressed person thinks about comes to no avail to the point of a blockage of the spirit." The extraordinarily astute Chinese clinician also noted a characteristic feeling of "great or excessive hollowness as if one has absolutely no substance." Similar expressions are often heard from individuals in the acute throes of grief and mourning (Osterweis et al. 1984). Zhang Jiebin goes on to describe depression in the culturally particular terms of classical Chinese medical theory as first a blockage and later an overwhelming loss of *qi* (vital energy). But much of his account could be assimilable to classical descriptions of depression in the West.

Qing Yue's Medical Text cites an even earlier source for *yu* disorders, Ju Runxiang's *Dan ji xinfa zhiyao,* which was first published in the Yuan Dynasty (1271–1368 A.D.) and republished in 1484 in the Ming Dynasty. Ju, we are told, divides *yu* into no less than six etiological types: *qiyu* (depression in vital energy), *shiyu* (damp depression), *reyu* (heat depression), *tanyu* (phlegm depression), *xieyu* (blood depression), and *shiyu* (dietary depression). These categories indicate that even though *yu* appears to map a phenomenon roughly equivalent to depression, it parses the phenomenon differently, using a changing indigenous conceptual system. The traditional meaning of *yu* in China is distinct from depression in the West, and there is no way of knowing, in the absence of ethnographic data, whether its modern derivative carries this traditional signification.

In modern times the indigenous Chinese category, *yu,* has not been widely used, in either traditional Chinese medicine or the popular culture. The

Western category, depression, has also been infrequently applied by psychiatrists in China, who employ a largely medical approach to mental disorder, emphasizing disorders of brain more than psychogenic explanations.[6] Moreover, the actual practice of contemporary Chinese medicine, which has assimilated aspects of biomedicine, emphasizes organically oriented, reductionistic somatopsychic models over earlier, holistic psychosomatic approaches. Hence the psychological and social aspects of disease, including depression and neurasthenia, are not highlighted in China's medical system. Chinese cultural idioms of distress and popular symptom terms tend to emphasize physical, not emotional complaints (Kleinmen 1980:119–78). For example, a common metaphor for depression, *men,* used by physicians and patients in Taiwan and China, conveys the idea of something physically "depressing" into the chest. These points are treated at greater length in chapters 3 and 7, where I discuss some of the cultural barriers to the use of the term depression in Chinese society and offer an explanation of why neurasthenia is preferred.

DEPRESSION CROSS-CULTURALLY

Cross-cultural research provides substantial evidence both for a core depressive syndrome that psychiatrists throughout the world diagnose and agree on and for major cultural variations in depressive mood, symptoms and illness experience.[7] Using the World Health Organization's ICD-9 diagnostic criteria, Sartorius and his collaborators (1983) have shown that core symptoms are present among depressed patients in societies as different as Japan, Iran, Canada, and Switzerland. Where earlier investigators, who possessed neither linguistic nor cultural competence, claimed that depression was rare in Africa, more recent research has disclosed the high prevalence of the core depressive symptoms among African patients (cf., Orley and Wing 1979; see also the special issue of *Psychopathologie Africaine* devoted to depression.) Moreover, the widespread use of antidepressant drugs worldwide has convinced mental health professionals that response to treatment is fairly similar, despite some biological differences in the metabolism of antidepressants among different racial populations (Lin 1983).

Anthropologists, however, have provided data demonstrating significant cultural variations. "Dysphoria"—sadness, hopelessness, unhappiness, lack of pleasure with the things of the world and with social relationships—has dramatically different meaning and form of expression in different societies. For Buddhists pleasurable things of this world and valued social relationships

are the basis of all suffering; renunciation and the deliberate choice of dysphoria are the first steps on the road to transcendence of suffering and sal-
vation (Obeyesekere, 1985). For Shi'ite Muslims in Iran, grief is a religious
experience, the tragic consequences of living justly in an unjust world; the
ability to experience dysphoria fully is viewed as a marker of depth of person
and sensitivity (Good, Good, and Moradi, 1985). Some societies, such as
the Kaluli of New Guinea, value full and dramatic expression of sadness
and grieving (Schieffelin 1979); Balinese, by contrast, "smooth out" emotional
highs and lows to preserve pure, refined, and smooth interior self (Geertz
1983). Members of such societies vary in how they express dysphoric emotion; they also seem to experience forms of emotion that are not part of the
repertoire of individuals in other societies. Because the cultural worlds in
which people live are so dramatically different, translation of terms for emotion involves much more than the identification of semantic equivalents. Describing how it feels to grieve or be melancholy in another society leads
straightway into analysis of different ways of being a person in radically
different worlds (cf. Lutz, 1985).

The available anthropological evidence discloses differences in the experience of depression as mood and in the illness experience and symptomatology of depressive disorder as well. For members of many African societies, the first signs of illness are dreams in which a witch may be attacking
one's vital essence. For members of many American Indian groups, hearing
voices of relatives who have died is considered normal, not a sign of sickness
as it is among Caucasian Americans (Manson et al., 1985). For members of
other societies, hallucinating or dreaming of spirits may indicate a member
of the spirit world is seeking a victim or demanding to establish a relationship
with one who will become a follower and perhaps a healer. Perception and
communication of bodily complaints associated with depressive illness dramatically differ cross culturally, indicating forms of experience not available
to members of our own society. Nigerians complain that "ants keep creeping
in parts of my brain" (Ebigbo 1982), while Japanese complain of exhaustion
of their nerves, use naturalistic metaphors of gloomy weather, and fear that
some aspect of their personal presentation—blushing, unpleasant body odor,
stuttering—will appear reprehensible to those with whom they come in contact (Kasahara 1976; Reynolds 1976). In most societies depressive disorder
is not associated with the profound guilt and intense feelings of sinfulness
that often are central to its illness experience in the Judaeo-Christian West.
We do not have research studies that examine if the course of depression
is different in different societies; since there is considerable evidence that

outcome in less-developed societies is better for schizophrenia, a disorder that carries a much better documented genetic loading and brain pathology, this question deserves cross-cultural comparison among depressive patients.

We do know, however, that the concept of depression differs enormously across cultures. In some societies neither a category nor lexical terms exist for anything bearing a family resemblance to depression (Kleinman and Good, 1985; Leff 1982). In other societies depressive affect and disorder are categorized along a continuum, in yet others as the same thing or as qualitatively different states. Psychologists, psychiatrists and anthropologists also disagree on these points. Thus, cultural differences in construing depression are matched by differences among disciplines and theoretical schools. Among two small-scale preliterate societies—Ifaluk and Ilongot—Lutz (1985) and Rosaldo (1980) show that depressive emotion is not conceptually divided from thought the way it is in the West. Diagnostic criteria of depression in Western psychology imbed cultural values that often are not shared by non-Western societies. Lutz (in press) avers that "joylessness" (anhedonia) in the American Psychiatric Association's diagnostic system is predicated on the core American cultural belief in the right to the pursuit of happiness. Lack of joy is not a chief concern of depressed individuals in many non-Western societies. Provocatively, Lutz suggests we had best regard psychology as a particular ethnotheory inseparable from the cultural categories and value orientations of Western society. Her point is that psychology is implicitly ethnocentric and psychocentric. The cross-cultural differences become even more striking when cultures are compared for their views of the causes of depression and its appropriate treatment.

The chief methodological problems that cross-cultural researchers studying depression and neurasthenia face concern the translation of diagnostic criteria into epidemiological and clinical research instruments that are valid and reliable in cultures whose illness categories and linguistic and other symbolic idioms of illness expression differ markedly from those in the West (Marsella et al., 1985). An example is the work of Orley and Wing (1979), who have conducted one of the more rigorous attempts at the cultural translation of meaning, not just the wording of questions on psychometric questionnaires. These investigators asked Ugandans in the Luganda language, "Do you sometimes blame yourself for something that was a mistake?" They considered a positive answer among patients, as in London, to be evidence of "pathological guilt." Would not pathological guilt in this African society, however, be more likely to be expressed as self-accusation of witchcraft? The ethnographic data for African societies suggest that this would be a more culturally valid means of eliciting the relevant information. This is but a single illustration of a prodigious problem in the translation of meaning cross-culturally.

The failure to adequately assess cultural differences in cross-cultural research commits a *category fallacy:* namely, the ethnocentric imposition of one culture's diagnostic system and the tacit beliefs and values it contains on the illness experiences in another culture, whose indigenous diagnostic categories and the tacit beliefs and values they express may be radically divergent (Kleinman 1977). This fallacy has beset many of the cross-cultural research studies on depression. A purposefully absurd illustration will help explain why.

Obeyesekere (1985) writes that if a researcher who came from South Asia, where popular culture and traditional medical systems maintain a category of a semen loss syndrome, were to set out to conduct a scientific study of the prevalence of this syndrome worldwide, he would doubtless find cases with semen loss symptoms (for example, drastic weight loss, weakness, sexual fantasies, hypochondriasis, night emission, urine discoloration) in most societies. He could develop refined diagnostic criteria with inclusion and exclusion operationalized, draw up a relevant research instrument translated into the world's major languages, back translate it for semantic equivalence, validate it for differential distribution among normal and psychiatric patient populations, and derive prevalence rates for various societies. What would he have accomplished? If he claims this to be a universal psychiatric disorder, affecting patients in societies in which there is no coherent illness category of semen loss, then it is an impressive illustration of the category fallacy. But are these methods significantly different from those employed by psychiatric studies conducted by Western investigators or indigenous researchers using Western categories in non-Western societies? A large number of them, regrettably, are of this type. Those that are not have struggled in various ways to negotiate between "local meaning" (Geertz 1983) and scientific categories.

By using different kinds of research approaches, researchers have successfully overcome this problem of cultural bias in the study of depressive disorder cross-culturally. For example, to establish semantic equivalence the studies in China described in chapters 4 and 5 not only translate questionnaires from English into a local language, but back translate them into English from the local language by different teams of mental health professionals linguistically competent in both languages and expert in psychological assessment in the local language. Various techniques have then been used by researchers to establish the reliability of questionnaires and their replicable use by different investigators. This is accomplished by comparing their diagnoses to those of indigenous clinicians for unambiguous, mutually agreed on cases of depression, through comparison of the diagnoses derived from different investigators using the same questionnaire with the same cases, and through comparison of evaluations of the same patients using different research instruments, including those for which reliability in the local culture has already been established.

Other techniques include development of indigenous questionaires based on native illness categories (say, Chinese diagnostic criteria for neurasthenia or depression) and their comparison with translated Western psychiatric interview schedules for which validity and reliability have been established (Manson et al. 1985); triangulation between questionnaires, clinical interviews by indigenous clinicians, and ethnographic description that collects detailed case histories and conducts discourse analysis of the talk of illness in the local culture to determine how such cases are evaluated in terms of local categories (Good, Good, and Moradi 1985); and epidemiological surveys that compare symptom clusters (for example, neurasthenic weakness, fatigue, headaches) derived from factor analysis of complaints elicited from local populations with those from established cross-national samples (Good, Good, and Moradi 1985; Beiser, 1985). Using the latter two techniques, Good, Good, and Moradi (1985) impressively demonstrated both a unique Iranian cluster of depressive symptoms and the presence of the core depressive syndrome in a sample of recent Iranian immigrants to the United States. The findings from these and other studies now offer overwhelming evidence of universal *and* culture-specific aspects of depressive disorder. Hence the depressive disorder category does appear to map an authentic phenomenon of human distress found cross-culturally, but one for which beliefs, norms, and experiences differ. The situation of neurasthenia is much more uncertain, only in part because it has attracted a great deal less research interest. There is little cross-culture agreement on definitions, diagnostic criteria, or standard instruments for assessing neurasthenia.

Even when we limit our concern to depression as emotion, not disease, the cross-cultural differences are balanced by surprising cross-cultural similarities. Ekman (1980:87–88), for example, writes

> emotion refers to the process whereby an elicitor is appraised automatically or in a ponderous fashion, an affect program may or may not be set off, organized responses may occur, albeit more or less managed by attempts to control emotional behavior. What gives an emotion its particular flavor, is the

particulars of the elicitor, the appraisal, the part of the affect program set off, and those parts of the response systems which go unmanaged or managed.

For Ekman the structure of this process is an interaction of cultural and physiological events, neither alone being sufficient to produce what we think of as the emotion of being depressed (cf. Averill 1980).

From a developmental perspective, Shweder (1985), an anthropologist with training in both child and cognitive psychology, shows us that young children can express specific emotions even before they acquire language, but that these are not necessarily the same as what adults feel. There are both culture-specific and universal elicitors of emotion, but Shweder asserts there are fewer universal elicitors for adults than for children. He argues that cross-culturally children experience loss as distress and frustration as anger, and that they interpret such universal experiences with respect to ideas of "natural law" and sacred obligations, the transgression of which are universally felt on a continuum of shame-guilt-terror. The view that though emotions have meanings that influence how we feel, affective meanings may be universal—for example, there is a seemingly universally understood emotional language of facial expression, voice register, and body posture that is understood even by three-year-olds—is upheld by the cross-cultural literature. For Shweder the development of emotions and cognition is not as many have held them to be, from undifferentiated states to differentiated ones, but the other way around. The young child, he contends, does not lack "complex differentiated mental structures but the knowledge and representational skills needed for talking about and making deliberate use of the complex structures available to him." Culture, in Shweder's model, provides the knowledge and representational skills, and thereby applies universal and culture-specific meanings to the constitution and expression of experience. Like Osgood, he regards emptiness as having universal implications and connotation (cf. Osgood et al. 1975). This and other universal meanings of emotions Shweder conceives to be articulated in all societies in three ways: via a language of causal responsibility, a language of concomitant mood metaphor, and a language of physical consequences. The most common cross-cultural understanding of emptiness, Shweder provocatively asserts, is not sadness but "soul loss," which has perceptual, legal, and moral significances that vary but for which there is a universal substrate. Ordinary language utterances tell one how to feel soul loss; regulations and rules for social roles carry with them obligation to feel soul loss in certain situations and manage the emotional experience of emptiness. Soul loss, then, is an appropriate basis for a cross-cultural phenomenology of the emptiness and other feeling states associated with depression.

To illustrate the value of a semantic approach to emotion, Shweder presents a phenomenology of depression, echoing Sartre's (1948) phenomenology of emotions, as soul loss. He suggests that where soul loss is still a leading component of the local cultural code (and it is in much of the non-Western world), this is how depressive affect is constituted and expressed. Virtually all the phenomenological details of emptiness and the loss of soul, even where this shared public idiom is unavailable, are central to the actual experience of depressed emotion (see Kleinman 1980:119–178 for examples from Taiwan.) The differentiated "emotional keyboard," possessed by four-year-olds worldwide, that enables this common dirge to be played is the basis for this universal signification. Because of the effect of culture-specific meanings and complex social relationships on this panhuman keyboard of emotions, in adulthood the emotional scores that get played diverge considerably: here loss is expressed as depressive mood, there as neurasthenic fatigue. This is his model for what happens with depressive affect as it is transformed from a psychobiological universal to a culturally shaped emotion (neurasthenic exhaustion, existential despair, or possession state).

Shweder's phenomenology of the *lost soul* upsets the conventional wisdom of ethnographers and experimentalists alike and should offer clinicians wedded to "atheoretical" descriptive psychiatry a looking glass whose images challenge the fundamental assumptions of the universal phenomenology of depression as *sadness*. To be adequate, phenomenology must begin not with professional categories but with panhuman (read, cross-cultural) lay experience.[8] When more than three-fourths of the world's population live in non-Western cultures, and greater than ninety percent are unfamiliar with psychoanalytic and other clinical constructs, symptom phenomenologies—if they are to be valid—must begin with central meanings and experiences that may seem alien to educated, middle-class, white North Americans and Europeans. These phenomenologies have been normative for most of human history, including the West, and spring from a shared human nature and condition. Admittedly soul loss may not be the best way to integrate the divergent experiences of depression among Western and non-Western groups, but it does illustrate the biases in Western existential understanding of the phenomenology of depression and offers the possibility that a more adequate cross-cultural phenomenology can be developed based on available research.

Cross-cultural studies disclose, therefore, that depression (both as emotion and disease) should be understood as the product of an *interaction* between biological processes, psychosocial situations, and cultural versions of the world from which both the *shared* and the *peculiar* dimensions of the depressive experience emerge.[9] This is a framework that also can be employed to recast questions about neurasthenia. Is neurasthenia best configured as a disease, an emotional state, or a behavior? What are its universal and culture-specific aspects? But more problematically, we are left with a large question: If depression is so common in the West, and neurasthenia in China, and if what was once called neurasthenia in the West is now called depression (as well as anxiety and other things), could neurasthenia be depression? Or are neurasthenia and depression distinctive idioms of some third phenomenon?

Three
★
Somatization

So long as pain experience is intensely personal, it is necessarily shaped, as
it were, by the forms of life of those who . . . articulate it.

Tu Weiming (1982:64)

Experience has taught, however, that between physiological and
psychological phenomena no absolute contrast exists, but a mutual
(dialectic) relation which is constituted in the course of personal existence.

Buytendijk (1974:74)

SOMATIZATION CROSS-CULTURALLY

The third term that mediates the relationship of neurasthenia and depression
can now be introduced. Before we draw on it to edify our discussion of
neurasthenia and depression in China, we first must come to understand
what it is, what its sources are, how salient the problems it poses cross-
culturally for health care systems are, and how it relates to Chinese and
American societies.

In many non-Western societies *somatization* (the presentation of personal
and interpersonal distress in an idiom of physical complaints together with
a coping pattern of medical help-seeking) has been shown to be the predominant expression of difficulties in living.[1] That is to say, individuals experience serious personal and social problems but interpret and articulate
them, and indeed come to experience and respond to them, through the
medium of the body. Loss, injustice, failure, conflict—all are transformed
into discourse about pain and disability that is a metaphor for discourse and
action about the self and the social world. The body mediates the individual's
perception, experience, and interpretation of problems in social life. Mental
disorder is a prime instance.

High rates of somatization in depressive disorder, for example, have been found in studies of psychiatric clinic patients in Saudi Arabia (Racy 1980), Iraq (Bazzoui 1970), West Africa (Binitie 1975), India (Teja et al. 1971; Sethi et al. 1973), the Sudan and the Philippines (Climent et al. 1980), Taiwan (Kleinman 1977, 1980), Hong Kong (Cheung et al. 1981), and in other non-Western societies. Matched comparisons of Peruvian and North American depressed patients and East Africans and Londoners show higher rates of somatization among Peruvians and East Africans, respectively (Mezzich and Raab 1950; Orley and Wing 1979). Marsella's review (1979) of the cross-cultural literature finds the somatic expression of depression to have higher prevalence generally in clinical samples in non-Western societies. Styles of somatic complaints unique to a particular culture have been demonstrated by Ebigbo (1982) for Nigerians, Good (1977) for the Turkish population in Iran, Finkler (1985) for rural Mexican women, El-Islam (1975) for Qatari patients, and Wen and Wang (1981) for Taiwanese.

A WHO survey disclosed that of a sample of 1165 adult patients in primary health care facilities in India, Sudan, and the Philippines, at each center 11 to 18 percent of cases had psychiatric disorders. Fewer than one-third of these were recognized by health workers and appropriately treated. Most complained of physical symptoms: headaches, other pain, weakness, dizziness (Climent et al. 1980). These authors, like those cited above, emphasize the importance of early diagnosis and specific treatment of depression and other forms of psychopathology to prevent chronic illness behavior and its accompanying overutilization of health facilities, polypharmacy, addiction to narcotic drugs, costly and unneeded biological tests and surgery, and iatrogenesis. Other WHO surveys show that the problems labeled somatization are more common than serious infectious disease in primary care clinics in the Third World.

The research literature indicates that depression and most other mental illnesses, especially in non-Western societies and among rural, ethnic, and lower-class groups in the West, are associated preponderantly with physical complaints. Thus a recent clinical report listed the chief complaints of depressed North American patients in decreasing order of frequency as impaired concentration, weakness, agitation, daytime drowsiness, headaches, excessive perspiration, dizziness, dry mouth, rapid breathing, blurred vision, constipation, tinnitus, dry skin, delayed ejaculation, flushing, slurred speech, premature ejaculation, chest pain, excessive salivation, weight gain, amenorrhea, impotence, and so forth (Mathew et al. 1981). The reader will note that many of these complaints, as well as those reported by Climent et al. and other authors already cited, appear in Beard's original list of the neurasthenia symptoms among his New York patients in the late nineteenth century.

SOMATIZATION AMONG CHINESE

Cheung and her collaborators in Hong Kong (1981) studied the symptoms that depressed Chinese patients presented to a general medical clinic. These patients acknowledged the following complaints on a symptom checklist: feelings of sadness/downheartedness (82%), agitation and restlessness (80%), irritability (74%), tension and nervousness (86%), inertia or retardation in thoughts and actions (70%), guilt or an inclination to self-reproach (61%), suspiciousness of others (37%), suicidal ideation (17%), insomnia (65%), early morning waking (62%), loss of interest in social (68%) and sexual (43%) activities, anorexia (53%). But the three symptoms they checked most frequently were feelings of tiredness and fatigability (90%), pains and aches (89%), and gastrointestinal/cardiovascular symptoms (87%). The chief presenting somatic complaints in decreasing order of prevalence were sleep disturbance (31%), tiredness/malaise (29%), headache (20%), dizziness (20%), menopausal complaints (20% of women), abdominal pain (14%), anorexia (14%), weakness (13%), palpitation (13%), fearfulness (11%), epigastric pain (10%). The main source of symptoms was the central nervous system; after that patients complained of gastrointestinal, gynecological, cardiovascular, respiratory, and urinary problems in decreasing order.

Not all depressed Hong Kong patients were aware of their depressed mood; few complained primarily of their emotional distress. Their wide range of symptoms was similar to those experienced by nondepressed patients with medical disorders in the clinic. But the depressed patients were more likely to communicate vague and diffuse somatic difficulties in a pattern the authors interpreted as a "somatic facade (that) concealed the depressive-ridden state of mood." When directly questioned about their mood, however, most of the depressed patients admitted to feelings of sadness. They also expressed anxiety complaints. Cheung and her colleagues suggested different psychological causes of somatization as a manifestation of depression. Depressed Chinese patients, they conclude, simply may not experience sadness as a salient symptom. Even if aware of dysphoria, they may suppress and disguise their depressed feeling owing to fear of the powerful social stigma attributed to mental illness in Chinese culture. Or somatization may reflect difficulties in verbalizing inward feelings. "For most working class Chinese who are used to more concrete modes of expression, conceptualization at the psychic level may seem too abstract." (This notion is close to the psychoanalytic concept of alexithymia, a clinical theory that certain somatizing patients are unable to express emotions or fantasies verbally.) Because many of their patients recognized and admitted psychological symptoms of depression when directly asked, the Hong Kong authors explain somatization among this group of Chinese depressives as a cognitive style of communicating inward feelings in outward somatic terms. For them it is not usually the result of unconscious denial, nor did it reflect differences in gender. Elsewhere Cheung and her co-worker Lao (1982) also disclose that situational factors strongly influence whether somatization occurs. Students in Hong Kong are less likely to express distress in a somatic idiom when they are with close friends and more likely to do so when in a clinic where this idiom is expected.

Headaches, dizziness, and insomnia, which figure prominently in the diagnosis of neurasthenia among Chinese, and which are on Beard's list of the core neurasthenic complaints, were described as early as the Han Dynasty in China as leading symptoms of mental disorder (Ch'eng and Chang 1962) and are especially salient complaints in contemporary Chinese culture. As was pointed out in the previous chapter, these symptoms were specifically associated with depression in a Qing Dynasty medical text (Zhang Jiebin 1710). Weakness and loss of energy (exhaustion), which are usually thought of as the essence of neurasthenia, are key symptoms in traditional Chinese medicine where they relate to lack or blockage in the flow of *qi* (vital energy) and imbalance between *yin* and *yang*. Xu Youxin and Zhong Youbin's (1983) diagnostic criteria for neuroses in China give a prominent place to somatic symptoms for each of the neuroses he describes; and other authors from the People's Republic attest to the prominent place of somatic complaints among a wide range of Chinese psychiatric patients (see relevant chapters in Lin and Eisenberg 1986; Zheng and Young n.d.).

In an earlier volume, I set out a cultural explanation for somatization among Chinese on Taiwan based on my research there (Kleinman 1980:133–75). I pointed out that culturally shaped psychological processes lead Chinese to suppress distressing emotions. These processes include valuing the harmony of social relations over the expression of potentially disruptive and ego-centered intrapsychic experience; a situation orientation that emphasizes state appropriate emotional expressions over trait appropriate ones; cognitive coping mechanisms that systematically employ externalizing idioms of distress over internalizing ones; strongly negative valuation of the open verbal expression of personal distress outside close family relations, which is viewed as embarrassing and shameful; the use of a rich cultural code of bodily metaphors of psychosocial problems; and a desire to avoid the strong stigma that attaches to families with members labeled emotionally ill. Moreover, help-seeking in Chinese society is legitimized for bodily complaints, but not for psychological complaints. Physical complaints have social cachet, psychological complaints do not. Traditional Chinese medicine associated health with emotional balance, and illness with emotional excess and incontinence. Emotion in traditional Chinese literature is portrayed subtly and indirectly via body movement, dress, environmental description, allusive language, and not by direct verbal expression, which is regarded as insensitive and uncouth. These and other traditional cultural concepts and norms, I reasoned, overdetermine a somatic idiom for the expression of personal and social distress among Chinese.

SOMATIZATION IN THE WEST

What tends to get lost in discussions of such studies, however, is, first, that somatization is also very common in the West, and second, that somatization is not limited to depression and other psychiatric disorders. Indeed, it may not always represent pathology or even maladaptation. While population-based studies to support the last point are lacking, many research reports substantiate the other two. These studies show that cases of somatization account for between one-third and three-fourths of patient visits to primary care physicians in the United States and the United Kingdom (Collyer 1979; Regier et al. 1978; Hankin and Oktay 1979; Goldberg 1979; Hoeper et al. 1979; Widmer et al. 1980; Katon et al. 1982, 1984). In the West somatization correlates with lower socioeconomic and educational levels, rural origins, active religious affiliation, traditional value orientation, and behavioral ethnicity—that is, where ethnic background really influences diet, habits, friendship patterns, and activities of daily living (Katon et al. 1982; Harwood 1981).

Prior to the emergence of an increasingly psychological idiom of distress among the Victorian middle class, somatization appears to have been even more prevalent in the West. This psychologizing process, which has gained momentum since the First World War, seems related to cultural transformation, in which the self has been culturally constituted as the now dominant Western ethnopsychology (cf. Romanyshyn 1982; Lasch 1979; McIntyre 1980; Gehlen 1980:75). It is quite possible this psychological idiom, one of Western culture's most powerful self-images, is the personal concomitant of the societal process of *rationalization* that Max Weber saw as modernism's leading

edge, "the process by which explicit, abstract, intellectually calculable rules
and procedures are increasingly substituted for sentiment, tradition and rule
of thumb in all spheres of human activity" (Wrong 1976:247). From the We-
berian perspective, the conception and experience of "affect" among the
middle class in the contemporary West is culturally shaped as "deep" psychological experience and rationalized into discretely labeled emotions
(depression, anxiety, anger) that were previously categorized and felt principally as bodily experiences. As bodily experience, "feeling" was expressed
and interpreted more subtly, indirectly, globally, superficially, and above all
somatically.

Inasmuch as bodily experiences are understood through the social categories that establish them as "natural" symbols (Douglas 1973; Helman 1984,
1985; Turner 1984), both psychologization and somatization can be conceived
as cultural constructions of psychobiological processes. Psychologization is
the result of the Western mode of modernization that now influences the
elites of non-Western societies; somatization is the product of more traditional
cultural orientations worldwide, including that of the more rural, the poorer,
and the less-educated in the West. Counter to the established views of Western mental health professionals, from the cross-cultural perspective it is not
somatization in China (and the West) but psychologization in the West that
is unusual and requires explanation. Furthermore, it is important to remember
other cultural idioms of distress of which these two are part, including cos-
mological (divine retribution), moral (sin, evil), interpersonal (envy, greed,
revenge, other kinship problems), and political (governmental oppression)
idioms that also serve to communicate demoralization and other types of
distress in culturally salient and socially approved terms.

In recent years political scientists, economists, and other social scientists
interested in the disability system in North America have noted that somatization accounts for a large share of disability payments and missed
workdays, and is also frequently an emblem of worker dissatisfaction, demoralization, and alienation (Stone 1979a, 1979b; Yelin et al. 1980; Figlio
1982; Alexander 1982). Disturbed family processes and problems in the medical care system itself have been found to help maintain and intensify chronic
illness behavior in medical as well as psychiatric disorder (Alexander 1982;
Helman 1985; Lock 1982; Plough 1981; Stewart and Sullivan 1982). Chronic
pain syndrome, one of the major causes of disability in the United States,
has been shown to be encouraged and maintained by marital, family, work
and health care relationships (Turner and Chapman 1982; Sternback 1974;
Fordyce 1976; Keefe 1982, Keefe et al. 1982; Roberts and Reinhardt 1950).

For Stone (1979a, 1979b) chronic illness behavior has become a key to the American system of distributive politics: the illness test has replaced the means test as a way to control access to social welfare resources; while for Yelin and co-workers (1980) conditions in the workplace are a better predictor of return to work than biomedical tests and measurements for patients with chronic disability.

Paradoxically, the biomedical health care system has become a dangerous place for chronic pain and other somatization patients. It encourages addiction to narcotic and analgesic drugs, polypharmacy with drugs that can have serious side effects, overuse of expensive and risky tests, and unnecessary surgery. The system thereby creates anger and frustration for patients, families, and physicians (Katon et al. 1982; Rosen et al. 1982; Turner and Chapman 1982). To reduce the prevalence of somatization and its negative consequences, its psychological and social sources must be addressed along with its biological bases. Health professionals are trained professionally to somatize inasmuch as they are taught to reinterpret (medicalize) personal and social "troubles" as medical problems (cf., Pilowsky 1969; DeVries et al. 1983). To understand and successfully prevent the negative effects of somatization, a dialectical model of its origins is crucial. Nowhere are the inadequacies and distortions of the reductionistic biomedical model more apparent and dangerous.

Chronic somatization is a major source of disability—the failure to perform normative social-role activities because of functional limitation (for example, weakness, fatigue, limited movement, pain). In the United States in 1970 all expenditures on disability came to more than 25 billion dollars; disability expenditure as a percentage of personal income was 3 percent (compared to 9.3 percent for all government social insurance and public assistance payments); and programs for physical invalidity per se cost 2.8 billion dollars. By 1977 all expenditure on disability had soared to 63.5 billion dollars (an increase of 150 percent); disability expenditure as percentage of personal income grew to 4.2 percent (5.6 percent in 1980); all government social insurance and public assistance payments had increased to almost 13 percent of personal income; and the cost of the invalidity programs had reached 11.5 billion dollars (an increase of 400 percent)! (Berkowitz 1981, personal letter; Congressional Budget Office 1982).

In 1976, the U.S. National Health Interview Survey found that 7.3 percent of the noninstitutionalized American population was seriously limited in work, housekeeping, or attending school, and an impressive 14.3 percent were disabled if recreational, social, and civic activities are included. In 1969, 9.3

percent of the American work force aged 16–64 were disabled for work for
six months or more, and the figure is believed to be significantly higher today.
It is estimated that at present 12 percent of the population is limited in living
activities, including 5.3 percent who require assistance in basic activities of
daily living. (Albrecht and Levy 1984:45–106). Chronic illnesses are the major
sources of disability worldwide, but chronic pain syndromes, psychosocial
concomitants of physical disease, and mental illnesses, either occurring together with or independently of medical disorders—in other words, the key
causes of somatization—create much of the burden of disability. From the
figures cited, disability in turn can be seen to be a great financial and social
burden in the United States. Figures on disability are not available for the
People's Republic of China, but leading members of China's biomedical system routinely report in private that work disability is perhaps an even greater
problem in socialist countries than in capitalist ones, and that China faces
a serious problem with work disability. Somatization and its social sequelae
are thus a significant problem in both Western and non-Western societies.

THE CAUSES OF SOMATIZATION

Depression relates to somatization in several ways. It produces somatic
symptoms as a psychophysiological component of the core depressive disorder (Katon et al. 1982). It can be a consequence of medical disorders,
especially severe medical illnesses such as renal failure, cancer, and heart
disease, when patients become hopeless and give up. Patients with Cushing's
syndrome, diabetes, or thyroid disease often suffer depression, which is a
common secondary psychophysiological manifestation of these disease states.
In fact Cushing's syndrome (a pituitary-adrenal abnormality that increases
the secretion of cortisol) has been shown to produce many of the symptoms
of the major depressive disorder (Starkman et al. 1981). A significant (though
not as substantial as originally claimed) number of depressed patients have
endocrine abnormalities, most commonly failure to suppress on the dexa-
methasone suppression test of hypothalamic-pituitary-adrenal axis function
(Carroll et al. 1981) and to a lesser extent a blunted response to the thyro-
tropin-releasing hormone stimulation test of hypothalamic-pituitary-thyroid
axis regulation (Targum et al. 1982). There is also convincing evidence of
autonomic nervous system and limbic system abnormalities (Depue 1979;
Kupfer and Foster 1972; Whybrow, Akiskal, McKinney 1984). More recently,
grief and depression have been shown experimentally and clinically to seriously interfere with immunological responses (Osterweis et al. 1984:145–

78). Hence depression provides the physiological substrate for the amplification of somatic symptoms.

Somatization has been defined (cf. Katon et al. 1982; Kleinman 1982; Rosen et al. 1982) as both the expression of physical complaints in the absence of defined organic pathology (for example, conversion symptoms and hypochondriasis) and the amplification of symptoms resulting from established physical pathology (for example, chronic disease). The amplification of existing symptoms usually occurs as subjective reports of disability (both symptoms and social impairment) that strike medical observers as excessive and unexplained by the existing pathology. Other psychiatric disorders are also associated with somatization, including anxiety disorders, hysteria, schizophrenia, chronic personality problems, and factitious illness. Social scientists have reported somatization in the absence of mental illness as a process of communicating and coping with social and personal distress (Good 1977; Katon et al. 1982; Kleinman 1980). Mechanic (1980) has conducted one of the only longitudinal studies of somatization. His findings indicate that "developmental experiences are particularly relevant in directing attention to inner experience and in forming an inclination to monitor the body."

> The extent to which this actually occurs in later life depends on the occurrence of illness, adverse life experiences that result in psychophysiological changes, and personal stresses that reinforce a tendency toward self-attention and evaluation. . . . Although the relationship between attention on internal states and reports of discomfort may be more substantial in the case of psychological symptomology . . . psychological and physical symptoms are not clearly distinguished and tend to occur concomitantly. Thus psychological distress may produce bodily discomfort, increase body monitoring and make persons more sensitive to changes. (Mechanic 1980:154)

Mechanic (1984) presents evidence that *introspectiveness* is a multi-determined sociopsychological process that encourages somatization in certain circumstances, and combined somatic and psychological complaining in others (Mechanic 1983, 1984). This line of empirical research conflicts with established psychoanalytic speculation, which has traditionally held that somatizing patients lack introspection (defined by psychoanalysts as psychological mindedness). Mechanic's important contribution is to demonstrate that what he calls introspectiveness involves monitoring of both bodily and psychological experiences, as well as amplification of somatic *and* cognitive-affective complaints. Mechanic's data support an integrative, nondualistic framework of emotions as embodied experience that encourages a more sophisticated, dialectic model of somatization.

Parker (1981) compared field dependence (a cognitive style) and the differentiation of affective states. Field dependence, which did not affect the overall level of symptom intensity, did influence individuals' differentiation of neurotic symptoms and their association with particular emotions. Subjects shown to be field-independent discriminate symptoms associated with particular emotions to a greater degree, especially cognitive and somatic ones. Field-dependent subjects, in contrast, experience global and diffuse disturbance rather than discretely distinguishable patterns of cognitive or somatic experiences. The field-dependence cognitive style is more common among women than men, among members of lower social classes, and among individuals in traditional non-Western societies. Although it is uncertain what this measure of perceptual style signifies, it does lend experimental support to the gaining contention that culturally and socially organized cognitive styles may significantly determine which symptoms are perceived and elaborated.[2]

The research on cognitive style has resulted in at least four hypotheses to explain somatization. In addition to the well-known thesis that somatization is caused by suppression of the affective component of psychophysiological arousal, a second hypothesis is that somatization results from the amplification of normal sensations. Yet another hypothesis holds that somatization occurs because the somatic symptoms of affective arousal are misattributed and labeled as illness. A final proposition holds that somatization results when introspective, cognitive coping processes centered on the body are used to handle stress, and thereby create a final common cognitive-behavioral pathway along which is channelled attempts to cope with dysphoria or disease (cf. Barsky & Klerman 1983; Cheung and Lau 1982; Katon et al. 1982; Kleinman 1982, 1984; Mechanic 1980; Pennebaker and Skelton 1978).[3] Social situation and cultural learning, researchers repeatedly reaffirm, can influence these cognitive processes such that perception, attribution, labeling, coping, and communication styles will support a somatizing mode of behavior. It is important to emphasize that in the perspective of behavioral science, unlike that of psychiatry, somatization need not result from or represent psychopathology. Instead it is seen as a particular cognitive-behavioral type whose adaptive or maladaptive consequences involve assessment of social, cultural, and personal variables. Only population-based community surveys and ethnographies will determine whether somatization is less often associated with pathology than clinical studies disclose, or whether somatization at times even has certain adaptive effects.

CLINICAL CATEGORIZATION OF SOMATIZATION

To specify more precisely the relationship between sociocultural and psychobiological interconnections in somatization, it is useful to have a categorization of different types of somatization. One such categorization is organized in terms of its course: acute, subacute, and chronic (Rosen et al. 1982). Acute somatization lasts days or weeks, and most frequently develops out of acute stress syndromes. General autonomic nervous system arousal, including activation of neuroendocrine system, gives rise to combined psychophysiological symptoms. Somatization in this case can be said to occur when the affected person (abetted by the family and health professionals) systematically focuses on and thereby amplifies the physiological symptoms (pain, weakness, rapid heart rate, hyperventilation, gastrointestinal complaints, and so forth), while at the same time he minimizes and thereby dampens their affective and cognitive concomitants. As a result a psychophysiological reaction becomes defined and is experienced chiefly as a physical problem; help is sought for treatment of what patient, family, and health professionals consider to be a medical sickness. Subacute somatization lasts several months. It originates in a more prolonged stress response or an actual psychiatric disorder; most commonly depression and/or anxiety disorders.

Chronic somatization, lasting many months to years, may result from physical complaints accompanying chronic psychiatric disorder (for example, chronic depression or anxiety, hysteria, personality disorder, schizophrenia, or chronic factitious illness), or from amplification of symptoms and disability in the course of chronic medical disorder (for example, heart disease, asthma, arthritis, diabetes, or epilepsy). In the former instance the bodily symptoms of psychiatric disease (insomnia, appetite and weight loss, energy disturbance, pain, weakness, dizziness, and so forth) are emphasized, expressed, and dealt with, while their psychological concomitants are deemphasized, regarded as secondary, and therefore left untreated. In the case of chronic medical disorder psychosocial stress in local contexts of power (for example, family conflict over access to insufficient resources, work problems stemming from abuses of employer power or quests for empowerment by workers, school and examination failure, or community problems) can be the chief source of symptom amplification and the exacerbation of disability, though depression and anxiety secondary to physical illness or chronic situations of high stress and inadequate support may mediate this reaction.

But chronic somatization has other sources. Illness behavior in acute or subacute somatization may become prolonged and eventually frozen into a longterm sick role in which complaining about bodily symptoms and preoccupation with illness form a central part of one's everyday behavior and a means of negotiating with other people, as in chronic pain syndrome. Here, it has been argued, psychological and social factors behaviorally condition physical symptoms—for example, in the operant conditioning paradigm— and bring these bodily complaints under the control of concrete environmental forces in the local systems of power. These forces maintain the illness behavior in spite of medical treatment, which may remove the underlying disease process (stress response, depression, anxiety, acute biomechanical low back strain). The illness behavior becomes a crucial relationship in the ecology of the local system (for example, maintaining the stability of a pathological family system). Indeed, at times, medical treatment itself may become one of those concrete environmental forces conditioning chronic illness behavior. In such a circumstance, the underlying disease may remit in response to pharmacological or other treatment while the illness behavior persists in response to the environmental factors that encourage it (say, an overly dependent clinical relationship).

Alternatively, chronic somatization may occur in the absence of any medical or psychiatric disorder as an habitual coping style or idiom of distress that is learned via childhood socialization in the family, in school, and in the other sectors of local systems. A somatic style of coping with stress and of articulating distress is widely shared in many societies where it is indirectly and often inadvertently supported by family, school, work-disability, health care, and other social institutions.

When medical or psychiatric disease or stress do not provide the biological substrate of somatic amplification, normal physiological processes seem to be the source. For example, Demers et al. (1980) showed that normal American adults experience what they call "symptoms" roughly once per week. The great majority of these complaints are minor and either quickly disappear, are regarded as insignificant and forgotten, or are monitored internally until they can be normalized. A very few complaints may be amplified. Research shows that under psychosocial stress, or owing to a habit of somatic introspection, or where such complaints fit into a culturally shaped and socially legitimated coping style and idiom of distress in a particular local context of power, such physiologically based headaches, dizziness, fatigue, and so forth are a ready source of chronic somatization.

This clinical model of the forms and sources of somatization complements the cognitive, social-psychological hypotheses by suggesting a broader array of contributing factors. One important factor deserves considerably more elaboration: the system of cultural meanings which, anthropologists hold, orients individuals in groups to the world around them and to their own inner body-self experience.

LANGUAGE, MEANING, AND SOMATIZATION

In the first half of this century colonial European psychiatrists working in Africa failed to diagnose depression among their indigenous patients, as they often loudly proclaimed. Later investigators, both Africans and Europeans fluent in local languages, have diagnosed some of the highest levels of depression in the world. This discrepancy is indicative of the crucial role language plays in somatization. Leff (1981), building on the recognition that verbal equivalents of anxiety and depression are absent from a number of languages in the non-Western world, reasons that there is a historical and cross-cultural development of words for unpleasant emotional states. His argument can be epitomized as follows: At an early stage a single word designates the somatic accompaniments of dysphoria; the somatic experience is relatively undifferentiated so that a range of words is unnecessary. At the next stage of linguistic development, the semantic network of the word broadens to encompass the psychological as well as the bodily experience of emotions. Since the psychological experience is as undifferentiated as the bodily experience, however, a single term suffices to express it. The next level of cultural development brings a shift away from somatic to psychological experience. Thus, in European languages anxiety and angina take origin from the same progenitor term that expressed a similar bodily feeling of chest discomfort. "Eventually," Leff (1981:45) avers, "the root word split into a number of phonetically related variants as the global psychological experience of unpleasant emotion was differentiated into several distinct categories." In this evolutionary explanation most non-Western languages remain at an early developmental stage, "Lacking words for depression and anxiety and instead possessing words for the bodily experience of emotion which are relatively undifferentiated."

Leff's reading of the cross-cultural data-base views the *psychologizing* of emotion as more recent and therefore worthy of being highlighted against the older background of somatization. To support his thesis Leff shows that depression and anxiety have no direct equivalents in Yoruba, a Nigerian language; that the Xhosa people of South Africa have no word meaning depression, but instead refer to this state by a word meaning "his heart is sore''; and that the same holds for Luganda, an Ugandan language. I have already remarked on the use of *men* in Chinese to convey a sense of something pressing on or depressing into the chest and heart. Leff cites this point along with Marsella's (1979) data that a number of non-Western societies possess no concepts of depression as disease or symptom. Although Leff recognizes that some non-Western languages do possess highly differentiated psychological terminology, he regards these to be exceptions. He also presents other interesting evidence in defense of his thesis, including data indicating that unpleasant emotions seem to be less well differentiated in non-Indo-European language groups that participated in the WHO International Pilot Study of Schizophrenia than in Indo-European ones. Leff takes this to mean that "languages with a restricted vocabulary of emotions do impair patients' ability to express emotions in a well-differentiated way" (Leff 1981:48). Leff's findings also show that psychiatrists from the more developed societies tend to impose greater differentiation of the emotions on patients from developing countries, perhaps because this is what they have come to expect from patients in their own culture. Leff reasons this may hold for psychiatrists in Western societies, especially when they work with lower-class, less well-educated, and ethnic patients.

Ebigbo (1982), gathering information with an indigenous psychometric questionnaire that assesses local cultural symptom terms, documents that Nigerians use somatic terms that are culture-specific (for example, a peculiar crawling sensation in the head), and which convey unique meaning pertinent to their particular cultural context even if they refer to shared experiences. Good (1977), working in Iran, has shown that there is a specific semantic network of meaning associated with the somatization term "heart distress," and that this network conveys key social and psychocultural information (especially about problems in female sexuality and the oppressions of daily life) to its indigenous members, information that holds considerable cultural significance and serves social and personal functions. In chapter 2 I reviewed the writings of a number of anthropologists that offer ethnographic evidence to support the cultural relativist view that emotions are inseparable from the way they are categorized and used in a particular society's practical discourse of daily life. Even where there is an equivalent word for depression or anxiety, those emotions *mean* and therefore *are* different experiences in distinctive groups who hold divergent collective representations of what the self, the body, social relations, normal behavior, and illness signify (cf. Heelas and Lock 1981; Rosaldo 1980; White 1982).

Leff's formulation, along with others like it, has run into a great deal of criticism from anthropologists working from such a meaning-centered perspective. For them it is both empirically and conceptually flawed. They point out, for example, that Buddhism contains highly sophisticated psychological terminology and conceptualizations, which held importance from the earliest historical period. (In fact Buddhism might be regarded as the only great religion that is founded on a psychology, not a cosmology.) Furthermore, many non-Western languages, such as Tamil in South India, possess no Cartesian dualistic separation between psychological and somatic aspects of experience.[4] Language usage integrates both. For these anthropologists assuming that overt somatic complaints are any less "real" than allegedly hidden psychological problems is an ethnocentric example of Western dualism. When Western psychiatrists and psychologists say that the former "mask" the latter, we perceive a popular instance of this ethnopsychological bias that misrepresents a much more complex reality.[5] These critics further argue that Leff's historical linguistic reconstruction is wrong even for the Western world. While medical discourse in the past has been limited psychologically, religious discourse has always been rich in the sophisticated use of psychological terms (for example, acedia). For the proponents of cultural relativism it is the study of subtle and changing meanings in real life—not generic words, not the frozen artificial prose of dictionaries—that makes the psychological and social significances of illness and emotions comprehensible. Universally occurring illnesses and emotions may be present in all human societies, but because of the particularities of culture, situation, and person they will be distinctive (cf. Kleinman and Good 1985).

A cross-cultural illustration should make this anthropological criticism of the orthodox psychiatric paradigm clearer. The Afghan psychiatrist Waziri (1973) reported that Afghans with depression generally "had no words to describe their feelings of sadness," though they could differentiate it from grief. They complained of a feeling "as if a strong hard hand was squeezing" their hearts. This symptom was the one most highly emphasized in his interviews with patients, the one for which patients principally sought relief. Waziri did not examine the semantics of this term, nor did he explain its place in the Afghan system of rules and norms, yet it has a striking resemblance to the symptom of heart distress for which Good (1977) conducted a semantic analysis in a Turkish area of Iran. This culturally salient Afghan expression would have been an ideal subject for an interpretative account. Instead the term is adduced to demonstrate somatization, with the assumption that its real meaning is an underlying affective disorder (in the Western sense). The related assumption in much of the psychiatric literature on non-Western peoples is that psychological-mindedness comes with higher education and Westernization, in the form of a new language learned to express previously unrecognized or unstated emotions, and that it represents a higher stage of cognitive development. Researchers writing from this perspective are often Western-educated members of indigenous communities. The suspicion lingers that such writers are cut off from (and perhaps embarrassed by) their own native cultures and tend to see things only from a decidedly Western professional mental health perspective. This is why anthropological field research on the cultural meanings of illness behavior and emotions is needed to complement biomedical and psychological studies. Only an ethnographic field approach is likely to elucidate the culture-specific significance of a symptom that "like reality, is multiple and evanescent, and no one account of it will do" (Goodman 1984).

Izard (1979) shows the discourse on somatization to be even more complex. He builds on studies begun by Darwin to offer a universalist alternative to the evolutionist and relativist interpretations. Cross-cultural psychological studies of the facial expression of emotion, Izard shows, indicate that the same emotional experiences are detectable in a wide variety of cultures and appear to derive from basic neurophysiological correlates of human and animal behavior. These, he says, have the same somatic, affective, and cognitive expressions across cultures. Thus, he and others suggest that depression may occur in nonhuman primates, and Suomi et al. have (1978) produced depressive-like reactions in young rhesus monkeys by repeated separations. Impressively, the affected monkeys showed more improvement when an antidepressant drug was administered than they did when a placebo was given. Hence the major cross-cultural interpretations of emotions seem to fall into three distinctive interpretative frameworks. Each can be (and has been) applied to elucidate somatization, and each seems to have its appropriate place.

Based on the findings from our Hunan studies, chapter 7 presents an interactionist theoretical position that oscillates between the cultural construction of depressive experience and the universal core depressive disorder, but one that sees the oscillations as always tending more toward cultural difference. Neurasthenia is interpreted as culturally shaped somatization, illness experience, and behavior that elaborate depression and other disorders which form its psychobiological template. Somatization, then, links neurasthenia and depression. The three terms triangulate the symbolic bridge connecting symptoms to self and society. Somatization varies in its prevalence and patterns across cultures and historical periods. Under the pressure of major societal transitions it intensifies and proliferates, in part because depression and other forms of distress increase, in part because of its social and personal uses. But somatization is around us all the time and in every society for which we have adequate ethnographic and clinical information. Where social structure is more tightly organized, institutions of social control (religion traditionally, political surveillance more recently) limit the discourse on self and society, and ideologies of collective experience and expression emphasize bodily and other idioms of distress over psychological and social ones, somatization flourishes. But it is not all members of a local cultural system who are at equal risk of developing somatization. The local cultural context mediates the effects of society on individuals, of culture on illness. Neurasthenia in Chinese society illustrates each of these points. To understand neurasthenia among the Chinese, however, it is necessary to go beyond psychological and physiological explanations. The social sources and consequences of somatization must be analyzed together with the sources and consequences of depression, through empirical findings and case studies.

Another point toward which I hope to lead the reader is that translation from cultural discourse and forms of experience in a particular social system into universalist language and forms of experience must occur if there is to be a cross-culturally valid science of human behavior and clinical work. *But* translation must always be the very last step on a pathway that begins with and spends most of its course in the particularities of the cultures under study. That is what I take to be the essence of an anthropological approach to cross-cultural psychiatry. It is also my apology to the reader for the three chapters in which the findings of our field research are presented in an intensive analysis of the individual experiences of Chinese patients. In chapter 7 the unraveled threads are tied together in a synthesis of somatization, neurasthenia, and depression in Chinese society and society in general.

Four
★
Clinical Research: China, 1980

Liang was moved to inquire about his health. Mao replied that although someone once told him that he had tuberculosis, he had been examined by a doctor who denied it. He did admit, however, to occasional nervous exhaustion (neurasthenia).

Guy Alitto, *The Last Confucian: Liang Shu-ming and the Chinese Dilemma of Modernity*

That he [Mao Zedong] ruminated aloud on extraphysical factors in illness is suggestive in light of the striking coincidence of Mao's own bouts of sickness with setbacks in his work.

Ross Terrill, *A Biography of Mao*

I undertook an empirical study in the People's Republic of China in the summer of 1980 to elucidate the connections between neurasthenia, depression, and somatization in Chinese culture and thereby to help clarify the conceptual issues in the relation of culture and affect.[1] One hundred patients with the diagnosis of neurasthenia who attended the psychiatric outpatient clinic, Second Affiliated Hospital, Hunan Medical College, were selected for the study once they met inclusion criteria: eighteen to sixty years of age; attending the clinic for the first time with their present complaints; free of major medical illnesses (diabetes, thyroid disease, multiple sclerosis, mitral valve prolapse) and organic mental disorder; willing and available to participate in the study and return for follow-up. At each weekday morning clinic, the first two or three patients (depending on whether sufficient time was available to complete the assessment of three patients) who met the criteria entered the study. Since patients at the Hunan Medical College and in China generally carry their own medical records, including reports of laboratory tests and documentation of medication and other treatment received, we reviewed the medical records in full and requested all relevant data, including the report of patient's initial interview and physical examination in the psychiatry clinic and in other of the hospital's clinics they had attended. In a few cases where there was a question of an underlying medical or organic mental disorder not fully worked up in the recent past, pertinent blood chemistries, X-rays, and neuropsychological tests were obtained.

Each patient took part in an interview lasting several hours and consisting of a complete description of symptoms, course, illness behavior, help-seeking, and ethnomedical beliefs associated with the current illness. Each received a psychiatric assessment using the *Schedule for Affective Disorders and Schizophrenia* (SADS, Third Edition, Part 1), which had been modified to yield DSM-III diagnoses for major depressive disorder (serious clinical depression), dysthymic disorder (chronic neurotic depression), cyclothymic disorder, manic-depressive disorder, panic disorder, generalized anxiety disorder, phobic disorder, obsessive-compulsive disorder, somatization disorder (hysteria), conversion disorder (acute or episodic hysterical reactions), schizophrenia, and substance abuse disorder.[2]

This instrument was translated into Chinese by psychiatrists who are bilingual in both standard Chinese and the native Hunanese dialect, then back-translated into English by other bilingual members of our research group, and finally tested for validity and reliability in a pilot sample of ten subjects, whose diagnoses had been established through lengthy and detailed clinical interviews following both Chinese psychiatric evaluative procedures and standard American mental status evaluation and psychiatric diagnostic assessment.

Interviews were administered by the author together with at least one native-speaking postgraduate psychiatrist. In addition each patient was interviewed about past experiences with symptoms covered by the SADS and with the psychiatric disorders listed above, as well as about past medical history, work, educational, family, marital, and personal histories. A questionnaire was constructed to gather information on stressful life events in the six months prior to the most recent exacerbation. It also inquired about coping, social support network, patient explanatory model of the illness, perceived social impairment, and significant psychosocial problems (family, marital, work, school, financial, and doctor-patient, hereafter referred to as *illness problems*) associated with the illness experience and its treatment. Stressors, social impairment, and illness problems were scaled on a five-point Likert scale of perceived severity. Following these assessments each patient underwent an open-ended ethnographic interview to determine the social significance and uses of their symptoms in their day-to-day illness behavior in concrete work, family, and community contexts. When family members and/or co-workers were available, they were queried about many of the same points and also asked to provide whatever additional information they were willing to contribute.

Patients were asked to return five to six weeks following the initial interview for follow-up assessment, which consisted of review of current symptoms, illness problems, help-seeking, and compliance. Each was scaled as in the initial interview. Ethnographic interviews were repeated to reassess the social significance and uses of illness behavior. Post-treatment explanatory models were collected, and in a few cases psychological and biological tests were performed to rule out medical disease or organic mental disorder. Family members and co-workers who accompanied patients to the follow-up also were queried about these issues.

Seventy-six patients returned for the full follow-up interview, and twenty-three of these returned for a second follow-up. The major reason for not returning was living at too great a distance from the hospital. Several patients who failed to return sent back replies about their current condition, or their local doctors did so. But these data, which were quite incomplete, are not included in the outcome data. The research team was responsible for providing treatment for the patients in the study, which consisted almost entirely of psychopharmacological medication.

ETHNOGRAPHIC SETTING OF THE CLINIC

The building that housed the psychiatry clinic at the Second Affiliated Hospital in 1980 is striking in comparison to the building that contains all the other clinics. The latter is an impressive, white-plastered, five-story structure that is new, clean, and modern, readily comparable to medical clinics in American hospitals. The hallways are large; there are sizeable waiting areas; and it is well-lighted owing to the large windows that face either outward onto the busy street in front of the hospital or onto a pleasant, if plain, inner courtyard. In sharp contrast, the psychiatry clinic was housed in an old, somewhat derelict, two-story brick structure that is shabby, dark, damp, and unattractive. It is, moreover, noticeably hidden behind and to the side of the clinics' building. In fact, one needs to walk down a flight of stairs to reach the psychiatry clinic, which literally (as well as symbolically) is on another level.[3] It possesses four or so small, poorly-lighted, crowded rooms. The main piece of furniture in each is a long wooden table bearing the scars of heavy use and age, at either end of which sits a psychiatrist. The psy-

chiatrists wear white gowns and hats, like other doctors in the hospital, sym-
bolizing their medical orientation. Adding to this impression is the pile of
diagnostic equipment before them on the table (stethoscope, blood pressure
cuff, neurological reflex hammer).

The rooms are crowded, each with about a dozen patients and family
members. While two sets of families and patients are seen simultaneously
by the psychiatrists at either end of the table, other patients and families
observe and listen, and occasionally talk among themselves or with the nurse.
Hence the consultations are public, noisy and, because of the great press of
patients and very limited time, short (about five minutes for return patients,
twice or three times as long for new ones). The psychiatrists (and the patients)
are sensitive to the crush of clients—around 100 at each half-day clinic—
waiting to be seen by the seven or eight psychiatrists working in the clinic
at any particular session, each of whom interviews thirty or more patients
over the tiring course of the seven-hour workday, divided into morning and
afternoon clinics. The style of interviewing is paternalistic, interrogative,
and medical. Each consultation ends with either a prescription or a referral.
Treatments, including electrical acupuncture, injections, counseling, are given
openly in the room. This highly public setting constrains the talk about personal or social problems, as does the fact that patients keep their own records
(which over time become dirty, torn, crumpled), which encourages clinicians
to use euphemisms or stick to symptomatic rather than etiological terminology
in their brief case write-ups.

A small number of nurses help to keep order and control the flow of
patients. Before patients and the family members or friends who accompany
them enter the examining room, they have usually been in the hospital for
a long time: queuing on the lengthy line for registration, sitting in a large
covered shed, which serves as an outside waiting area until the clinic opens.
There are ten half-day clinic sessions each week, including one on Saturday
morning. The staff devotes Saturday afternoon to academic and personal
pursuits, and one afternoon each week is given over to a political meeting
for the entire department of psychiatry, followed by academic lectures.

During the course of our 1980 study those patients who met the inclusion
criteria and gave their informed consent left the clinic and walked with family
or friends to the locked gate surrounding the equally old and dilapidated
psychiatric inpatient unit. After entering they walked to a very small room
at the rear of the inpatient unit, used by physicians to write reports and see
patients and families, where they sat at a desk across from me and one or
two of my Chinese colleagues. Our research interviews lasted approximately

two hours each, sometimes longer. At the close of the interview my colleagues and I consulted and prescribed treatment for the patient. This generally consisted of a prescription for medication, almost the only form of treatment available in the clinic, along with suggestions about which current medications to stop or continue. Follow-up interviews were conducted in the same setting. All interviews were conducted in standard Chinese, though some involved periodic rephrasing from the Hunan dialect that some patients were more comfortable in using to talk about themselves. The psychiatric unit at the Second Affiliated Hospital is described in more detail elsewhere (Kleinman and Mechanic 1981).

As a number of interviews ran over the two-hour period, especially in the morning, we invited patients and their family members to visit with us in our apartment, either after lunch or before dinner, during which time we engaged in a more leisurely exchange, unencumbered by questionnaries and procedures for structured interviewing. At the time of the 1980 follow-ups we engaged in more of these informal interviews, and also spent more time with patients in the interviewing room. This was even more true of our 1983 follow-up study. At that time, we spent half a day with each patient and family members; for several of the cases reported in chapter 6 the time was even longer.

Besides the lengthy questionnaires we filled out during the interviews, we recorded the responses to open-ended questions in our field notes along with lengthy commentary based on our observations, those of our Chinese colleagues, and our discussions together, in which we tried to make sense of the life histories and illness reports we had elicited. I wrote up each of the follow-up patients as a case report, and these reports were discussed by members of the research team who critiqued, emended, and helped revise the report. These cases, both individually and collectively, came to dominate our thoughts. We discussed them, making sure to protect patients' anonymity, with our friends and colleagues at the Hunan Medical College who were not engaged in the project, and with other Chinese acquaintances, to check the accuracy of events that had been described to us from the Anti-Japanese War, the civil war, the early post-Liberation period, the Great Leap Forward, the period of starvation in the early 1960s that followed upon the excesses of the Great Leap, and especially the Cultural Revolution. These case discussions acted as a kind of projective test, provoking deeply felt personal accounts from our neighbors and friends. Indeed, they led to lengthy personal (and illness) accounts that were often comparable in emotional intensity, moral purpose, and personal significance to the accounts of our patients. I have not included these materials in the book, but they lend additional support to the validity of our case illustrations and interpretations. After leaving China we had much the same experience with scholars from the People's Republic who were visiting the United States.

RESULTS

The chief findings are summarized in tables 3–34. (Consult Appendix at end of book.)

DEMOGRAPHY OF THE SAMPLE

As table 3 shows there were more men (52) than women (48). This finding is surprising in cross-cultural psychiatry research, since evidence from many cultures reveals that women more commonly suffer from depression, anxiety states, and various somatization syndromes than men. But it is in keeping with the demography of the psychiatry outpatient clinic at the Hunan Medical College, where in a one-week period there were 184 men and 177 women in attendance. Again this finding is unusual in cross-cultural perspective, since in most societies women predominate in psychiatric clinics. There is not enough information available at present about the demography of psychiatric clinics throughout China to know how generalizable this finding is.

Another surprising finding was that in the initial visit many more patients were unaccompanied than accompanied by family or co-workers. This also is contrary to help-seeking patterns in other Asian and non-Western societies (including other Chinese settings), where most patients tend to be accompanied so that the doctor-patient interaction is at least triadic and frequently involves several family members and friends. Again, I do not know if this finding holds for other psychiatric clinics in China. One reason that it occurred was that some patients did not want others to know they had visited a psychiatric clinic or to hear their personal problems. These patients complained of feelings of stigma and shame. Slightly more patients were self-referred or referred by family or friends to the clinic than were referred through the formal medical system, but most patients, on their way to the psychiatry clinic, did pass through biomedicine and Chinese medicine clinics. This finding seems to hold for patients with psychological problems in all Chinese communities. General physicians recognized that there was some sort of psychiatric problem, since nearly half the patients received a psychiatric referral. This recognition rate is similar to the figure we cited for somatization patients treated in primary care in the West, but we did not determine if in the other cases there was a failure, as in the West, to identify psychiatric problems. Our impression, and that of our Chinese psychiatric colleagues, is that there is such a problem in China too.

We did not include children or the elderly in the neurasthenia group in order not to have to deal with childhood psychopathology and dementia. In both the neurasthenia and general psychiatry clinic groups there is a preponderance of patients in the twenty-six to forty-five years age range.

There are a few major differences in occupation. Peasant-farmers are markedly underrepresented in the neurasthenia sample compared with their general prevalence in the psychiatry clinic, and students are also slightly underrepresented. Housewives (who are uncommon, since most women in China work) accounted for 8 percent of patients in the psychiatry outpatient clinic, but do not appear in the neurasthenia group; and there was only one retiree (a worker). The latter were doubtless excluded by the age criteria. Professionals (especially health professionals) are overrepresented in the neurasthenia group. It is worth noting that in spite of the fact that the excess of professionals and teachers fits with the Chinese stereotype of neurasthenia, which holds that it is an affliction especially of intellectuals, the large number of workers and the sixteen cadres with neurasthenia indicates that this health problem affects major segments of the urban Chinese population. Rural research should determine whether the very small number of peasant-farmers in our sample is due to less frequent diagnoses among members of this group or means that neurasthenia patients, unlike schizophrenia cases, are not brought to the psychiatry clinic because this problem is not deemed serious enough to warrant travel and time away from a very busy season of agricultural work.

PSYCHOPATHOLOGY

The striking finding among the DSM-III diagnoses of the one hundred neurasthenia patients (see table 4) is that depression was far and away the predominant form of pathology. Of the ninety-three cases who were diagnosed as suffering from clinical depression of one kind or another, eighty-seven, an impressively high number, met the strict diagnostic criteria for major depressive disorder. As can be seen in table 8, moreover, most of the patients easily met the cut-off criteria of at least four vegetative symptoms required to make the major depressive disorder diagnosis. The mean number of symptoms per case was almost six, only 10 percent of cases had the minimum,

62 percent experienced six or more, and 13 percent demonstrated all eight diagnostic symptoms. Moreover, these patients perceived themselves as impaired and sought help for their symptoms (see tables 11 and 12). Thus most of the neurasthenia patients we studied could be rediagnosed using American psychiatric criteria as cases of depression.

One-third of the Hunan patients with major depressive disorder gave evidence of melancholia (see table 7)[4], a particularly severe form of the disorder, and in 60 percent the depression was chronic (more than two years' duration), in keeping with the chronic course of neurasthenic complaints among most patients in the sample. A history of recurrence was not uncommon. The vast majority of patients with major depressive disorder complained of dysphoria (97 percent) as it is defined in DSM-III (see table 8) and 61 percent voiced anhedonic (joylessness) complaints, though as I shall show below most of these complaints were not spontaneously expressed but rather were elicited in response to specific inquiry.

Anxiety disorders were diagnosed in sixty-nine cases, with panic disorder (thirty-five) the most frequent. The overlap of anxiety and depression has often been reported in the clinical literature. While it frequently could not be determined with certainty which had occurred first, most of the anxiety problems seemed to be secondary to depression. A quarter of the sample were diagnosed as cases of hysteria, using the much narrower definitions of DSM-III's somatoform disorders category as conversion disorder (episodes of hysterical symptoms: for example, blindness, aphonia, paralysis) and somatization disorder (a lifetime pattern of hysteria involving most bodily systems with history of vague, difficult to diagnose, and dramatic symptoms). Again there was some overlap between hysteria (especially conversion disorder) and depression. Because the depressive and anxiety disorders were often long-standing, it is difficult to determine if the cases should be diagnosed with somatization disorder as a separate disease, or if this is an artifact of chronic affective disorders and their psychobiological consequences.

In keeping with what is known about psychopathology among Chinese generally (Lin et al. 1982), the single case of alcoholism indicates what a small problem it is in Chinese culture. Chinese seem to be protected by their culture against alcoholism, which is one of the commonest mental health problems worldwide, although recent reports from Taiwan and Hong Kong indicate a rising, if still fairly modest rate, and there is concern in China that the same phenomenon may be in an early phase there. The single case of sedative-hypnotic drug intoxication and addiction, along with the absence of narcotic drug problems, is an impressive contrast to the drug abuse problem that afflicted China as a major plague before 1949. It is still significant in Hong Kong and among overseas Chinese, but is now extremely well controlled on the Chinese mainland.

The reader should be aware that the DSM-III decision rules are unclear about multiple psychiatric diagnosis. While DSM-III encourages a single diagnosis for each patient at any given time, clinicians worldwide recognize that, as in this study, that objective is usually very difficult to achieve. In our study, 80 percent of patients were given two diagnoses, and almost one-third three or more diagnoses. Also, as already mentioned, I generally accepted depression as the primary diagnosis when more than one diagnosis was made for a patient. This is somewhat arbitrary and likely skewed our results toward an excess of depressive diagnoses. Another source of inflation for the very high number of cases of major depressive disorder is the difficulty of determining if the clinical depression was an intercurrent problem in the longitudinal cause of some other disorder—for example, dysthymic disorder (chronic neurotic depression), personality disorder, or a chronic anxiety problem—which could not be adequately assessed because of the current predominance of depressive symptoms. In the next chapter the reader will see that there is some evidence from the three-year follow-up to support the conjecture that, for the reasons noted, we overdiagnosed major depressive disorder among the patients in our 1980 sample. Nonetheless, if the figure of 87 percent is uncertain and likely to be exaggerated for major depressive disorder, there is no doubt that this diagnosis was by far the most frequent diagnosis among this group of patients, and that a substantial number of neurasthenia sufferers were depressed.

Forty-four of the neurasthenia patients were suffering from chronic pain syndrome (pain in a single site or several sites lasting for more than two years and causing disability with social impairment in family or work settings). None had previously been diagnosed as suffering from this disorder, since it is not part of the Chinese nosology, though they had received frequent medical attention for specific pain complaints, had undergone numerous diagnostic tests, and had been prescribed many different types of pain medication. Similarly, none of the fourteen patients exhibiting culture-bound syndromes had been diagnosed as such. These syndromes have been reported in the literature for Chinese in Hong Kong, Taiwan, Singapore, Malaysia, and other overseas Chinese communities, but to the best of my knowledge not by psychiatrists in the People's Republic of China, though privately they admit to seeing these cases. Eleven cases of *shen kui* syndrome (a culture-specific psychosexual neurosis) demonstrated the classic complaints of excessive loss of semen via urination, masturbation, intercourse; fear of lack of energy, infertility and impotence; sexual inhibition and abstinence, guilt and anxiety; and a range of hypochondriacal preoccupations including dizziness, blurring of vision, cold sweats, memory disturbance, palpitations, and alleged discoloration of urine (cf. Wen and Wang 1981:365 for data from an empirical study of this syndrome in Taiwan). The eleven patients all believed they were suffering from *shen kui* (kidney weakness), had been diagnosed as such by friends, family, or Chinese-style doctors, but had not previously reported these ideas to their Western-style doctors or psychiatrists. This disorder is inseparable from the traditional Chinese medical belief that vital essence, derived from the body's limited supply of *qi* (vital energy), is stored by the kidney in the semen and that its excessive loss will lead to weakness, illness, and eventually death. Three other patients fit the pattern described by psychiatrists in Taiwan as fear of cold *(pa leng)* or frigophobia (Chang et al. 1975) in which, based on the traditional belief in the balance between *yin* and *yang* and "hot" and "cold" components of the body, patients develop a morbid fear that their bodies are excessively cold owing to loss of "hot" substance and depletion of *yang*. These patients bundle up even in warm weather, fear "catching cold," avoid going out of doors, eat only "hot" foods and tonics, refrain from eating "cold" substances, and organize their hypochondriacal preoccupation around this culturally constituted fear to such an extent that they suffer significant disability. (One case in our sample wore a long-sleeve shirt, sweater, and outer jacket on a day when the local temperature was an uncomfortably hot 37 degrees Celsius and made us switch off an electrical fan and close the windows to the examining room because he feared "catching cold.") The fact that my Chinese colleagues implicitly understood these complaints suggests that the failure to report them is most likely due to a systematic effort to translate them into biomedical equivalents and not to use traditional Chinese medicine concepts in the day-to-day practice of psychiatry. Such cases, I was told, are seen in large numbers in traditional Chinese medicine clinics—the setting where culture-bound syndromes should be studied in China. Few of the patients used the Chinese medicine terms in their presenting complaints; it is plausible that patients themselves translate between biomedical and indigenous medicine terms in the appropriate setting and thereby actively contribute to divergent social constructions of disease in these distinctive clinical settings.

We can compare the diagnoses of these patients to those of fifty-one cases with somatization attending general medical clinics and folk healers' shrines in Taiwan, whom I studied in 1976 (Kleinman 1980, and see table 5). Almost all of the latter carried the diagnosis of neurasthenia. Only 43 percent of the Taiwanese subjects made the criteria for major depressive disorder, however, a statistically significant difference that is best explained by the high probability that patients attending a psychiatric clinic will demonstrate more serious psychopathology than patients in primary care. A more appropriate comparison would be a neurasthenia sample in a primary care clinic at the Hunan Medical College, a study reported in chapter 5 that confirms this hypothesis. The difference also doubtless partially reflects the different diagnostic methods used. In the Taiwanese study diagnosis was made by a Taiwanese psychiatrist using a standard clinical interview, mental status review, and the Zung Depression Scale. His diagnoses were later transformed by the author from the local diagnostic system into equivalent DSM-III diagnoses. Nonetheless, the comparison suggests that the population of neurasthenia patients we studied needs to be regarded as a psychiatric sample that differs in important ways from the great bulk of neurasthenics in primary care clinics, who are likely to possess less major depressive disorder and other forms of psychopathology. Because two patients in the Taiwan sample had no mental illness, we should be cautious about assuming that neurasthenia can be regarded simply as an expression of underlying mental illness, though it frequently does appear to be accompanied by it. Epidemiological surveys in local communities would inform us about the frequency of neurasthenia as social behavior independent of psychopathology, but we have not been permitted to undertake such research as of yet, nor have others reported this data. Unlike the Taiwan study, where the assessment was made from clinical impression, we did not systematically assess for personality disorder in the Hunan sample because we felt there is no reliable instrument for assessing these disorders in China. It was my clinical impression, however, that about half the sample had personality problems, usually not of a severe kind, relating either to the personal experience of chronic depression and anxiety or to the difficult social situations that they had experienced for substantial periods of their lives. The chief personality problem for most was a usually long-standing negative self-concept and feelings of lack of confidence, fears of incompetence, and sense of being socially ineffective: in other words, a picture of personal demoralization. A concomitant was morbid absorption with bodily processes as part of a pervasive brooding on self and circumstances, a self-defeating introspection, and an alienating preoccupation.

PAIN

Table 9 documents the enormous burden of physical pain complaints in the neurasthenia sample: 90 percent had some form of pain. Eighty-seven percent of the patients with major depressive disorder exhibited pain—a finding similar to studies of pain and depression in the West. The data in table 10 show that headache was the primary form of pain in 87 percent of the pain patients, while back pain, chest pain, neck pain, limb pain, abdominal pain, whole body pain, and still other forms of pain were the primary source of pain in the remainder. This is a clear cultural difference when compared to U.S. findings, where there is less chronic headache and much more low back pain, but it is in keeping with the high incidence of headaches in Chinese culture discussed earlier. What we are seeing here is the great prevalence and cultural significance of a single type of somatic complaint, one many patients viewed as most bothersome. The tendency of practitioners in the Chinese medical system was to avoid focusing on the symptom of pain as a particular syndrome but to view it as an expectable component of the neurasthenia syndrome. Here is an illustration of how two distinctive psychiatric systems configure the same phenomenon in divergent categories that socially construct two different disorders: in China neurasthenia, and in North America chronic pain syndrome associated with depression or anxiety. Yet in both societies there is a similar process of psychosomatic and sociosomatic transduction from psychic pain and the pain of demoralizing social circumstances to the embodiment of pain as a physical experience.

PRESENTING COMPLAINTS

Reviewing the presenting complaints (those symptoms that patients' spontaneously express when asked what problem brought them to the clinic) of one hundred neurasthenia patients in table 11, we see that each patient volunteered a mean of seven complaints, of which five were somatic and 1.8 psychological. This finding quantitates the somatic preponderance of neurasthenic complaints. Out of the psychological complaints there were slightly more affective than cognitive ones; but thirty-nine patients expressed no affective complaints and thirty-eight no cognitive ones. The chronicity of neurasthenia is well illustrated by the 7.8 years mean length of time that the chief presenting complaints were experienced.

Turning to just those patients with major depressive disorder (N = 87), we note again the somatic preponderance and focusing, this time in illness idioms (see table 12). Thirty percent of patients complained entirely of somatic symptoms, and 70 percent of somatic and psychological complaints together but with a decided emphasis on the former, a somatopsychic illness idiom. Remarkably, none of the patients, though all knew they were in a psychiatry clinic, complained entirely or even mostly of psychological symptoms.

Table 12 lists the chief presenting complaints in all ninety-three cases of depression (major depressive disorder, manic-depressive disorder, dysthymic disorder, cyclothymic disorder). It is interesting to compare this list to the lists of complaints cited above for neurasthenia patients in nineteenth-century America, depressives in primary care in Hong Kong, patients with mental illness in primary care in the WHO collaborative study in several non-Western societies, patients with Cushing's syndrome (Starkman et al. 1981), and in the Mathew et el. (1981) survey of the physical symptoms of depression. These lists contain many of the same items, though the frequencies differ. Together they describe the phenomenology of somatization. A psychiatrist or psychologist reading the lists is struck by symptoms of autonomic nervous system and neuroendocrine origin. A nonpsychiatric observer will be struck by the preponderance of similar somatic complaints in depression and other psychiatric disorders, and will wonder why these are not listed among the DSM-III criteria of major depressive disorder and related psychiatric disorders. The diagnostic criteria of psychiatrists in America have clearly emphasized psychological complaints over somatic complaints that seem to be even more common in psychiatric disorders, but which are regarded as epiphenomenal when one holds a psychological orientation. Seen from a general medical perspective, however, the psychological complaints would be regarded as less frequent and less important. I will return to this conflict in cultural construals of somatization in chapter 7, where I compare American and Chinese psychiatric formulations of this problem. Somatic features of depressive experience obviously are not well studied and understood. Further phenomenological research should help determine if other psychiatric disorders present the same wide range of somatic complaints or if there are particular patterns of complaints with different disorders, such as is the case with the well-recognized vegetative complaints of the major depressive disorder and the physiological concomitants of panic disorder in the hyperventilation syndrome. The co-occurrence and interdigitation of psychological and somatic complaints illustrate the psychophysiological integration of the illnesses we are studying. This finding also suggests that just as a fairly narrow spectrum of psychological reactions limits the range of outcomes of cultural patterning of emotions, so too a relatively restricted range of physiological signs and symptoms of emotional arousal and pathology limits the cultural shaping of somatization.

Table 14 analyzes the presenting affective and cognitive complaints in all the cases of depression. Anxiety was spontaneously expressed much more often than was depressive affect. The latter was complained of in only eight of the ninety-three cases. Nonspecific, undifferentiated, or poorly differentiated affects were expressed in even more cases than these differentiated ones. The former included irritability, displeasure-unhappiness, general or vague fear, and restlessness. Many of the neurasthenic patients were thus better able to differentiate somatic than affective states, in keeping with their priorities of what was the chief problem and what required most attention. The commonest cognitive complaint, loss of or poor memory, has been shown to be a neuropsychological concomitant of depression, a characteristic and measurable cognitive deficit in brain functioning.

In contrast to presenting complaints, where psychological symptoms were spontaneously expressed relatively infrequently, a number of psychological symptoms were elicited from the depressed patients during specific questioning regarding each symptom, using a symptom checklist. Hence dysphoria (defined here differently than in DSM-III to include nonspecific displeasure and unhappiness, but excluding hopelessness) was found to be present in all patients with depression, anhedonia in 61 percent, hopelessness in 50 percent, helplessness in 42 percent, and low self-esteem in 60 percent. Even if we use the DSM-III criteria of dysphoria, there was no patient with a depressive disorder who did not admit to feeling either dysphoria or anhedonia! That is to say these depressed patients recognized, even if they did not freely express, problems with inner feelings. Irritability, hopelessness, and displeasure-unhappiness were more frequently elicited from these patients than were specific complaints of depression or sadness, which further supports our conclusion about affective undifferentiation. (It was no surprise that the DSM-III dysphoric complaints—"blue," "low," "down in the dumps"—were not expressed by any of the Chinese depressives and are clearly culture-specific Americanisms.) These findings demonstrate that even though dysphoria or anhedonia must be present for a case to make the DSM-III diagnosis for major depressive disorder, all the neurasthenics with major depressive disorder met this criterion. Hence it appears that, at least in this sample, we can say that Chinese depressives *suppressed* affective complaints. (Such suppression is one possible reason why clinicians routinely fail to diagnose depression among Chinese.) Difficulty concentrating, making decisions, or in thinking generally was elicited in 84 percent, again underlining the importance of perceived cognitive changes in depression. Half of the depressed patients maintained marked hypochondriacal preoccupation, including fear of brain tumor in thirteen cases and of going "crazy" in seventeen others;[5] these were almost somatic delusions in several of the cases (cf. Kleinman 1980:161–63).

As has been shown in the past, few Chinese suffering depression admitted to feelings of guilt. Yap (1965) reported this finding for Cantonese. (Surprisingly Cheung et al. (1981) found guilt *or* self-reproach in a relatively high proportion of their Hong Kong sample. But they do not say exactly how common guilt was, and in our sample feelings of worthlessness were also relatively common, though guilt was uncommon. Could many of their patients have been Westernized Christians?) Sethi et al. (1973) noted little guilt among Indian patients, as did Rao (1973); and the same has been reported for Iraqi (Bazzaui 1970), West African (Binitie 1975), and many other patients with depression in non-Western societies. Murphy et al. (1967) associated guilt with Christianity, and others have added Islam (El-Islam 1969); guilt is not associated with Buddhism, Hinduism, or African religions.

But this cross-cultural distinction has been challenged. Rao (1973) refers with some disquiet to karmic guilt among depressed patients in India, and more recently Orley and Wing (1979) present evidence that there was more guilt among depressed subjects in Uganda than among a depressed cohort of Londoners (cf. Lebra (1976) on guilt among Japanese women). Guilt in non-Western samples has also been said to be more prevalent with higher social class, education, and modernity. But anthropologically sophisticated analyses of the meanings of guilt and depression in local cultures have yet to be conducted, and in their absence we should be cautious of making too much of the findings of superficial psychiatric surveys lest we repeat the kind of fiasco created by the naive early distinction between guilt and shame, a distinction found untenable in many populations. Because I did not explore the meaning of guilt among those few patients who reported it, or its absence among most of the depressed patients in the present study, I am unable to say if guilt means the same thing it does in the West, or whether the same meaning may not be conveyed in the semantic field of other Chinese terms. For this reason the reader should not place too much importance on our findings that only 9 percent of depressed neurasthenics admitted harboring feelings of guilt, while 60 percent reported low self-esteem or worthlessness. Some studies have correlated reduced rates of low self-esteem and feelings of worthlessness with the relative scarcity of guilt, while others like our own have demonstrated that these psychological symptoms vary independently of each other.

Suicidal thoughts, plans, and attempts were impressively few in number among the depressed Hunan patients. While some patients may have suppressed such preoccupations, it is intriguing to consider the possibility that somatized depression may involve less suicidal behavior, perhaps because it is principally an experience of bodily distress rather than intrapsychic alienation and existential despair. Suicidal ideas have been reported as less prevalent in a number of studies of non-Western depressives, but the explanation given is because guilt is absent, the depression these patients experience is less serious. The hypothesis put forth here suggests that if lack of guilt plays a role in reducing suicidal ideas and actions, it does so only because the depressive experience among patients with a somatic focus is not psychological. Somatization, in my formulation, is the main factor affecting suicide, and perhaps somatic preoccupation explains why there is so little guilt. This is a testable hypothesis awaiting further study.

Table 16 lists a number of culture-bound complaints (complaints so embedded in traditional Chinese cultural beliefs that they are virtually untranslatable when removed from their indigenous semantic network) experienced by neurasthenic patients (cf. Kleinman 1980:84–86, 140–45). Sixteen patients used *men* to refer to depression as a somatic experience of something physically pressing or depressing into their head or chest, but the cultural connotation was clearly of psychological depression. This might be regarded as a somatopsychic (body affecting mind and person) metaphor understandable only in a Chinese context. *Huoqi da* is a complaint with two distinctive physical meanings and one specific emotional connotation. It can refer to a sensation of burning in the upper abdomen or lower chest, what Western physicians might regard as dyspepsia, gastric irritation, or esophageal reflux, as well as a sensation of bad taste in the mouth or tenderness and swelling of the gums, which in biomedicine might be associated with an upper respiratory infection or flu syndrome. The psychological connotation is irritability owing to irascible disposition. While the idea of ghosts can be expressed directly in English, for the Chinese in our sample this fear included the possibility of spirit possession and bad fate. *Suan* is a special form of bitterness best rendered as sour or vinegary; it is part of the Chinese tradition of systematic symbolic correspondences between the microcosmic body-mind and the macrocosmic social-physical environment. It is occasionally used to indicate the physiological component of grief when referred to the heart. (I have treated several Chinese patients with depression whose first symptom of exacerbation or recurrence was a feeling of *suan* in the upper abdomen in the absence of evidence of gastric acid hypersecretion or any other gastrointestinal pathology.) These culture-bound symptoms were not spontaneously expressed, but were elaborated only when patients were questioned about them.

EXPLANATORY MODELS

Tables 17 and 18 summarize patients' explanatory models of neurasthenia— the beliefs they articulated about the nature, name, cause, expected course, and desired treatment for this episode of their particular problem. Here again we see evidence of these patients' strong somatic orientation. Despite the fact they were in a psychiatric clinic, 78 percent of patients held that their disorder was wholly or partially organic. Only 22 percent regarded their problem as principally or wholly psychological. Forty-four percent named their disorder neurasthenia, 27 percent called it a neurological disorder, and only 18 percent classified it as a minor psychological problem. Notably, none labeled it depression. Not too surprisingly, given the biomedical setting, no patient volunteered traditional Chinese medicine or folk-healing terminology for their disorder. (On direct questioning forty-one patients were either unfamiliar with or could not articulate a traditional Chinese medical assessment of their problem, while of those who could do so half claimed not to believe in Chinese medical theories. Our subjects, like most urban Chinese I have encountered, were oriented to biomedical ideas.)

Importantly, by far the most frequent attribution of cause was work problems (61%), followed by political problems (25%), separation (of work sites, not divorce) (25%), marital and family problems (20%), exam and school problems (16%), and so forth. Only a small number of patients thought their neurasthenia was due to another disorder (13%), nutritional problems (9%), or heredity (5%). An equally small number (12%) specifically attributed their illness to emotional causes. Although psychosocial stressors were listed as causes, they were perceived as producing organic disease. Patients seemed quite familiar with a stress model of physical disease, but one somewhat different than in Western psychiatry. Psychosocial stressors like grief or job dissatisfaction or school failure were thought of as bringing about bodily change directly, just as an accident or physical illness might, and were held to bypass emotions.

Most patients expected a chronic course, and that is what they had experienced, but almost a third feared their illness would progressively worsen. Only 2 percent felt their illness was improving at the time of our initial interview. In table 18 we see that 40 percent of patients left the choice of treatment to their doctors, but the rest wanted medicine or diagnostic tests of one kind or another. That Chinese medicines were requested more than Western medicine in a psychiatric clinic is not unusual in China, since the former are widely used in such clinics, often to contain cost, and are popularly regarded as more effective for treating chronic illness. It is surely noteworthy that few patients wanted psychotherapy, which is neither routinely legitimated nor available as a treatment in China, and that only two patients *openly* expressed a desire to change work so as to improve their illness.

HELP-SEEKING AND ILLNESS BEHAVIOR

Tables 19–22 present data on the help-seeking and illness behavior of the neurasthenia patients. As has been found for patients in Taiwan (Kleinman 1980) and in the United States (Demers et al. 1981), self-treatment was quite popular in our sample. But unlike Taiwan, where most patients in an earlier study resorted first to self-care (Kleinman 1980:183), only a third of the Hunan neurasthenia patients did so. This discrepancy most probably reflects the ready access to inexpensive care in the People's Republic. In spite of active suppression of religious healing in China, almost a quarter of our sample engaged in such treatment and, even though the study took part in a large city, 14 percent had sought help from shamans, sorcerers, and other religious experts, suggesting that folk healing is still actively pursued in China (cf. Parrish and Whyte 1978 for other findings pointing toward the same conclusion). Special foods, tonics, dietary changes, traditional Chinese medicine, and Western exercises, in that order, were by far the most common self-treatments. Lay resort to self-prescribed Western medicinals, either from patients' own supplies or from pharmacies, was quite limited. Perhaps patients were reluctant to admit such use to the researchers, who were themselves biomedical physicians, or perhaps self-prescription of Western (biomedical) medicaments is more tightly controlled in China than in Taiwan or Hong Kong, where this form of self-care is common.

The neurasthenia patients' illness behavior was considered excessive by local standards. They made on the average almost two visits to doctors per month (see table 21), a high figure for patients at the Hunan Medical College. Moreover, they perceived themselves as sick 75 percent of the time during the preceding year, and one-third of patients regarded themselves as sick 100 percent of that time. More than half regarded their illness as interfering with work, school, personal, and/or other relationships and believed it prevented normal social activities. Fifteen percent of patients were so seriously socially impaired because of the illness that they were unable to work, attend school, or carry out normal social activities and relationships in their work unit or family. This degree of disability seemed excessive to their physicians based on the observable pathology, and contributed to some patients' being regarded as complainers who were overly demanding and failed to get better— in other words this subsample was regarded as problem patients in the Chinese health care system.

Table 22 indicates that virtually all patients had consulted Western-style (biomedical) physicians for their illness and that a great many had also sought care from traditional Chinese doctors. But for most the chief source of care was physicians of biomedicine. In spite of this fact, however, patients were receiving mostly traditional Chinese medications, which were being prescribed by biomedical as well as by traditional Chinese medical practitioners. The biomedical practitioners seem to employ Chinese medications for treatment of vague, nonspecific complaints and for chronic conditions unresponsive to Western drugs. It was a surprise and a concern to learn that 58 percent of patients had received sedatives in the past year, and that almost half had received benzodiazepines (for example, valium, librium). Patients were receiving polypharmacy (more than three drugs per person) with traditional herbs, sedatives, and antianxiety agents, along with vitamins, tonics, and pain medicines. This situation is encountered often with chronic pain and other somatization patients in the United States and is consistent as well with this sample's high utilization rate and history of frequent changes in caregivers and medical regimens. This pattern of care in both societies indicates frustration on the part of both practitioners and patients over chronic problems that fail to respond to specific therapeutic interventions and which thereby challenge the physicians' coping skills as much as they do the patients'.

FAMILY HISTORY

More than a third of patients had a family history of neurasthenia, and in 70 percent of those with an affected family member it was the patient's mother (see table 23). More than half gave a family history of chronic illness, a quarter had chronic pain patients in their families, and approximately the same number had a positive family history for mental illness (54 percent of the time affecting the patient's mother). Depression accounted for 62 percent of all mental illness in the family. Sixty-four percent of patients reported significant psychological problems in their families, 35 percent substantial family discord, and 12 percent reported stepparents (owing to remarriage) with whom they had often maintained poor relationships. In 28 percent of families a member was working in the health field.

In the absence of a control group or valid community data, it is difficult to know how to interpret these findings. It was the impression of my psychiatric colleagues that these would be unusual findings for most Chinese families, since they indicated high rates of physical and mental illness, family pathology, and contact with the health care professions. Although I cannot rule out a genetic basis to neurasthenia, and there is good evidence from many studies for a genetic contribution to depression, these data can be interpreted to support a social learning hypothesis of neurasthenia as chronic illness (somatization) behavior. Patients grew up with family models of chronic illness, pain, depression, and neurasthenia, particularly from their mothers. This burden of illness behavior and the reported high levels of personal and family problems may well have seriously affected parenting and social support, and offered a family language of bodily complaints and perceptual style of bodily preoccupation (somatic introspectiveness) as a dominant response to stress, as Mechanic (1980) hypothesizes for American somatizers. Perhaps this ecological setting of chronic distress also provided an ethos of demoralization and hopelessness (cf. Brown and Harris 1978) that impaired the development of a sense of personal and social efficacy while fostering vulnerability to despair and depression (cf. Beck 1971; Minuchin et al. 1978), chronic help-seeking (especially from the medical system with which these families were so familiar), and poor adaptation. These are hypotheses that can neither be refuted or confirmed because of insufficient information. More detailed studies of family and personal background may help explain why these patients developed neurasthenia, whereas other Chinese exposed to the same stressful life events did not.

Because of the lack of a matched control group and a valid Chinese measure of stressful life events, we also have difficulty interpreting the data contained in table 24 on the types of major stressors (both new events and chronic sources of stress) experienced by the one hundred neurasthenic patients in the six months prior to illness onset or, in cases of chronic illness, most recent exacerbation. Patients experienced 3.3 stressors on the average that they themselves reported as major during this period. Work stress affected 75 percent of the sample, separation owing to work site 57 percent, financial problems 45 percent, significant political problems 31 percent, death of spouse or other family member 20 percent, school and examination stress was reported by 26 percent, and major family stress by 19 percent. Thus, as was consistent with patient perceptions of the most important cause of their problem, work stress was the single most frequent stressor. Separation of spouses, or less often parents and children, because of different and distant work sites was an impressive stressor with a mean time of separation of 6.2 years and a history of only a few, usually brief, visits home each year. There were only several cases of actual divorce in the sample. The Chinese psychiatrists who collaborated with me thought that these patients had in fact experienced substantial stress, but they also were quick to point out that the same stressors had been experienced by large numbers of individuals in China. Separation owing to different work sites may strike Westerners as unusually stressful, but it has been accepted by Chinese historically for economic reasons and probably conveys different cultural and personal significance than in the West, though it still is perceived as difficult and undesirable. Only the development of culturally valid, indigenously scaled instruments to measure perceived stressful life event change that can provide substantial data for normals and patients suffering diseases other than neurasthenia will allow the relationship of stress to neurasthenia to be accurately assessed. The Chinese are just beginning to research and write about stress (Zheng and Yang 1983; Xu 1984), and it may be a few more years before valid methods are available, and therefore even longer before we achieve a more discriminating understanding.

Even then it will not be easy to know what to make of "stress" in China. During the Warlord and Nationalist phases of the Republic, chaos and oppression reigned. In the Anti-Japanese War, more than 20 million Chinese were killed, and more than 100 million were uprooted. The Civil War saw further turmoil, forced migration, and death. The Chinese suffered one million casualties in the Korean War. The period of starvation that followed the errors and excesses of the Great Leap Forward was one in which thousands (perhaps tens of thousands) starved to death. The Cultural Revolution left few families untouched by tragedy: broken families, physical separation, humiliation, torture, and, for thousands, death. Looking back over half a century of the severest kinds of human misery, what does stress mean? Looking back over the millennia in China, or the West, makes one wonder how to compare the measurement of present misery with what had been experienced before. That most Chinese seem to have coped and did not succumb to neurasthenia or other mental illnesses does not mean that these stressors have not had profound effects. Interviewing urban residents makes it apparent that people felt betrayed by their leaders, particularly Mao, who had been accorded the status of an emperor during the Cultural Revolution, and that at present, amid impressive economic growth, increasing material prosperity, and liberalization there is, especially among the intelligentsia, widespread cynicism, demoralization, and alienation. These collective traumas have deeply affected individuals. This is no less serious a stress than the threat to personal life that was also widespread in the nightmare years of the Cultural Revolution. But how do we evaluate either the historical background or the current social context of stress?

Have periods of intensified societal stress witnessed increased prevalence of personal distress? The impression, in the absence of empirical data, is that this may well have happened. Have these same periods led to a more prolonged time in the sick role among those who became ill? This too seems plausible. Is this the reason neurasthenia is so prominent in China? Are the social sources of neurasthenia more powerful determinants than psychological vulnerability and biological predisposition? Is this situation all that different from what we find in other cultures? In chapter 7 I attempt to respond to these questions, but the reader is forewarned that definitive answers are largely unavailable. Our contribution is to sharpen the focus, specify more precisely the line of enquiry, and shift the way we think about the relationship between social structural change and illness.

ILLNESS PROBLEMS

I have summarized the illness problems (psychosocial accompaniments of sickness and treatment) suffered by the members of the neurasthenia sample (see table 25). There was a mean of 3.4 illness problems (family, marital, financial, work, school, doctor-patient problems) per patient. Moreover, only four of the hundred patients were assessed as coping adaptively with their illness; the rest exhibited evidence of varying kinds and degrees of mal-adaptive coping, ranging from excessive utilization of medical services and noncompliance with treatment regimens to giving up—what in many cases Pilowski (1978) would call abnormal illness behavior. Perhaps that is why these cases of neurasthenia ended up in a psychiatry clinic: depression and anxiety, personal and social problems undermined coping responses.

Almost three-fourths of the patients either were in process of using or had already used their neurasthenic illness behavior as a reason to change jobs, or to return from separation due to different and distant work sites, or to go on sick leave to avoid or reduce work. This key finding illustrates both the important social consequences of chronic illness and the problems they pose for society and the medical profession. In many societies, including China and the United States, illness once legitimated places the individual in a sick role that release him or her, at least temporarily, from routine social responsibilities. Over time these social responsibilities must be renegotiated with employers, co-workers, family, and agencies of the state. Our data suggest that Hunan is no different than Seattle or Boston in this regard. Nonetheless, a number of large questions are provoked by this finding, which requires much further study. Field investigations in medical anthropology could help determine to what extent neurasthenia offers important social leverage on local work-disability systems; how changing work owing to chronic illness behavior is handled by medical, work, and political institutions; what are the other chief somatic modes of social negotiation besides neurasthenia; and whether psychiatrists or other physicians play a special role in this process as negotiators between patients and families on the one hand, and cadres, co-workers, and members of other social agencies on the other. I will return to the serious social implications of this finding in chapter 7, where I also will review additional findings on this topic gathered in our 1983 studies (see chapter 5).

Table 26 shows that patients' illness behavior was accompanied by work problems in 90 percent of the cases and by family problems in 80 percent. School and marital problems also were prevalent in more than half of cases, while illness was associated with financial problems in 45 percent of cases. Although only 15 percent of cases involved doctor-patient conflict, the number of patients with neurasthenia in China is so large, and such conflicts are otherwise so uncommonly observed in its health care system, that if this finding is substantiated, the total number of such conflicts may be quite substantial and neurasthenic patients may represent a large portion of "difficult or problem patients." Characteristic illness problems included inability to carry out one's job, marital strain, family conflicts and breakdown, school and examination failure, substantial financial loss, and conflicting medical and lay views of what is wrong and what should be done. These problems illumine the burden of illness experience in the context of everyday life. Since it is not always easy to separate antecedents (stressors) from consequents (illness problems), the real issue is the burden of daily living in China that relates to a number of misfortunes, only one type of which is health problems.

ILLNESS MEANINGS

In the initial ethnographic interviews, and for most patients also in the follow-up interviews, ninety-eight of the neurasthenia patients were assessed for the significance of illness, and in each case it was possible to work out at least one meaning associated with the illness behavior and frequently additional ones as well (see table 27).

The single most common significance (in 93% of cases) was to express personal or interpersonal distress or unhappiness, followed by manipulation of interpersonal relations (in 74% of cases), time off from work or other social obligations (73%), and receive love and care from family and friends (66%). All the rest were present in half or less of the cases: personal threat (55%), personal loss (46%), and so forth. Illness significances included both keeping together a family or marriage (26%) and breaking them apart (4%), sanctioning failure (22%, especially examination failure), and receiving financial compensation (9%). These meanings are clearly superficial and mostly social, since it would take long-term relationships of trust and greater familiarity with informants' life situations to elicit deep personal meanings, as occurs in psychotherapy. Ethnographic and psychodynamic data, limited as they were, do tend to support each other, but no attempt was made to gauge the validity of these results which are best regarded as merely initial impressions and tentative interpretations. As such they are, nonetheless, provocative because they suggest that besides a limited number of culture-specific meanings that only make sense in Chinese culture, it is possible to specify illness meanings in contemporary China that are not greatly different from those in other societies, including the United States.

From an anthropological perspective the symptoms our patients experienced can be viewed as multivocal symbols expressing different social meanings and exerting distinctive effects in local relationships of power, a theme developed in chapter 7. From a psychiatric perspective, these cases of somatization resemble those in the West described in chapter 3, and call to mind the important uses of neurasthenia in the Soviet Union to gain leverage over a highly controlled work and political system (Gluzman 1982).

OUTCOME

When patients with major depressive disorder, all of whom were treated with tricyclic antidepressant drugs, the only treatment for depression available in the clinic, were asked at time of follow-up to assess their symptoms, 82 percent regarded themselves as at least slightly *improved,* while 65 percent evaluated their symptoms as substantially improved (see table 28).[6] Nine percent did not feel there was any improvement, and 10 percent felt their symptoms had worsened. On the whole this is an expectable response of the symptoms of major depressive disorder to antidepressants, and it is cor-roborated in the assessments made by my Chinese colleagues and me as depicted in table 29. Here 87 percent of patients were assessed by us as having experienced symptomatic improvement (at least slight), whereas the symptoms of 70 percent were evaluated as substantially improved. Only 4 percent exhibited no symptomatic improvement, while 9 percent appeared worse. Eighty-two percent of major depressive disorder patients returned for follow-up. Several of those who did not wrote that they lived too far away to return for follow-up, but we do not know why others failed to return. This unaccounted-for proportion of nonreturning patients should caution against overinterpreting the outcome data.

A smaller percentage of major depressive disorder patients assessed their social impairment as less (37 percent; see table 30). Not only did 34 percent experience no change in social impairment, but notably 30 percent viewed themselves as more impaired after treatment. Thirty-seven percent of patients, moreover, engaged in further medical help-seeking from practitioners of tra-ditional Chinese medicine and biomedicine, as well as from their families and selves (see table 31), despite the fact that 82 percent regarded their symptoms to be at least partially improved and all were scheduled for follow-up in psychiatry. These patients made thirty-four visits to clinics outside the psychiatric clinic. These outcome findings indicate that perceived social im-pairment, and to a lesser extent help-seeking, did not improve as much as symptoms did; or, put differently, that in spite of symptomatic improvement there was less change in help-seeking and especially in perception of social impairment. The improvement in illness behavior apparently lagged well be-hind the improvement in disease manifestations, and patients maintained the sick role even as their disorders got better. This finding supports the notion that illness in many members of this group performed a positive social func-tion. There is nothing unique to China about this finding. Much concern in our society and in Europe centers on those social features that defeat treat-ment and maintain the course of chronic illness behavior.

Among patients with major depressive disorder, almost two-thirds of those with maladaptive coping (noncompliance, doctor shopping, giving up, passive-hostile behavior, unwillingness to carry out normal social activities, with-drawal and isolation, failure to successfully mobilize or alienation of social network supports, and so forth) either stayed the same or became worse (see table 32). A substantial number of work problems either remained un-changed (35 percent) or worsened (20 percent), and, to a lesser extent, the same was true of family and school and financial problems. Almost as many marital problems stayed the same or worsened as improved. These findings would seem to indicate that although antidepressant drugs may have significantly benefited symptoms, they frequently did not have a major effect on illness problems. Again there is evidence of much less improvement in an important psychosocial aspect of illness. These data demonstrate that medical treatment for chronic conditions without significant psychosocial intervention exerts only a limited effect on the overall illness.

What would be the appropriate therapeutic response to neurasthenia in the People's Republic, or to neurasthenia-like work-related disability problems in the United States? Since illness behavior seems to result from a set of environmental conditions which are harsh and difficult to modify, what is it a Chinese (or American) psychiatrist can do for his or her patients? Furthermore, when psychiatrists address social problems, how do they intervene? Are such interventions legitimate medical actions, or a sign of medicalizing social problems, and therefore disguising their sociopolitical, cultural, and economic roots? What will keep the social psychiatrist out of political difficulties in socialist and capitalist societies? These disquieting therapeutic and preventive implications of our findings will be discussed in the epilogue.

The penultimate table shows that compliance varied directly with perceived symptom improvement. That is to say, the better patients felt, the better they adhered to the treatment regimen. This finding could be interpreted to argue against a major role for social determinants of noncompliance in this patient sample. But we simply did not collect sufficient information on this topic to go beyond a superficial level of analysis, and our measure of compliance (patient reports) was indirect and rough enough to render even this conclusion uncertain. This may simply be another example of the well-known fact that you cannot accurately assess compliance by having the providers of patients' care ask them about compliance in the very setting in which they are being treated. A vast literature on compliance in the West shows that there are numerous other sources of patient failure to follow medical orders besides treatment response (Haynes and Sackett 1979). But it may be the case that Chinese are particularly likely to decide whether to continue to comply based on their strongly pragmatic tendency to judge the quality of treatment in terms of the outcome.

All patients diagnosed as suffering major depressive disorder were informed of this diagnosis before treatment and were even given a biomedical explanation of depressive disease. As has just been discussed, most of these patients experienced symptomatic improvement after taking drugs identified to them as antidepressants. Yet only 11 percent reported at follow-up that their disorder was depression, while 69 percent held to the notion (or came to believe!) they were suffering from neurasthenia (see table 34). That is to say, there was only a 7 percent change in explanatory models from neurasthenia to depression notwithstanding explanations to the contrary and positive response to treatment identified as specific for depression. Surprisingly, a larger percentage of patients called their disorder neurasthenia after treatment than prior to it. Indeed most patients denied that their disorder was depression when we tried to suggest that it might be.

Thus, patients actively rejected the psychiatric label "depression" and reaffirmed the organic medical label "neurasthenia." Not only did the traditional Chinese cultural factors already noted seem to foster this behavior, but so did newer political considerations. During the Great Proletarian Cultural Revolution, all mental illness, including most notably depression, had been called into question by the Maoists as wrong political thinking. This penumbra of meaning still affects the term depression, which also connotes withdrawal and passivity, behaviors that in China's often passionate context of aroused political energy seem suspiciously like disaffiliation and alienation. Such connotations spelled disaster during the Cultural Revolution and even in the pragmatic political atmosphere of present-day, post-Maoist China these are not public attributions with which patients and families wish to be associated. Indeed, neurasthenia is a much safer, and more readily accessible and widely shared public idiom of frustration and demoralization to which Chinese continue to resort in great numbers. Though most demoralization relates to local issues of work and family, for some this is a dual discourse (overt physical complaints, covert political ones) to express dissatisfaction with the broader political situation. Because these insights are not unknown to Chinese psychiatrists, though they are not talked about, it is even more difficult for them to transform neurasthenia into depression and examine certain of the wider social structural sources of this form of human misery.

The findings I have reviewed in this chapter have been taken by some psychiatrists in the West and in China to support our initial hypothesis that neurasthenia sufferers in China can be diagnosed as suffering depression (and other psychiatric disorders) when assessed with standard North American evaluation techniques and diagnostic criteria. But from an anthropological perspective neurasthenia and depression are seen as examples of the social construction of clinical reality.

Our analysis suggests that in spite of the undoubtedly great international professional pressures on Chinese psychiatry to recast neurasthenia as depression, neurasthenia and depression have a much more complex relationship, and the former—not the latter—is (at least at present) a more socially suitable and culturally approved diagnostic category in Chinese society.

Why is neurasthenia still so prominent, then, in China? Is it because the prevalence rates of the disorder are actually higher? Is it because it is a potentially acceptable way for mental health personnel to deal with depression and other serious psychological problems? Is it because China's psychiatrists have not modernized their society's diagnostic system for categorizing and responding to mental health problems? Both our 1983 studies at the Hunan Medical College and our description of real cases suggest some answers.

Five
★
Clinical Research: China, 1983

The Medical Board continued for some years to recommend me for a
disability pension. My particular disability was neurasthenia; the train
journey and the first-class Army railway-warrant filled out with my rank and
the regiment usually produced reminiscential neurasthenia by the time I
reached the Board.

Robert Graves, *Good-bye to All That*

In April 1983, my wife and I followed up twenty-one of thirty cases from
the 1980 sample who were suffering from both chronic pain syndrome and
major depressive disorder and who lived near enough to the Hunan Medical
College to return for interviews. (Nine patients declined to participate because
they lived far outside the city. They wrote back to our letter of inquiry,
answering that they were too busy with agricultural or other work activities
to be interviewed).[1] We conducted this study to determine to what degree
somatic complaints among these patients were amplified or dampened in
response to work, family, and other social problems over a period of years,
and to what extent both chronic pain and depression had responded to medical
treatments. We hypothesized, owing to our original data, that the social context of illness would be the major determinant of persistent somatization.
We wanted to study that context in more depth to obtain a better understanding of the life experiences of our patients. What, for example, was the
influence on the long-term course of their illness experiences of major political, economic, and other large-scale social change in China? What role
did their local situations play in influencing how their illness experiences
were affected by such macrosocial transformations?

Two-thirds of the patients were women; most were middle-aged workers
and teachers (see table 35). Using the same diagnostic interview schedule
we had employed three years before, we determined that only one-third of

the patients made the DSM-III diagnostic criteria for major depressive disorder, far fewer than in 1980. A quarter of the sample made the criteria for dysthymic disorder (chronic neurotic depression, a less severe form of clinical depression). For many of the patients depression had become a less severe but very chronic problem; for others it had remitted, but often without return to normal health inasmuch as physical complaints persisted. The same percentage, but not always the same patients, were suffering from anxiety disorders. Nineteen percent had no mental illness at all. Thus, almost one out of five psychiatric disorders remitted over the three years, while others displayed a more chronic low-grade character (see table 36).

Over the course of the three years, one-third of the patients experienced no change in their chronic pain and other symptoms, just under half were somewhat improved but still experienced pain as well as other somatic symptoms, and only 14 percent were greatly improved. Only one patient had experienced a complete cure (table 37). Most patients still complained of pain and other symptoms. Eight (38 percent) had changed work since 1980, and altogether ten (48 percent) had changed work at some point in the preceeding five years (see table 38). This compared with no reported history of work change during the past three years among twenty-five patients with various non-neurasthenic neurotic disorders in the psychiatric clinic at the Hunan Medical College, who were matched with the patients in our sample for age, sex, and occupation. Three other chronic pain patients (14 percent) had retired from work during these three years.

Those patients whose chronic pain complaints improved had either changed work, retired, or undergone some other significant change in those social situations that had been identified as a source of significant stress in 1980. For example, four (19 percent) were reunited with family after separation owing to different and distant work sites; two (10 percent), who had desired to do so for some time but had previously met with substantial bureaucratic and family obstacles, had married; one (5 percent) had earned a much desired university degree; and in one case a conflict-ridden home situation was resolved when a contentious mother-in-law moved out of the family's small apartment. Each of the retired patients had experienced symptom improvement, whereas 20 percent of the patients who changed jobs experienced no symptom improvement, and another 20 percent had experienced a worsening of complaints (see table 39). Each of those whose complaints had worsened, however, described current work problems (especially involving relations with supervisors and co-workers) as more severe than in the previous job. Of those whose change in work was self-perceived as an improvement over their prior work, four experienced symptom improvement, one had no change in symptoms, and none had a worsening of complaints. Of the three patients who informed us their change in work was neither more nor less stressful, the symptoms of two improved, one stayed the same, and none were worse (see table 40). Thus, though our sample was very small, there was substantial support for the conclusion that symptom amplification reflected worsening of work problems, symptom dampening improvement.

When family problems were evaluated, the picture was the same (see table 41). In one case, when a daughter who was the major support of the family had left home, her mother's chronic pain persisted, as it did in a woman whose marriage had deteriorated so badly that she was actively contemplating divorce—a stigmatized and infrequent act in the People's Republic. In contrast, of the six cases who resolved major family problems, two-thirds had undergone symptom improvement. We have demonstrated, therefore, a close relationship between persistence of complaints and persistence of social sources of distress, and diminished disability and perceived improvement in social life, including most notably retirement, reunion after separation due to different work sites, work change associated with improved work situation (usually described as better work relationships and less stressful), and improvement in family situations.

Ninety percent of cases in 1983 still experienced headaches, by far the most common complaint, though frequently these were less disabling than in the past. Other symptoms of neurasthenia (both in Beard's classical account and those the Chinese chiefly associate with the disorder) also persisted (see table 42).

Patients' accounts of work continued to disclose a strong association of symptoms with work problems. Unlike our initial interviews in 1980, when patients hesitated to complain openly of work, nine (43 percent) at the time of the three-year follow-up felt free enough in their relationship with us to state openly their dislike for their work, and of these seven (33 percent) expressed a strong desire to change work. Altogether twelve patients (57 percent) believed that illness affected their work, while the nine already mentioned viewed their illnesses as worsened by work. Most of these patients were either considering efforts to change work or were already actively doing so. We were also greatly impressed when almost one in five patients stated they had significant economic problems greater than those of co-workers, a quarter perceived themselves as having significant marital problems, and more than half described a serious family problem that was still incompletely resolved.

Over the three years since our first contact, only two patients (10 percent) had come to regard their sickness as depression, while nine (43 percent), the same number as in 1980, still thought of it as neurasthenia. This further supports the argument that neurasthenia is a more acceptable diagnosis than depression in China. But our understanding of why this is so was altered by a finding we had not anticipated. In 1980 all the patients regarded their pain as either entirely or primarily organic in origin, but by 1983 52 percent regarded their pain as chiefly or entirely psychological. This change in viewpoint almost certainly reflected the researchers' having communicated a psychosomatic stress model of patients' illnesses, and that model had also become more widely used in the psychiatric clinic. Surprisingly, in spite of cultural sanctioning of organic explanations the patients came to accept professionally proffered psychological ones. The switch in explanatory models was associated with an interesting change in help-seeking. Of those whose views of their illnesses became more psychological or psychosomatic, 70 percent decreased medical help-seeking, whereas of those few whose views of their illness became more organic, only a third decreased contact with the medical care system. Thus, change to more psychological explanations had the important effect of reducing the overutilization of medical services.

When 38 percent of the follow-up patients expressed a wish to be treated with psychotherapy—a treatment intervention which is neither well-developed nor prevalent in psychiatric care in China, and one that goes against the grain of the group orientation and somatic idiom of both traditional Chinese culture and the ethos of the People's Republic—our reaction was one of even greater surprise.[2] To make sense of this provocative finding, we wondered whether psychiatry is contributing to the advance of modernism in the clinic, a form of Westernization of Chinese culture by "rationalizing" (explaining and legitimating) psychological idioms and self-images and thereby transforming neurasthenia into a disorder of "affect." This sea change in the cultural code of communicating distress has not yet overtaken the popular culture in the People's Republic, but on the basis or reports for Chinese in the United States, Hong Kong (Cheung et al., in press), Taiwan (Rin 1982), and other overseas communities, it is apparent that it is happening in Chinese populations as they undergo rapid modernization and that psychologization can be expected to emerge. Our data suggest that psychologization is already beginning to gain ground on the mainland, at least among the more educated class of teachers and professionals. Indeed, it is our impression that the term *psychological* is appearing with increasing frequency in the Chinese psychiatric literature and in Chinese academic publications generally.

Of the patients in our sample, not one had experienced a cure due to medical treatment, nor had a new medical diagnosis (for example, endocrinological disease, cardiovascular disease, neurological disease) been established over the three years for any patient that had explained his or her pathology or changes in the level of disability. None of the psychiatric diagnoses (depression, anxiety, no mental illness) predicted positive treatment response, though clearly diagnoses of both "neurasthenia" and "chronic pain" were associated with relatively poor outcomes. The only robust predictors of course were the social indicators of work, family, and other social problems. We take this to be an impressive confirmation of the hypothesis that motivated our follow-up, though the small size of our sample and the absence of studies to replicate our results means that caution must be applied when generalizing from the findings. Because the data are similar to those from the West (for example, Yelin et al. 1980; Stone 1979a, b), however, a call for further research with larger samples in different clinical sites in China seems warranted.

The depressed pain patients in our sample were labeled "problem patients" by their medical system. We can make this claim inasmuch as almost one-third had experienced some important conflict in their relationships with practitioners, a complaint rarely mentioned among patients in China. They were viewed by their physicians as "problem patients," we suspect, for much the same reason that chronic pain patients are so viewed in health care settings in the United States and the United Kingdom: because they fail to get better, persist in seeking medical attention, and make treatment demands on their health care system that cannot be fulfilled (cf. Helman 1985). Again as in the West, the psychosomatic label enables practitioners to shift responsibility for the poor therapeutic outcome from themselves to their patients. (In fact the label chronic neurasthenia seems to convey the same relatively frustrating message to many physicians with whom we discussed this problem in China).

In each case we worked out an interpretation of the meaning of the illness experience that extended beyond work and family problems to the broader sociocultural context (see table 43). For four patients (19 percent) chronic pain and other somatic complaints appeared to provide a cultural sanction for *failure* (in college entrance examinations, in achieving career goals, in returning from the countryside to their urban homes, and in other aspects of social life). For five patients (24 percent) the pain was a palpable symbol, a physiological index, of their own personal tragedies during the Cultural Revolution, though, as in the general population, many more had experienced some problems (usually less serious ones) in that dangerous and chaotic period without their taking on such overwhelming significance. The validity of both sets of meanings of illness are vividly illustrated by the case vignettes in chapter 6. To our minds almost half the sample appeared to regularly and fairly successfully use their chronic pain to control spouse, children, or parents. Among four patients (19 percent) pain effectively sanctioned the expression of anger which otherwise could not be expressed openly, including anger at the political system. For six others (28 percent) pain seemed to less availingly legitimize expression of chronic frustration and demoralization over unresolved problems in the local community, including political ones. Two patients' pain appeared to successfully sanction time off and away from what they perceived as enervating responsibilities in the community, giving them otherwise unavailable time to rest. (Indeed, two other patients with serious work stress were able to persuade the Chinese psychiatrists in our research team to provide certificates to take time off from work in order to "rest"!) For 19 percent of the sample physical pain complaints grew out of the context of bereavement over the loss of a close family member, and in several other patients pain complaints seemed to express a more complicated set of losses (health, youth, confidence, education, Communist Party affiliation). Two patients justified isolation and nearly total withdrawal from sources of life stress via their pain complaints. Thus, for the patients we studied, pain, as in the original 1980 study, held substantial social cachet. Pain complaints routinely symbolized more than one personally or socially significant meaning, a point discussed in chapter 7, where the social sources of neurasthenia, depression, and somatization are reviewed.

CHRONIC PAIN IN PRIMARY CARE AT
THE HUNAN MEDICAL COLLEGE

Did our results apply to neurasthenic patients generally, or only to that special group referred to a psychiatry clinic? Since the chronic pain patients in our 1980 and 1983 studies were all attending a psychiatry clinic, we could not answer this question until we had studied a primary care clinical sample. Therefore, in July 1983 a study was conducted in the general medical clinic of the Second Affiliated Hospital at the Hunan Medical College, a primary care clinic which daily saw many times the number of patients in the psychiatry clinic and which would enable us to compare our findings with the data on somatization in primary care in the West. First we surveyed the clinic to determine what percentage of patients complained of the two most common chronic somatization complaints in China: headaches and insomnia, in the absence of a medical diagnosis of specific physiological pathology. A chief complaint of headaches without documented biomedical disease was expressed by 11 percent of all patients surveyed over a two-day period, while insomnia was the chief problem, unexplained by diagnosis of an organic lesion, for 10 percent of the 658 patients attending the clinic during those two days.[3] These symptoms, which frequently occur together, were written as single diagnoses on patients' records problems and by and large these diagnoses did not overlap. Using these problems as a very conservative estimate of somatization cases suggests that about one out of five outpatients in this primary care clinic may have been somatizing. Of the 658 patients, 7.4 percent were diagnosed as neurotics or neurasthenics, and this group was composed almost entirely of patients suffering from headaches or insomnia.

After the survey was completed, a clinical study was undertaken. Twenty-six patients, who were diagnosed as suffering from chronic pain (here defined as more than six months of pain perceived by the patients themselves as disabling, not the two-year criterion applied in the 1980 study), were selected roughly consecutively and interviewed in the same manner as in the earlier studies.[4] Two-thirds were middle-aged women, almost half workers, the rest mainly teachers, cadres, and professionals (see table 44). All suffered headaches as their site of pain, though half had other pain sites as well. Fifty-four percent of the sample made the DSM-III criteria for major depressive disorder when interviewed with a modified version of the SADS diagnostic interview translated into Chinese, though none had been diagnosed by the clinic's internists or consulting psychiatrists. Almost a quarter (23 percent) were determined to make the criteria for dysthymic disorder (chronic neurotic depression), which also was not diagnosed in the clinic. A third of patients, mostly those who were depressed, also made the criteria for various anxiety disorders. Notably, seven patients (27 percent) were assessed to have no mental illness (see table 45). Thus, as our Taiwan findings had earlier suggested, serious psychopathology (including depression) was less common among neurasthenic patients in primary care than among neurasthenic patients in the psychiatry clinic.

The other findings are in line with those from the chronic pain study in the psychiatry clinic. Women predominated in both groups. (In our 1980 survey of the one hundred neurasthenia patients, men had a very slight predominance, as they did in the psychiatry clinic generally. But even at that time women predominated in the chronic pain-depression subsample, as they do in the West.)[5] Teachers and others who belong to the intelligentsia were overrepresented, but workers (especially skilled workers) were well represented. The elderly were not overrepresented. If these findings are replicated in larger samples and in community surveys, somatization may turn out to affect a wide segment of the Chinese population. In the absence of population-based figures, it would seem that women, especially middle-aged women, teachers, other members of the intelligentsia, and skilled workers may be at greater risk for somatization.

Depression and anxiety disorders, as in the follow-up study, were found to be common concomitants of chronic pain, even in a general medical clinic, although more than one out of four patients had no mental illness. That both the follow-up study and this study contained a significant minority of patients who exhibited no evidence of mental illness on a fairly rigorous assessment schedule indicates that somatization is not always mediated by psychiatric disorder, though it does seem almost always to be associated with social problems.

These chronic pain patients had visited medical services an average of fifteen times over the preceding twelve months, which is a high utilization rate for this clinic and for China generally. Headaches and other pain were accompanied by dizziness in more than half the cases, insomnia in more than three-quarters, weakness in one-third, blurring of vision in more than one-quarter, and tiredness in one-quarter. This constellation of complaints can now be regarded as the "classical" symptom picture of neurasthenia in China. Not surprisingly, 73 percent of the patients either had been diagnosed as suffering from neurasthenia by the doctors they visited or had labeled themselves with the term. No patients called their sickness chronic pain, and only 2 (8 percent) called it depression. More than a quarter of patients had family members with a history of chronic pain or neurasthenia, which was true of the psychiatry clinic sample too. Is this a genetic or socially learned vulnerability factor? Again, as in the 1980 sample, the answer is uncertain, and will have to be assessed in future research. In the meantime it is reasonable to assume that both may make a contribution.

More than half the primary care sample experienced serious work problems. Fifteen percent had significant marital problems, and almost one-third had severe family distress. Thirty-eight percent of patients described themselves as being in serious economic difficulties, and nine patients (35 percent) had experienced difficult political problems in the past or were experiencing them at present, most usually related to the Cultural Revolution. Five patients (19 percent) were separated from their families because of distant work sites. Once again severe social problems of the same type described in the follow-up study were an integral part of the illness experience (see table 46).

As in the earlier studies we drew on the interviews to interpret the meanings of the often not so covert chronic illness behavior. We found that ten patients (38 percent) wanted to change work, and their illness seemed to legitimize their efforts to do so; four (15 percent) were actively negotiating time off and away from work and from what were perceived as overwhelming family responsibilities, from which they sought "rest." The spouses and family members of two patients clearly treated them better when they were ill. For two others the pain complaints crystallized and expressed deep frustration over a strong desire to obtain divorce in untenable marriages that were deemed unsuitable for divorce by work unit *(danwei)* leaders and family members. For another patient the language of pain sanctioned personal failure; for yet another it gave voice to a cry for help in a situation that was impossible to alter (see table 47).

The picture of the social origins and cultural construal of somatization in this primary care clinic is thus quite similar to what we described for the psychiatry clinic. It adds information about the symptomatology and the social context, and lends further support to the interpretation of somatization in China that emerges from our research. The question now is to develop a more fine-grained image of the processes that constitute the symbolic reticulum bridging neurasthenia and Chinese social reality.

Six

★

Cases

Because the body is the most potent metaphor of society, it is not
surprising that disease is the most salient metaphor of structural crisis. All
disease is disorder—metaphorically, literally, socially and politically.

Turner (1985:114)

Night, day, dusk reverse,
With face and countenance altered;
My spirit diminished,
Heart boiling and burning (with resentment).
One change leads to another,
Nothing in the world coming to settle.
Alas, my wisdom and counsel are not ample,
All I fear is my soul and breath will tumble away.
All my life I have been treading on thin ice;
Does anyone know how my heart scalds?

Ruan Ji (210–263 A.D.)
Songs of Sorrow (82 poems), J. Kleinman, trans.

The real persons and life stories behind the statistics are presented below
in brief case synopses of neurasthenia patients. These case vignettes (in which
names and identifying details have been changed to protect anonymity) illustrate various of the findings described previously,[1] and provide a deeper
sense of the social sources of personal and family distress in China. The
cases selected are not meant to be representative; instead they are ones for
which sufficient information is available to illumine the web of richly complex
interrelationships between social reality, affect, and somatization that is only
partially evoked by numerical description and inadequately explained by statistical correlations.

The thirteen cases are grouped in several sections, the first of which contains brief examples of neurasthenia patients who make the diagnostic criteria

of major depressive disorder and whose symptom pictures represent somatic and psychological modes of expression of distress. The second section describes cases that exemplify different social and psychological meanings of neurasthenia, and also some of the more important uses of this illness behavior in Chinese society. Section three contains case histories of psychological casualties in the Cultural Revolution. The cases in the last two sections especially should broaden and sharpen understanding of the social sources of psychological distress and mental illness in China.

CULTURAL AND SOCIAL INFLUENCE ON ILLNESS EXPERIENCE

Major Depressive Disorder with Melancholia, Partially Psychologized

Case 1   Qian Xiaozhang is an eighteen-year-old male, senior middle school student who one year before unexpectedly failed an examination and as a result was moved out of a special high-level, academic group in his class and placed into a lower group. As a result of exam failure, his parents, both of whom are high-ranking provincial cadres who hold great expectations for their eldest son, scolded him, blaming him for not working hard enough in school and severely criticizing him for his poor test performance. They told him he would have no future if he did not work harder. At the same time his schoolmates laughed at him for falling from a special group being primed for the university entrance exam down to a mediocre group who were not expected to go on to university.

Qian felt demoralized and humiliated. Even before this time he had harbored self-doubts about his own academic skills and ability to achieve at the high level expected by his parents. After failing the exam he became depressed, felt hopeless and worthless, lost interest in things that previously were pleasurable, thought of death, and experienced insomnia with early morning waking, headaches, dizziness, loss of energy, poor appetite, weight loss, poor concentration, and marked anxiety. He developed a haggard look and felt dizzy and complained of dry mouth and constipation. Unlike most of the patients in our study, he quite openly expressed his demoralization and sad mood, and in his explanatory model related his dysphoria to stress and his own psychological make-up. But fascinatingly, even though Qian and his family regarded his problem to be a psychological one and sought out appropriate counseling and psychiatric care, his illness idiom was still dominated by somatic complaints, which they viewed as more worrisome than the psychological complaints and for which they sought out medical care. His explanatory model, furthermore, was somatopsychic, since he regarded stress and his personality as affecting his brain and thereby producing organic pathology that was responsible for his mood disturbance and also his poor performance in school.

Major Depressive Disorder with Somatization

Case 2 Lin Zhen, a thirty-five-year-old female physician who works in a local factory clinic and graduated from the Wuhan Medical College, presents with a history of chronic headaches. In 1968 Lin Zhen decided to end a budding relationship with a fellow medical student in order to heed the Cultural Revolution's call to serve the people and forsake personal interests. Within a year she felt that she had made a mistake and at the same time began to experience headaches, palpitations, insomnia, and agitation. She grieved the loss of her boyfriend, who in the meantime had become engaged to another classmate. Dr. Lin underwent several medical work-ups for her headaches, all of which were reported as "negative." These headaches continued over the subsequent decade, worsening when she was under personal stress, or when she was criticized in the Cultural Revolution by her co-workers and unit leaders for not assuming enough responsibility. The headaches have become particularly severe in the past several months, following an order that she transfer to a new and smaller clinic in a distant suburb, something the patient, who grew up and presently lives in Changsha, has expressed a strong desire not to do. For the ten years her headaches have been diagnosed as part of a neurasthenia syndrome.

During the past two months she has had lack of energy, insomnia with early morning waking, difficulty concentrating, poor memory, loss of interest in her work, marked restlessness, and a sense of being in a hopeless situation that makes her feel worthless. Under gentle questioning she admitted to feeling depressed, but attributed this feeling to the inability to control her worsening headaches, which she regards as her real illness. These symptoms all were present a decade ago at the onset of her problem. She has tried more than ten different drugs and visited five different clinics in the two months prior to our initial interview in pursuit of an effective remedy for her headaches. Lin Zhen decided to visit the psychiatry clinic after reading a paper in a medical journal on Pavlov's view of neurasthenia as due to "negative localization in the brain." Dr. Lin believed she had organic brain pathology and requested an electroencephalographic assessment. Six weeks later, at the time of follow-up and after treatment with a tricyclic antidepressant, she had normal sleep and appetite, greatly improved social funtioning at work and home, and felt her mood was "70 percent" better. Though her headaches were still present, they were described as "60 percent" better. Lin Zhen is still trying to avoid transfer to a new work site on the grounds of her health problem, which she calls "neurasthenia." She is actively negotiating a modified work schedule to accommodate her illness, one that she reports is feasible at her current work site but not in the new clinic she has been asked to head.

Case 3   Qin Zijun is a forty-year-old female factory worker, mother of three children, and has a two-year history of dizziness, headaches, weakness, and marked lack of energy. Qin Zijun's husband, who comes from a landlord background, has had recurrent problems with the leading cadres of his factory; two and a half years ago he was sent to a factory in another city to work. His wife failed to receive bonuses and promotion, she believes, because of her husband's problem. She has been very unhappy with her husband's separation from the family, and also dislikes her work as a machine operator. For the past eigthteen months she has repeatedly asked to change jobs because of her illness, which has been diagnosed by different doctors as "neurasthenia." Qin Zijun has also requested that her husband be transferred back to Changsha to help care for her. She has stayed home from work the past several months and has received her full salary. Comrade Qin is uncertain if she will be able to return to work since her illness has not responded to treatment, and she is pessimistic that she will ever get well. She states that work makes her illness worse, and that she is hypersensitive to the noise and cold temperature at work. She admits to great anger and frustration over her situation. For two years she has had insomnia, poor appetite (which has worsened over the past half year with a ten-pound weight loss), felt both slowed down and restless, had difficulty with concentration, and thought about death without being actively suicidal. Comrade Qin also reports fear of leaving her house and being in groups of people. Under questioning she assents to feeling displeased, hopeless, helpless, and deriving no pleasure from activities which in the past gave her considerable pleasure.

Qin Zijun reported that she had felt low self-esteem and periodic hopelessness since childhood, and that she had always been regarded by family members as excessively concerned about her health and fearful of falling ill. She was briefly hospitalized with symptoms similar to those she now experiences after the birth of her second child. She lives with her husband's parents, with whom she has always had a poor relationship and who, she feels, fail to give her sufficient day-to-day support, although they do take care of her and of the family when she is ill. After treatment of her major depressive disorder and agoraphobia with imipramine, the patient experienced a substantial improvement in symptoms, but she still regarded herself as socially impaired and had not returned to work. At time of second follow-up she reported involvement in an ongoing negotiation with the leading cadres in her factory regarding change to part-time and lighter work and the possibility of her husband's receiving a transfer back to Changsha sometime the following year to help care for her and the household.

I ask the reader to leave aside for the time being the social questions raised by these three cases. Here I wish to focus only on the symptom pictures. Qian Xiaozhang (case 1) makes the diagnostic criteria for a severe clinical depression (see Chap. 2, note 1). The symptoms he reports include both psychological complaints (demoralization, sad mood, joylessness, anxiety) and physical problems (insomnia, loss of energy and appetite, headaches, dizziness, dry mouth, and constipation). Both his family and he regard the latter as the most important problem, and explain his psychological complaints as the result of bodily effects of stress on the brain. Hence both psychological and somatic idioms of distress and patterns of help-seeking (contact with internal medicine physicians and psychiatrists) are present, but the somatic idioms predominate. From the perspective of Chinese psychiatry this is a typical case of neurasthenia with virtually all the classical symptoms; yet from an American psychiatric perspective this is a classic instance of major depressive disorder, to which both longstanding psychodynamic and more recent situational sources of distress would seem to contribute.

In case 2 Dr. Lin Zhen has a lengthy history of headaches and seeking medical care to relieve them. She too believes that her headaches are symptomatic of a physical lesion in her brain. The symptom history she reports to her physicians centers on her headaches. She mentions feelings of hopelessness and worthlessness, but explains that they result from being unable to control her headaches. Only when specifically questioned does she talk about her depressed feelings and her work difficulty. For the internist the headaches are part of a neurasthenic syndrome, since they have no other organic basis and they occur within a symptom constellation typical of neurasthenia. Chinese psychiatrists would emphasize this syndromal pattern in treating Dr. Lin for chronic neurasthenia. For American psychiatrists the organic complaints look like the vegetative complaints of major depressive disorder. The affective complaints (hopelessness, worthlessness, sadness) are not viewed as secondary to the chronic physical problem, but rather are pictured as part of a psychiatric disorder—clinical depression—that has three groups of symptoms: affective (the sadness); cognitive (the difficulty concentrating and poor memory); vegetative (the energy and sleep disturbance and the headaches themselves). Moreover, for the American psychiatrist the headaches have become the centerpiece of a chronic pain problem that has seriously disrupted Dr. Lin's life. The fact that her symptoms improve with an antidepressant would likely convince American psychiatrists that this indeed is a depressive disorder. The fact that the symptoms have not entirely remitted and that the chief complaint, the headaches, is still present would likely make many Chinese psychiatrists stick to the diagnosis of neurasthenia.

Qin Zijun (case 3) illustrates the same problem in psychiatric diagnosis. Her disease can be viewed either as a psychological disorder in which the physical complaints are secondary in significance to the psychological ones or as a physical problem in which the psychological complaints are secondary. American mental health professionals would view her childhood history of psychological problems and her postpartum distress as indicators that her personality contributed to vulnerability to depression and to an earlier depressive experience. Their Chinese counterparts might well interpret these as vulnerability to and an earlier instance of neurasthenia.

Each case had serious social problems associated with their illness experiences (school and family stress, work difficulties, and problems related to separation of work sites). The cases below further illustrate the social uses and cultural and personal meanings of neurasthenic symptoms; they also describe instances of the social origins of illness that place certain vulnerable individuals and categories of persons at greater risk of developing illness in response to serious social problems.

SOCIAL AND PERSONAL MEANINGS AND USES OF ILLNESS

A. Work-related Problems

Case 4 Lin Hung is a twenty-four-year-old worker in a machine factory who complains of headaches, dizziness, weakness, lack of energy, insomnia, bad dreams, poor memory, and a stiff neck. Pain, weakness, and dizziness are his chief symptoms, along with bouts of palpitations. His symptoms began six months ago, and they are gradually worsening. His mother, who has had similar complaints for many years, has been diagnosed as suffering from "neurasthenia," and Comrade Lin fears he has the same problem. His factory doctors believe he has a heart problem, but repeated electrocardiograms at the Hunan Medical College have been normal. He states he has a serious bodily disorder, worsened by his work, that interferes with his ability to carry out his job responsibilities.

Lin Hung has all the symptoms of major depressive disorder as well as typical attacks of panic disorder (a type of anxiety disorder associated with waves of panic, hyperventilation, and rapid heart rate). He feels suicidal.

Until his father retired from the job Lin now occupies, he was a soldier living not far from home. He did not want to leave the army, but his father was anxious to retire so that he could move to a new apartment owned by his factory in another city. Fearing that his son would not be able to stay in the army and thereafter would not find work, Lin's father pressured him to take over his job, a job the younger Lin never liked or wanted for himself.[2] Lin Hung reluctantly agreed, but now finds that he cannot adjust to the work. He did not want to be a machinist, and cries when he recounts that this is what he must be for the rest of his life. Lin Hung, moreover, is despondent and lonely living so far away from his parents. He worries that he is not around to look after them in their old age, and that an older sister, who was sent to the countryside in the early 1970s, cannot get permission to move to the city to be with them. He has no friends at work and feels lonely living in the dormitory. He has a girlfriend, but he cannot see her regularly anymore, owing to the change in work sites. They wish to marry, but his parents, who have a serious financial problem because of a very low pension, cannot provide the expected furniture, room, or any financial help. The leaders of his work unit are against the marriage because he is too young. They also criticize him for his poor work performance and frequent days missed from work owing to sickness. He in turn does not believe he has the skill to work as a machinist and fears further ridicule for his shoddy work.

Lin Hung thinks that his health problem would resolve if he could leave his job, join his parents, and marry. But he regards each to be impossible. Lin tells us he is hopeless and helpless, yet he attributes these feelings to his physical symptoms not his social situation. He plans to seek sick leave so that he can rest and recover. His parents and he fear that he has a serious heart disorder, even though the physicians in the internal medicine clinic at the Hunan Medical College have reassured him that his heart is normal and that his palpitations result from anxiety attacks. Lin Hung rejects the diagnosis of a psychosomatic problem, "I am sad and agitated because of my physical illness! That is the real problem, my heart disease." Out of desperation he pleads that we give him a letter for his factory clinic indicating that he must rest and recuperate, preferably at his parent's apartment.

Lin's demoralization over his severe work problem, separation from his family, and inability to marry is an example of the powerful influences of social setting on psychological state. In Lin's case these problems contributed to the onset of his illness in a manner that we shall discuss in chapter 7 as the social production of neurasthenia-depression. Lin Hung's illness behavior, once created, however, is then taken up in the unique pattern of relationships that constitute his life world. Thus, his illness comes to express his social condition and to act as a potential lever on those social circumstances that have caused his distress. In contemporary Chinese society, where tight social control is diffused through the work unit, which is a type of total institution (where the individual eats, sleeps, forms his friendships, seeks permission to marry, and conducts most of the activities of daily living), illness gives the sick person some additional, if limited, personal control in a situation that easily can become oppressive. Symptoms can be used to get time off and away from work, to help change a job which, as in Lin Hung's case, is greatly disliked but which has been assigned to one for life, perhaps to change work sites or at least to have an excuse to join one's family, even if only for a limited time.

Of course, illness can and does serve the same social functions in the West, but I would argue that in the very tight social structure of socialist societies this social use of illness is intensified. I believe this is especially true of China, where until the recent period of liberalization, the work-unit potentially exerts near total control over individual's lives. In fact this control is a great deal less than it might be, in part because illness, along with other important circumstances in one's life, enables negotiations that mitigate the force of institutional authority. Much the same thing may well have taken place in Chinese society traditionally as a means of easing the impact of authoritarian controls on individuals in family, lineage, village and imperial settings. Thus, the traditionally oppressive relationships between husband and wife, mother-in-law and daughter-in-law, landlord and peasant, emperor and subject probably have always been negotiated, to some extent, based on personal circumstances, of which illness is a powerful instance. Since in sociocentric, hierarchical China, individual rights and privacy have always been subordinated to collective responsibilities and institutionalized authority, it is hard to gauge to what extent external oppression is perceived and experienced as internal distress. But our cases disclose that such distress does occur, and that close control over life choices in a setting of limited access to resources and inadequate protection from bureaucratic constraints can be a source of misery and illness.

The first three cases I described further illustrate the social uses and meanings of neurasthenia. In case 2, Dr. Lin's headaches played a key role in legitimizing her negotiations with her factory's leaders to avoid moving to a new work site to which she did not wish to transfer. In the past they had worsened precisely at those times when she felt much pressure, especially when she was criticized for not assuming increased responsibility at work. During the Cultural Revolution those individuals in positions of responsibility were particularly vulnerable to serious attack, so that there was good reason to avoid being placed in such a position. Lin Zhen's loss of a boyfriend during the Cultural Revolution was the event that seemed to precipitate her initial episode of illness and to place her at greater vulnerability to other politically motivated losses, for example, the threat of losing a secure low-level position and a work site near her home. Similarly, loss of self-esteem and parental and peer group support appeared to push Qian Xiaozhang, in case 1, into a downward depressive spiral for which his physical complaints especially elicited family support and provided a more acceptable excuse for his declining academic performance. Qin Zijun, case 3, suffered a sense of chronic persecution because of her husband's landlord background. Her personal history indicates that she had had longstanding depressive and hypochondriacal problems since childhood that made her more vulnerable to separation from her husband and chronic work problems. Her symptoms have produced substantial work disability, which in turn is a key component in her negotiations at work to change jobs and bring her husband back home from his distant work site.

Case 5   Wu Baihua is a forty-two-year-old principal of a senior middle school in a small city in Hunan Province who has suffered from headaches, dizziness, attacks of palpitations, and complaints of tension for five years, following upon the sudden, unexpected death of an elder sister in 1978. The serious clinical depression (major depressive disorder) diagnosed in 1980 is no longer present, but in 1983 it became apparent that Wu Baihua has been experiencing a chronic low-grade depression (dysthymic disorder) that developed imperceptibly and insidiously out of the grief for her sister.

This sister had been exceptionally close to Wu since the death of their mother, when both were adolescents, and had assumed a parental role toward her. When she married, she invited Wu to live with her and her husband. Several years before her sister's death Wu's brother-in-law had died in an accident, so that at the time of her sister's death their adolescent daughter had become orphaned. Thinking back to her own similarly tragic experience, Wu Baihua felt a strong need to adopt and care for her niece. Despite her husband's hesitancy, and the real difficulties of bringing a late adolescent into the three small rooms occupied by Wu, her husband, their three adolescent children, and her in-laws, Wu carried through her plan. Now twenty-four, her niece has been a constant source of family tension. She was a marginal student who got into trouble with school authorities because of her uncompromising, "autistic" (meaning, self-centered) behavior, and left senior middle school before graduating. Working at a menial job in a factory, which Wu's husband had arranged only with great difficulty, her niece quarrels frequently with her supervisors and co-workers. Wu Baihua is especially troubled that her niece has not been able to marry, because of her difficult, unbending disposition. Wu's eyes fill with tears as she recounts this part of her story. "Perhaps this is all my fault. I have not been able to devote the time to her upbringing that I promised my dying sister I would. I feel very badly that I have not performed this duty in the way my sister performed it for me. I have failed her."

In 1981 Wu was promoted from science teacher of a special class of advanced students being prepared for the university entrance examination to principal of her middle school. Although she had the full support of the leaders of her unit and her fellow teachers, she strongly resisted this promotion because she believed the position would be too stressful. Following the promotion Wu's fears were quickly realized. The school entered a period of major reorganization during which great responsibility was placed on her shoulders to reform the curriculum, reorganize the faculty, plan for new school buildings and the refurbishment of old ones, and oversee a gradual transition from nonprofessional cadres to professional teachers in the administrative hierarchy of the school. Wu felt that she had much too much work to do. She spent from early each morning until late in the evening at her job, forcing her husband, a cadre in another unit, to take over most of the household activities. Even when she is home Wu feels saddled with work responsibilities that she has to carry over into her home life. This situation would be difficult enough, Wu suggests, but a divisive relationship with the secretary of the local unit's branch of the Communist Party causes marked tension in her work.

An old soldier of peasant background, with little formal education and no professional training, the party secretary's post is a sinecure given in recognition of his early service to the party. He has been deeply threatened by the post-Cultural Revolution changes that have revivified professional interests and imperil the power structure of the school. As a result he countermands Principal Wu's plans at the last minute, after support from the faculty has been achieved following hours of difficult negotiations; changes faculty assignments without consulting her; and alters curriculum reform in unpredictable ways that undermine directives from local educational authorities but place Wu Baihua in conflict with her faculty. His actions undermine her influence and make even minimal reform extraordinarily difficult. For the past two years Wu Baihua, faced with this impasse in her relationship with the party secretary and feeling the growing tension in her relationship with faculty and local educational authorities, has tried to receive permission to resign as principal and return to science teaching, which she greatly misses. The leaders of her work unit and the local educational authorities have not agreed to her request. Instead they have complimented her for her sense of responsibility and hard work, while arguing that in time the party secretary will be transferred. But in the meantime nothing has happened to diminish his authority, and Wu has come to feel that it will be years before she is able to carry out the reforms she has assiduously planned.

An extremely competent women with a long record of effective leadership and great skills as a science teacher, Wu feels tremendous pressure to succeed in a situation that she is unable to control. Her co-teachers, she believes, are becoming demoralized, which is negatively affecting the ethos of her school. Her unit leaders and the local educational authorities she perceives as unable to protect her from the destructive decisions of the party secretary. Hence she views her situation as desperate and worsening. When she thinks about it she becomes enraged and displaces her anger onto subordinates and family.

Adding to her difficulty, Wu Baihua fears the serious impact her work problems are having on her family. She is unable to spend adequate time with her children, particularly her oldest, who is preparing for the greatly feared university entrance examination. Wu feels guilty that she, an expert in preparing students in science for this examination, cannot spend the time she should with her son to help him succeed in what she believes to be one of the most important challenges he will face. She feels equally bad about her husband, who must do the cooking and housework in addition to carrying his own heavy responsibilities as an administrative cadre in a large and busy factory. She thinks her work situation has made their relationship strained. Both her husband and children complain of her unavailability for family activities, her increasingly irritable disposition, and her obsession with her work problem. Hence, Wu Baihua blames herself for the family's disharmony, which in turn is worsening her health problems.

A final worry is that in a time of very rapid change in science teaching in China, she will soon no longer be competent to return to her former position as special teacher of the best science students. Thus, Wu Baihua feels trapped in a self-defeating situation that has slowly sapped her energy and compromised her competence and confidence, while worsening her health.

Wu Baihua sees only one solution open to her: to take time off from work to rest and recuperate at home. Because her health is clearly worsening, Wu believes that at some point she will be relieved of her responsibilities and allowed to be an invalid. In 1980, when we first interviewed her, she thought she would get better with the right treatment, but now she believes that no treatment can help her. Yet even here her work situation intrudes. Neither the unit leaders nor the party secretary believe her symptoms are serious enough to require disability leave. The former compliment her on her high sense of responsibility and effective performance *in spite of her illness,* while the latter pays no attention to her complaints. Thus Wu Baihua has entered a period of difficult negotiations about her disability status in which her own personality and moral standards seem to work against her self-interest, while her work situation has amplified her symptoms significantly. The symptoms, in turn, speak of her social dilemma and painful psychological reaction to it as much as they index problems with her bodily processes.

At the close of our final interview, this highly competent and responsible educator, speaking firmly and with emphasis, shared her personal conviction with us: "If I didn't have such a serious health problem, I could continue to work in the present situation, as bad as it is. But my health is getting worse, much worse, and because of this I will, at some point, have to be relieved of my duties. Otherwise my health will be permanently and seriously injured. This is too much to ask of me. I can do no more. I need rest and recuperation. Then I will be able to return to work as a science teacher and carry out my responsibilities as a mother and wife."

Like Lin Hung's problem, Wu Baihua's situation involves both family and work stress. Distress serious enough to cause disorder is often overdetermined by several sources. Here I wish to focus on the work-related context of Wu Baihua's neurasthenia. She is in a very difficult institutional situation that presently afflicts professionals in China. Authority within institutions is split between professional and political leadership. Increasingly, the demands of modernization have polarized these twin sources of control and intensified the structurally based potential for conflict. Politically, cadres are no longer unquestionably in authority as at earlier times. One of the effects of the Cultural Revolution was to seriously weaken the control of the party over work units. In the post-Cultural Revolution period professionals have come back with a vengeance. Now it is sufficient to be expert; one need not be "red" first. Nonetheless, professionals like Wu Bahua frequently do not control the work unit either. Conflict accordingly ensues between political cadres who resent the increased power of professionals and can slow down and even undermine reform, and professionals who are bent on modernizing their institutions in terms of technical, not political objectives. In medical schools and hospitals physicians struggle with political cadres over whether to upgrade technology rather than extend services, to decrease the number of students and give them longer, more sophisticated training rather than produce larger numbers of low-level medical professionals, to concentrate on research rather than teaching, or to base promotion on academic rather than political grounds.

In Wu Baihua's case we see an entire educational institution come to a halt because of controversy. Worsening her situation is the particular limitations and biases of an old political leader who lacks the educational background and technical knowledge to make informed decisions and is so threatened by the major socioeconomic changes around him that he undermines his colleague's plans. This situation seems typical of the present era and suggests a special kind of work stress for professionals, who, feeling they lost ten years to the political excesses of the Cultural Revolution, do not like to compromise. It is intriguing to recognize that Wu Baihua's disability not only expresses the difficulties of her work situation but actually plays a role in her struggle with the Communist Party secretary, and indeed may provide the extra bit of leverage she requires to force the regional educational authorities to remove the secretary from his position. Though reluctant to take on this cagy political opponent, the regional leaders are being forced to do so by the threat of losing a clearly outstanding school administrator.

B. Family Problems

Several of the cases have had significant family problems that contributed to both the onset and continuation of illness behavior. Lin Hung (case 4) deeply felt the retirement of his elderly parents to another city. His job failure took on heightened significance because it was his father's job and his father had retired early to help secure his future. Lin's desperation resulted from the feeling that his father had forced him into work he disliked and could not succeed in; therefore he saw himself forced into a double bind of being condemned for life to a job he could not tolerate, or losing or leaving the job and thereby risking his security and his parents' disappointment. Unemployment of adolescents and young adults is a significant problem in urban China, and Lin was not unaware of the perilous position in which he had placed himself. Adding to his distress was his financial problem, which made it impossible for him to marry. These social sources of distress were not separate stressors. Rather they worked together, enhancing each other's effect and placing Lin Hung in a local system of social constraints within which he felt trapped.

Wu Baihua's situation illustrates the same systematic relationship between family, work, and personal distress. Contributing to Wu's demoralization was guilt over her failure to successfully replace her dead sister as a mother for her wayward niece. She blamed herself for letting her sister down—the very sister who had taken over from their mother the responsibility for raising Wu Baihua. Her niece's work problems reminded her of her own, which she blamed for interfering with her family responsibilities toward her niece. Wu recognizes this same amplifying cycle of work responsibilities interfering with family obligations, which in turn worsen her feelings of frustration and demoralization, is beginning to affect her relationship with her children as they prepare for the immensely competitive university entrance exams—a particularly bitter feeling for a teacher who specializes in preparing elite classes for these exams. Her relationship with her husband is similarly affected by her work problems. In contemporary China, as in the West, women bear a double burden of career and family responsibilities that is heavier than that borne by their husbands or their mothers in the past; this double load seems to be as important a vulnerability factor for psychological problems in China as it is in the United States.

Case 6 Li Xiangu is a forty-year-old bus driver who has suffered from neck pain, insomnia, and waves of tightening in the chest and throat for six years. In 1980 we diagnosed major depressive disorder and panic disorder. In 1983 there was no evidence of mental illness. Though Li Xiangu still experiences his physical complaints, they are "70 percent better."

Six years ago Li had an accident. He drove his bus into a telephone pole while turning a corner. "I don't know how it happened. I'm a careful driver. But all of a sudden my mind was blank and the bus was against the pole." No one was injured, but after the accident Li began to experience panic feelings, palpitations, waves of tightening in chest and neck, tingling and numbness in his hands and feet, neck pain, and a premonition that something calamitous would happen. When he experienced these attacks he could not drive the bus.

Li blames his accident on the bad relationship between his wife and his mother. "They have never gotten along. My mother is a very difficult woman. She can't get along with my wife or my brother and his wife. For years she lived with my elder brother and his wife. But they couldn't take her anymore. Then she came to live with us. Everyday she would quarrel with my wife about the cooking, the housework, the children. I felt very bad. I am close to my mother. I feel sorry for her. I don't want her to be lonely and unhappy. When she gets angry I can't respond. I just look at the floor and keep quiet. But my wife won't stay silent. She argues with my mother. The night before the accident it was very bad and I was ashamed. I think I couldn't sleep. I couldn't concentrate. Maybe this is why I hit the telephone pole."

Li felt hopeless. He felt he couldn't get angry with his mother, because he was sensitive to her situation and feared she would blame him. She threatened to leave their home and live by herself, bringing shame on the family. Li believes that as this situation deteriorated, his relationship with his wife also worsened. She blamed him for failing to side with her and accused him of being less able than his brother to protect his wife and children from his mother's angry and selfish personality. His wife threatened to commit suicide and have her ghost haunt him if he failed to resolve the family problem.

Li became demoralized and depressed. He felt caught in a desperate situation without a clear way out. It was in this setting that his symptoms worsened. Because of them he would retire to his room after work, often eating by himself. He also took to visiting various evening clinics. But his sickness only made things worse. His mother blamed his wife for not providing proper care, and his wife, out of anger and frustration, avoided him and told his mother to take care of her son herself if she didn't approve of her daughter-in-law's behavior. Things got so out of control that the block committee held several meetings to arbitrate the family conflict, but these were unavailing, as was Li's request to his brother to mediate the problem. Indeed Li's brother would not agree to providing his mother with any support, saying this was now Li's responsibility, just as it had been his when she lived with him.

Finally, when Li felt the conflict was at its worst, the leaders of his unit stepped in. They pointed out that the family conflict was worsening Li's physical condition and seriously interfering with his job. They arranged for Li's mother to move to a small apartment near the work unit, where Li could see her daily and take lunch with her, but where she was some distance from the home. Initially Li felt guilty about this plan because he feared it would make his mother lonely and angrier. His wife, on the other hand, felt great relief and urged him to accept. His mother, much to his surprise, agreed. Now that the separation has lasted more than a year, the family situation is greatly improved. Li reports that his relationship with his wife has also improved, that she is more responsive than before to his health problems. He sees his mother regularly and believes that her spirits are also better. Li has worked out an arrangement with his brother to divide the support for his mother's living expenses. But he warns us, "perhaps if this is a big stress again in future, my neurasthenia will again get worse."

Li Xiangu's domestic tangle deeply affected him and his work. Both Li and his doctors recognized that the difficult triangular relationship between Li, his mother, and his wife worsened his health problem. Mother-in-law and daughter-in-law relationships are a classic source of family tension in Chinese society that continue up to the present, though with less intensity than in earlier times when daughters-in-law were viewed as brood mares for sons and little better than household slaves. As in Li's case the threat of suicide was one of the few sources of leverage a daughter-in-law had. But in the People's Republic (and indeed in modern Taiwan and Hong Kong) the classic situation has changed. Li's wife was not about to be passively dominated by her mother-in-law. Li's mother did not have control over all the traditional levers of power. Stymied by her daughter-in-law and elder son, she felt better living outside the family, an arrangement that would have been almost impossible in traditional Chinese society. That the leaders of Li's work unit stepped in to resolve the deteriorating family conflict shows both their formidable powers and the forceful constraints on them of serious illness and family problems. That this type of family problem is not unknown in a wider range of other societies suggests that, independent of cultural patterns of kinship organization, certain sources of family tension may be virtually pan human; that the frequency of such problems appears to vary significantly suggests that particular forms of kinship organization are, nonetheless, a powerful influence on the social sources of distress. In presentday China even the family is not immune to the political institutions of control, as the case of Li Xiangu discloses. In this instance the diffusion of political control into the family led to a "therapeutic" result. In other of the cases I shall describe it can be seen to exert an effect on the illness side of the equation.

C. Psychological Sources of Distress

Social influences on psychological distress and mental illness vary in the extent they can cause distress. For certain kinds of distress and illnesses the contribution made by social problems may be determinative; for others it is minimal. Psychological vulnerability, as noted in several cases, is an important mediator of the effects of social tensions on individuals. In the case that follows psychological vulnerability is indeed the major source of distress, that is, longstanding personality and behavioral problems grow worse and in turn worsen health, family, and work conditions.

Case 7   Xiao Guanglan is a twenty-nine-year-old unmarried worker with a ten-year history of vague, shifting, at times dramatic physical complaints, frequent visits to medical—and more recently psychiatric—clinics, and their equally frequent failure to diagnose or successfully treat her problem. In 1980, at the time of our initial interview, Xiao Guanglan complained of weakness, various pains, transient sensations in her body, dizziness, and a long list of other ailments. She feared she had a brain tumor, but her medical diagnostic work-up was negative, and she was diagnosed as suffering from a constellation of conversion disorder, somatization disorder (hysteria), and a personality disorder. In the 1983 follow-up she appeared profoundly depressed and complained of some of the same symptoms and many new ones.

Since early adolescence Xiao had had difficulty in making friends and a tendency to be withdrawn and solitary. Over time these traits were pointed out by friends and family as evidence of a personality problem. The youngest of four children born to a factory supervisor in Wuhan, Xiao obtained work in her father's factory, working on the night shift as a common laborer. After several years of night work, she complained to her father that it was bad for her, preventing her from meeting friends her own age and interfering with other aspects of her social life. She also blamed it for her frequent physical complaints and visits to the factory clinic. Her father played down these difficulties as minor and encouraged her to persevere. He refused to consider transferring Xiao to another job. Ever since childhood he had had a difficult relationship with this his youngest child, whom he regarded as eccentric and troublesome. He chided her for being a "complainer" unable to endure difficult life situations and told her he would show her no favoritism. At home Xiao began to routinely quarrel with her father about her dislike of night work, with her mother over what her mother regarded as a failure to carry out responsibilities in the home, and with both about her frequent illnesses and visits to clinics. As a result she left the family apartment and moved into the factory dormitory.

After several years the leaders of her factory agreed to a shift to day work in the factory nursery school. But after several months Xiao Guanglan decided she disliked the new work more than her old work, and she returned to the night shift. At this time her father became very angry with her, accusing her of exaggerating her bodily complaints and even malingering. He retired from his work but refused to agree to his daughter's taking over his job because he believed she was not capable of undertaking such responsibility. Between

1980 and 1983 Xiao's situation worsened. She was unable to negotiate another job change, yet came to describe the night shift as intolerable, believing it would ruin her chances to make friends and marry. The tensions in her family situation sharpened. Over time her co-workers, supervisors, and factory doctors came to doubt both the seriousness and even the reality of her symptoms. They began to treat her as a malingerer and rejected her claims to the sick role and disability status. By 1983 these attitudes had thoroughly demoralized her.

Xiao was profoundly depressed at our 1983 follow-up interview. She said her life had no meaning. She reported feelings of emptiness, hollowness, and loneliness. She believed that her personality problem prevented her from making good friends and kept her isolated. She anticipated not marrying because of this problem which she called "introversion." Xiao despaired that even her brothers and sisters failed to regard her health problem as serious and treated her as if she were feigning disability. "People can't touch or see my symptoms so therefore they don't believe they are real." For this reason she does not think that she can change work, because her only chance is to convince her unit's leaders that it has worsened her health problem, but she has not been successful in convincing them. Xiao believes her father has ruined her chances because he never treated her illness as a serious problem requiring attention and help, and he led others to the same denial and avoidance of her problem. For example, she recently entered the hospital for several days to have tests, but neither her parents nor workmates came to visit her. As a result Xiao Guanglan says that her condition is hopeless. She will die from her disease, she affirms, and then everyone will see that they have treated her unjustly.

Xiao Guanglan's pathetic story is the result of a deep-seated personality problem that has plagued her since adolescence. This problem came to dominate her life, creating havoc in family and work relationships, and in her relationship with the health care system. Part of this personality problem is a lifetime career of somatization (hysteria) that is personally and socially maladaptive. Xiao Guanglan has lost the support of family, work, and medical relations, all of whom have come to see her as a malingerer. So labeled, her illness behavior (for which in principle she is not held responsible) is no longer sanctioned, and therefore can no longer serve a legitimate social function (change jobs, obtain time off and away, elicit sympathy of family and friends). Here a mental illness first gives rise to somatic complaints, then undercuts the patient's efforts to bring those complaints to bear on her social situation. This picture is well known to psychiatrists around the world. It indicates that as there are social limits to the uses of somatization, so too there are psychological problems that limit its uses in daily life. Patients like Xiao are prisoners neither of society nor of the biology of medical disorder. Instead they are trapped in an iron cage of inner personal pathology; they are prisoners of a personality that is simultaneously illness-generating, self-defeating, and socially alienating and even stigmatizing. There is no firm evidence that such severe personality disorders have varied in prevalence with changing social circumstances in China. Since the impression exists that they are on the rise in the West (Lasch 1979), however, it may be that they are increasing in frequency in China too. Certainly the pace and power of modernization in the West have placed a greater burden on the resources of the family and undermined traditional patterns of nurturance; modernization has also contributed to the breakdown of affective bonds and moral sentiments, which encourages excessive individualism, alienation from societal responsibilities, and morbid introspectiveness both of the self (narcissism) and the body (hypochondriasis). There is currently great concern in China that both the policy of the one-child family and the turn toward a partial market economy, with its emphasis on personal consumption and material values, may lead to an increase in personality problems stemming from overindulgence and weakening of traditional Chinese cultural and socialistic values guiding child rearing. Whether or not such social changes actually do induce pathological patterns of the self, there is little doubt that personality problems may at times be serious enough to become the chief source of neurasthenia.

D. Psychological Casualties of the Cultural Revolution

Numerous large-scale sources of social chaos and personal tragedy in twentieth-century China (the Anti-Japanese War and outbreaks of epidemic disease and natural catastrophes during the Warlord and Nationalist periods in the 1920s and 1930s) have taken large numbers of lives and caused enormous migrations, but perhaps none has had a more disastrous effect on *individual experience* than the Cultural Revolution. For the legacy of the Cultural Revolution was not only to disrupt lives and place each individual in the society under great stress. It also created a delegitimation crisis unprecedented since the fall of the Qing, affecting the central values of the socialist state. By 1980, when the slogans of the Cultural Revolution had been turned on their head, the highly vaunted "new man" of the Maoist period—filled with revolutionary optimism, selfless commitment to serve the people, and negation of the "feudal" beliefs of the millenial culture—had become exhausted, sometimes hollow and bitter, cynical and alienated, grieving many losses, even broken. The delegitimation of an extremist Maoist ideology and even of Mao himself deeply affected the way individuals conceived of themselves, made sense of their past, and looked toward the future. Most were both victims *and* perpetrators, lending a complex ambivalence to the sense of loss that stood in marked contrast to the simplistic revolutionary emotions of the late 1960s. The policy of liberalization and improvement of people's personal material lives has made Chinese of the mid-1980s more optimistic. Yet beneath this brighter exterior, for some resides a darker interior fashioned out of pain and the crisis of disbelief that is the demoralizing legacy of the Cultural Revolution.

In the cases that follow, we witness what is probably not the average response to the Cultural Revolution, but rather special instances of profound psychological wounding. The individuals I shall now introduce developed serious mental illnesses and psychological distress in response to excesses of the Cultural Revolution. I do not suggest that each Chinese individual was as deeply affected. Yet even if these cases represent the extremes of a continuum of personal reactions to traumatic social stress, they are none-theless instructive. They edify us as much for what they suggest may be qualitatively less severe though structurally similar kinds of impacts (threat, loss, guilt, demoralization) as for what they tell us about the social sources of mental illness in China. These psychological casualties of the Cultural Revolution (and of its progenitors, such as the Anti-Rightist Campaign) are but the most extreme examples of experiences of distress undergone by tens, perhaps hundreds, of millions of Chinese. The illness behaviors of these patients share important similarities with the cases already described, several of which also had their antecedents in the Cultural Revolution. The Cultural Revolution led to no new forms of distress and pathology. Indeed the shared grain of our humaness means that there may be only so many forms of human misery. The reader is introduced to these cases because they show how powerful an influence social crises may have either on intensifying problems latent within the person (and his social network) or causing new suffering that those individuals (and their networks) are unlikely to have experienced otherwise.

Case 8   Wu Guangmei is a forty-nine-year-old former factory worker with complaints of swollen gums, headaches, dry throat, and poor memory, all of which have greatly improved after she took an early, disability-related retirement six months before. In 1980, when we first interviewed Comrade Wu, she was seriously depressed, but in 1983 there was no evidence of significant mental illness. At our first interview she reported frequent crying spells when reminded of the Cultural Revolution, at which time she would think with sadness of the death of Zhou Enlai, whom she regarded a great hero, one of the "fathers" of the nation. Thoughts of Zhou would lead her to thoughts of her own father and the effect of the Cultural Revolution on him. A prosperous merchant before 1949, whose two brothers had fled to Taiwan, he was punished during the Cultural Revolution for both his bad class background and his "overseas problem" by being sent to a terribly poor commune in the mountains. Comrade Wu was separated from her parents and sent to a commune in another province. The mother, sick with chronic rheumatic heart disease, stayed in Changsha. Comrade Wu's younger sister, who was only fourteen, was made to accompany her father. Comrade Wu worried greatly that her sister, who was frail and in poor health owing to the two years of starvation (1960–62) that followed the disastrous agricultural policy of the Great Leap Forward, would be unable to stand the rigors of life in the impoverished mountain commune and succeed in caring for both her ailing father and herself. As she feared, her sister "could not adapt to the very poor local conditions," became debilitated, contracted meningitis, and, before the first year of separation was up, died. During the period of bereavement, and up until recently, she blamed herself for what happened. Comrade Wu believed that if she had been more courageous and demanded that she replace her sister at her father's side she could have protected her sister and delayed the tragic cascade of events that followed. Six months after her sister's death she learned of the death of her father, and one year later her mother died as well. "I could not return for either my sister's or father's funeral. I did return for my mother's funeral, but by then it was too late. They were all dead."

When Comrade Wu thinks of these losses she feels great guilt and her somatic symptoms worsen. She becomes preoccupied by her physical complaints. In the past she would talk to her co-workers about them almost incessantly. But about her grief and despair she feels unable to talk to anyone. Her friends and daughter comfort her because of her illness, but their concern and support, she states, cannot relieve her grief or guilt. These she must "endure."

In 1959 Comrade Wu married a man much older than herself, a disabled soldier blinded in the Korean War. Their relationship has never been good. Her husband has always had a bad temper and frequently would curse her and beat her. She tried to divorce him on several occasions, but each time her unit's leaders brought great pressure on her to reconcile with him. In recent years he has periodically become enraged by her refusal to have sexual relations with him ostensibly because of menstrual problems which led to a hysterectomy. They have one child, an adopted daughter, now in her mid-twenties. In 1982 the daughter moved to Gansu Province in China's far west to live with her husband, a soldier. This year, when Comrade Wu's symptoms worsened to the point where she could neither take care of her husband or herself, her daughter returned to live with them. Shortly afterward Comrade Wu arranged early retirement because of her chronic disability. Since then her symptoms have greatly improved. She no longer experiences the same intensity of grief and guilt. With her daughter back in the home, she feels that all the family responsibilities are well handled and that she need be less fearful of her husband's anger. Indeed since her retirement he has been more solicitous and helpful. Her hope is that her son-in-law will be transferred back to Changsha to join them. The pensions she and her husband receive are more than adequate for their needs, and Comrade Wu looks forward to the birth of a grandchild, since her daughter is now pregnant. She believes the future will be better than the past, that the worse years are now behind her. "Sometimes I still think about my sister and my parents. But the pain is much less. Perhaps there was nothing I could have done. It was our fate. I am getting on better with my husband. My daughter takes good care of us. Things are easier now. When my daughter left for Gansu, my illness got much worse, I couldn't do all the work I had to do in the textile factory and at home. But now that I am retired and my daughter is again at home, my health is better and things are easier."

In Wu Guangmei's experiences during the Cultural Revolution we see the impact of loss. Her bereavement over the death of Zhou Enlai, with whom common people could identify because his great charm and personal warmth offered a more human, charismatic exemplar of Communist authority than the volcanically enigmatic Mao, symbolized a deeper, personal grief for her father and her sister, both of whose deaths resulted from the Cultural Revolution. This double bereavement (for Zhou and for her deceased family members) has persisted up to the present. The public mourning for Zhou helped legitimate the personal grieving for father, sister, and mother. Wu Guangmei had been orphaned by the Cultural Revolution, both literally and figuratively. Her grief continues in large part because of the guilt she feels. As the older sister she should have accompanied her father. Perhaps if she had done so, her thoughts obsess her, her sister and her father may have survived. The thought had become intolerable, intensifying and prolonging her grief, elaborating it into a general sense of hopelessness and despair. Her somatic preoccupation (the worrying over the physical complaints) is one of the few things that can distract her mind from its obsession with her family tragedy. On a psychological level, one might think of her somatization, then, as transiently helpful. Yet it is likely that over the long term it has contributed to the vicious cycle of prolonged grieving that dominates her life.

But Wu Guangmei's distress also has another source. She has had a very difficult marriage that may well have contributed significantly to her vulnerability to depression. Their troubled marital situation was eased by the presence of her daughter. It comes as little surprise that the loss of that daughter, who traveled to western China to be with her husband, led to a recrudescence of Wu's depressive symptoms, or that her return (because of the serious burden of Wu's physical disability on her home life and work) contributed to their improvement. Wu's somatization played as important a role in her daughter's return as in her own retirement. Both changes in her life have led to a remission of her depression and diminished the seriousness of her physical complaints and disability. Thus we see yet again the dialectic between changes in family and work problems and changes in chronic illness behavior, mediated by depression. Once having started upon a trajectory of chronic somatization, owing to prolonged grief, the serious stress of a conflict-laden marriage, the marriage and transfer of her daughter away from home, and the difficult negotiation over early retirement, all came together to maintain that illness trajectory. We might refer to these social sources of neurasthenia separately as proximal and distal, but it is the way they interconnect to form a sociosomatic system between feeling state (grief, sadness, physical preoccupation) and social life (repeated loss), that illustrates the point I wish to make.

Case 9   Huang Zhenyi is a worker from a rural county town in his late twenties with dysthymic disorder (chronic neurotic depression). He attributes his chronic headaches and dizziness to a traumatic childhood experience during the Cultural Revolution, about which he can talk only to his wife. During winter vacation from school Huang Zhenyi returned to the schoolyard to play. While there the then twelve-year-old noticed that on the rear door of the school building someone had tacked up a piece of paper. "Throw down Chairman Mao!" was written in bold characters across the paper. Not knowing what to do about this anti-Mao slogan, he ran to see his close friend, who told him to quickly inform their commune leaders. This he did, and those cadres responded by calling in the public security (police) agents. Three of them interviewed Huang Zhenyi at his school. They asked him who wrote the poster, and when he could not respond they accused him. The policemen threatened that if he didn't confess they would not let him return home. Frightened after being interrogated for several hours in a small room at the school, from which he was not allowed to go to the toilet in spite of a painful urge to urinate, he told the police that he had found the slogan but was not the one who wrote it. He was angry at his friend for not supporting his story by telling what had actually happened. Eventually, late at night, his interrogators allowed Huang to return home. There he found his mother distraught over his absence. He explained the problem to her and assured her he was not at fault.

The next morning the three agents came to Huang Zhenyi's home and took him to the public security building. Brutally, they assured Huang Zhenyi that this time he would never leave the small interrogation room until he confessed. Terrified that he would not be allowed to eat, relieve himself, or see his mother again, Huang Zhenyi signed the confession, accepting sole responsibility for writing the poster.

When he returned home he told his mother that he had written the poster, fearing that if he told her the truth it would only create greater trouble for her and for him. Huang Zhenyi still recalls with obvious pain his mother crying and cursing him, "If I knew before you'd end up like this, I wouldn't have wanted you." He remembers breaking down in tears, but he found himself unable to tell his mother the truth. "I felt like a coward. I couldn't tell her."

This experience recalled for him an earlier one. At age eight he had gone with several classmates to fish in a nearby pond, instead of walking to school. They were very late getting to class. The teacher punished them by locking the boys in a small mud-walled room. They escaped by knocking a hole in the wall and hid in a nearby cotton field. Their teacher, who was known for being a strict disciplinarian, ran after them and caught Huang Zhenyi's two friends but not him. "I was so frightened I froze in my place. I could not move." Later in the evening he returned home, and the next day went back to school. The teacher, greatly angered by Huang's behavior, ordered him to do menial work around the school rather than study. Huang Zhenyi refused to do the hard labor, and this led his teacher to criticize him severely in front of other teachers. After this experience, Huang Zhenyi reported "my liver became small, and I became frightened, cowardly." From this time onward he felt "paralyzed" whenever he had to "stand up" for himself before adults.

Because of his confession, the twelve-year-old Huang Zhenyi—who again felt "paralyzed," unable to break his silence before his adult accusers—was marched through the local county town wearing a dunce cap, carrying a sign around his neck in which he had written a self-criticism for the "terrible act," surrounded by thousands of local peasants and cadres, who cursed him, spat at him, and threw dirt and pebbles at him. The next day he was sent to work as a peasant at a local production team. He was expected to do the work of an adult. No one would talk with him at first. The heavy labor was so exhausting that Huang Zhenyi thought he would not survive. Each day he had to undergo self-criticism, while local groups of children jeered at him. In a big criticism session he felt himself go numb all over, as if paralyzed. He wanted to yell out the truth but couldn't get himself to do it, to break his silence. No one would believe him, Huang Zhenyi reasoned. He had been patient so far; he would endure the unendurable, since there was no way out. Finally, after a year of hard labor, a year during which he several times thought he could no longer stand the work and the isolation, his fellow peasants praised him for doing the work of an adult and enduring his punishment in silence. They pleaded on his behalf with the local authorities that he be allowed to return to school, which he did.

Eventually Huang left this commune and moved to a county town in another province, where he finished high school and where his past was unknown. He became a key worker and joined the Communist Party. He was able to do the latter since the local party officials, owing to the chaos of the time, knew nothing about his past and because of his highly regarded poor peasant background. He never told his mother his version of what had happened. When she was dying he thought of confessing to her the full story but decided against it. "I was too frightened to speak out and didn't think it would do any good." Huang's mother died not knowing of her son's innocence, a point he returns to again and again as a palpable reason for his current feelings of desperate shame and self-hatred.

Now looking backward, he feels depressed, hopeless, desperate. He retains great anger at the three policemen and at his classmate, who would not admit to the interrogators that Huang Zhenyi had told him he had found, not written, the anti-Maoist poster. He feels a searing sense of injustice, a feeling that he associates with a burning sensation in the head, dizziness and exhaustion. He is fearful that someone in the party will learn of his past and expel him on account of it.

Huang believes he will never recover from this event. "It has affected my character. I am withdrawn; I don't like to be too friendly with others. I am a coward. I cannot trust others." He sees his only hope as writing a novel about his experience that would fictionalize it to protect his anonymity and generalize it so that it comes to represent the "losses and defeat" his generation has experienced. "Like me we are a lost generation that has suffered so much." But Huang Zhenyi doubts he will accomplish this goal. He has no formal training or natural skill to write fiction. He actively fears the consequences of others learning about his past. He feels trapped. Each time he takes up a pen to write the story, he is overcome by a self-defeating lassitude, dizziness, and sense of his inefficacy. Hence Huang's physical complaints are amplified (perhaps created) by the literal embodiment of chronic frustration, inability to act—if we use his word, "paralysis", but of will not muscle—and the unbearable inner hurt of shameful "injustice" that he can neither publicly articulate (save through the personally unavailing neurasthenic pain) nor privately expiate.

Huang Zhenyi's own statement that his losses during the Cultural Revolution represent those of his generation signifies a collective awareness in China that the Cultural Revolution deeply affected the lives of entire cohorts of Chinese, in this case adolescents. Unlike the previous case, his losses during these terrible times were not the physical loss of close family members (his mother died after the Cultural Revolution). Instead Huang is talking about the loss of self-esteem, self-confidence, the normal developmental period of becoming an adult, the normal relationships with family members, and also of hope in his future and that of his society.

Doubtless there are parallels in pre-Communist China and in other societies, the United States included. I am not trying to suggest that what happened to Chinese in the Cultural Revolution is without precedent or cannot be compared to social sources of misery in other societies. But it is also the case that my argument is meant to implicate an entire generation in Huang's distress. His demoralization and anguish may be (and probably are) greater than that of others, owing to his personal vulnerability and the magnitude of the crisis he experienced. He developed a disorder; most others did not. Yet it is precisely because Huang's disorder exposes the inner hurt the Cultural Revolution caused that we may suspect this type of psychological wound is fairly widespread among the members of his generation. For most members of that generation the psychological effects of the Cultural Revolution are unlikely to have led to the despair that Huang experiences. We do not know with what intensity and quality of distress it has afflicted them. We can be sure it has left its mark, and that that mark is more like a wound than a blemish. China's leadership seems to have written this "lost generation" off, concentrating instead on the new generation of students, who are expected to be better prepared, educationally and psychologically, to take maximum advantage of the brave new emphasis on technological and economic growth (the so-called "Red Reformation").

Case 10   Hu Chengyeh is a thirty-seven-year-old cashier in a rice shop in a rural town who suffers from periodic bouts of headache, dizziness, and a burning sensation in the upper abdomen and chest. We diagnosed dysthymic disorder and a chronic personality problem in this sensitive but sullen, even haughty worker. He arrived at our three-year follow-up interview much as he had entered the intial interview: alternating between acting irritable, complaining (this time about the side-effects and lack of therapeutic effect of our treatment), and being silent, aloof, rarely smiling, with a defiant edge to his bearing and movements.

We asked him about his symptoms, but he disregarded the question, launching into his own account. He had come to tell us about something else, something he withheld at our first meeting. "My family is complicated. I was taken in by my step-father when my mother remarried after my real father died when I was very young. My step-father, who came from a landlord background, was sent to the countryside in the Anti-Rightist Campaign, where he eventually died of TB. I hate him. His bad class background deeply affected my life. Because he was my source of support I was labeled as having a landlord background.[3] My older sister, who stayed with my real father's relatives, who supported her, was assigned a very good class background, since they were poor workers and peasants. She benefited, went to senior middle school, joined the party. I was discriminated against. I couldn't go to senior middle school, was not given good work to do, couldn't join the party. My life was ruined. So I hate him."

In adolescence Hu remembers feeling deep shame about his class background and repeatedly experiencing discrimination because of the label "landlord," which he saw as pervasive, inescapable, and destructive of his "personality." The discrimination he thought he could hear in the casual words and see in the subtle expressions of his teachers, his schoolmates, his neighbors, and especially the leaders of his unit. On several occasions, when these leaders learned that he had made friendships with girls in the unit whose parents were cadres, they forced him to stop seeing them, leading Hu to feel tainted and unworthy. The effect of these experiences was to make Hu "hesitant, inadequate, helpless, and ashamed."

Hu also spoke of his problem as a great and irremediable "injustice." In spite of his stigmatized background, he asserts, he naively believed in his step-father, until he learned from other family members that his step-father resented having him in the family and spoke badly of Hu Chengyeh behind his back. Hearing these words, Hu felt even greater shame. His ambivalence was driven away; from then on, he reports, he felt only bitterness: a growing, unappeasable hatred that affected every part of his life. So all-pervasive and terrible did this hatred become that in recent years Hu Chengyeh visited rebuilt Buddhist temples to find peace of mind. He copied down Buddhist epigrams and wrote them out on scrolls which he hung in his room. But the admonitions to empty the mind of rancor, unhappiness, and vengeful desire and to forgive did not work for him. Bitterness and anger spilled over into all his relationships: with his wife and child, his co-workers, his neighbors, his physicians, even with us. Over the years he saw himself become sullen, withdrawn, alienated, implacably vengeful.

"I quarrel all the time with my wife: over what she wears, over being late for dinner, which happens often since she works late. Always over trivial things. I am irritable to my little daughter. I fear my anger will seriously affect her, hurt her, drive her away from me."

"Once when she was five, she locked herself in my neighbor's room. She was too little to understand how to unlock the door. I became furious, shouting at her. It frightened her more. She was too terrified and could not do what I yelled at her to do. My neighbor calmed her down and coached her through the steps of unlocking the door. Everyone present was greatly relieved. Not me. I felt such rage, I wanted to hit her. I still feel the rage surge through me when I think back to that event. It rises upward in my stomach and chest. I feel *huo qi da*." The greater the bitterness the worse his physical pain becomes. He believes the injustice he has experienced has ruined his emotions and health.

Recently Hu's physical symptoms have improved somewhat, following a work transfer from a distant rice shop, which necessitated that he live away from home for seven years, to one situated near enough to home so that he now again lives with wife and daughter. This transfer took him away from a tension-ridden work situation, one in which he daily squabbled with co-workers over work assignments and practices. But now he has begun quarreling more with his wife and especially with the neighborhood committee that oversees assignments of apartments. Hu Chengyeh regards his present room as unacceptable and has pressed the neighborhood committee to find him a larger and more healthy accommodation, but without success. Hu, his wife, and his daughter live in a very small single room that contains only one narrow window. In the furnace-like heat of the Hunan summer, Hu complains, it is too hot to sleep. The more he feels the situation is intolerable but unalterable, the more he finds himself quarreling with the neighborhood committee.

Anger and bad relationships also characterize his experiences with the personnel at the local county hospital. "The medicine is useless. They cannot find out what is wrong. They do no good. There is no sense in going back to them."

When his anger becomes unbearable, as Hu himself recognizes, his "neurasthenic headaches" and abdominal and chest complaints become much worse. Then he must lie down; he cannot help with housework or go to work. Sometimes his wife too must stay home to comfort and care for him. She treats him with great concern when his sickness worsens, fearful that he will suffer a stroke (like his biological father) because of his rage and pain. Both she and his friends attribute his anger to his neurasthenia, which has given an excuse of sorts for Hu's difficult behavior. Since changing work sites these episodes of sickness are less frequent. When they lived far apart for most of each month Hu would return home to his wife and child for days at a time when he was too ill to work. At such times he would read reprints of ancient Chinese medicine texts which extol diet, tonics, and herbal medicine to maintain health and thereby improve emotions.

But whenever he thinks of his step-father the burning bitterness returns.

"He ruined all my chances. I couldn't continue on in school, get a good job. I wanted to join the party, but how could I with the taint of a landlord label. It is a tragedy: my sister benefited from my real father's good class background; I have been ruined by my step-father's. There is no remedy. Sometimes I feel it would be better to be dead than to carry this curse any further."

Hu Chengyeh's anger is not the result of his experiences during the Cultural Revolution per se, but of almost a lifelong experience of discrimination because of his bad class background, much of it during the Cultural Revolution. I include it to show that besides major life events (for example, Huang Zhenyi's catastrophe), chronic long-term frustration can also deform the personality and diminish health. Hu's experience calls to mind the hidden injuries of class in the West, but with a vengeance. It is more like the implacable effect of caste in India (Freeman 1979) and of race in South Africa and the United States. Hu's bitterness about a real injustice conduces to a hypersensitivity that creates imagined injustice in virtually all his relationships. External oppression, no longer encouraged in China, is transformed into a ruinous inner oppression that will not cease.

Reading the previous case and this one, we see that in spite of the social sources of their illnesses both patients have problems that in principle can benefit from therapy. Yet neither one is able to find such treatment, since psychotherapy of the kind required for the treatment of serious personality problems does not exist in China. Mental health professionals cannot reverse the sociopolitical mechanism that has ground down each of these patients, but supportive therapy might enable each to come to terms with psychic effects of their trauma. Here is a direction for developing a culturally appropriate kind of psychotherapy in China. In its absence and in the absence of authorized traditional folk healers (shamans, fortune-tellers, Taoist priests [see Kleinman 1980]), who in an earlier era dealt with such problems, and still do in overseas Chinese communities, patients are abandoned to their own unavailing coping patterns, of which somatization seems to be a final common pathway.

The deep-seated anger Hu embodies must be present, albeit in less intense form, in many Chinese and in members of other societies, whose careers and personal lives have been systematically affected by bias. Riots in black ghettos and street crime may represent the eruption of this hostility on a group level. Perhaps in the Chinese revolution, generations of smoldering bitterness among peasants found an outlet in organized violence against members of the ruling class. We can only wonder what expression this terrible sentiment will receive in the People's Republic. The fact that millions of former "leftists," now out of power and confronted with a volte face in ideology, may harbor this powerfully long-lived and destructive emotion with little opportunity to transmute it, does not bode well for peaceful transitions in China's future.

Case 11   Comrade Yen is a forty-year-old teacher in a rural town, intelligent, articulate, and deeply depressed. She sits immobile on the wooden stool opposite us, looking fixedly at the floor. Her black hair tied tightly in a bun behind her face is streaked with white; her handsome, high cheekboned face is deeply lined with crow's feet radiating outward from each eye. She slowly recounts for us the story of her chronic headaches.

"There are several sources. Before the Cultural Revolution I was outgoing, active, had high self-regard. As a teenager I had been secretary of the local Communist Youth League. I dreamed of a career with the party and advanced education. My family and friends all expected great achievements. I had ambition and high goals. Then during the Cultural Revolution I was severely criticized. I had to leave my position in the Youth League. I went to the distant countryside to a very poor place.[4] I couldn't adjust to the conditions.

The work was too hard; too little to eat. Bad smells were everywhere, and nothing was clean. Terrible living conditions!''

All of this was made worse by the realization that her career aspirations were no longer tenable, that even return to an urban environment was unlikely. The daughter of intellectuals, with several generations of professionals in the family, Comrade Yen felt deeply the lost opportunity for a university education and career in the Communist Party, sources of social mobility in China. Cut off from family and friends, books and newspapers, yet not well accepted, at least initially, by the peasants among whom she lived, she grew aloof and solitary. As the Cultural Revolution accelerated she occasionally bore the brunt of self-criticism sessions. On one occasion she was denied an injection by a nurse at a rural county hospital who accused her of being a "stinking intellectual." She began to experience a change in personality. Comrade Yen felt constantly demoralized, and in place of her former optimism she felt hopelessness generalized to all aspects of her life. Comrade Yen expected only the worst to happen. She became introverted, sensitive to what she perceived as the rejecting and critizing eyes of peasants and cadres. She first began to depreciate her goals, then herself. Hesitant where she once had been assertive, lacking confidence where she once had radiated it, Comrade Yen regarded herself as inadequate and coped by narrowing even more her behavioral field and already limited options. She stayed to herself. Eventually she obtained a post as a primary school teacher in a rural town. When her native abilities became apparent to her fellow teachers, they wished to elect her the principal. But Comrade Yen declined becaused she feared the responsibility and did not want to expose herself again in a situation where she might well fail and suffer further losses.

She married a native of the region who is presently a peasant but previously was a cadre in a mine. They live apart, and it is clear she prefers it this way: he resides in a distant production team, while she lives in the small commune town. They have three children, two adolescent sons who live with their father, one daughter who still lives at home with her mother. Comrade Yen is angry that her husband has not been rehabilitated and given back his post as a cadre. It is aggravating to her that her husband has given up, declaring that he will never regain his former status. This is a chronic source of frustration, another difficulty about which she feels nothing can be done.

Her third source of anger is her daughter. "I really did not want to have her. I wanted to be alone. We already had enough children. When I was very pregnant I hit myself several times quite hard against the wall, hoping I might abort. But my husband wanted a child and I could not decide on an abortion at the hospital. Thus I blamed myself when I gave birth to a baby girl with a withered arm. I felt I caused it."[5]

The daughter grew up to be beautiful and very bright, an outstanding student. But her mother grieved for her because of her deformity. "In China normal people don't marry cripples. Even though she could do everything— cook, clean, play sports—I knew she would have trouble marrying." At this point in our interview, the patient silently cried, her gaze fixed on the cement floor beneath the table separating us. Her husband, who had accompanied her, looked much older than Comrade Yen and was wide-eyed in a provincial capital he had visited only several times before. His coarse peasant features may have contrasted with his wife's more refined face, but he joined her in weeping openly when she continued on about their daughter:

> There is no hope for her. Even though she is one of the best students in the senior middle school, she cannot take the examination to go to the university. Her school principal and the secretary of the local branch of the party decided that only completely healthy, normal children can take the examination. We appealed to the county authorities, but they upheld the decision. There is nothing that can be done. Our daughter will live at home and do what work she can.

There followed several minutes when the patient could not go on, but sobbed and wept. Finally she told us how she and her husband had arranged for their daughter to meet another "cripple" in a nearby town. But her daughter decided she would not marry someone else who was deformed; rather she would remain single.

Comrade Yen shared her full hopelessness with us. Often she thinks it would be preferable to be dead. Her headaches keep her to herself. She cannot face any more "stress", it is too upsetting. "My health is too un- certain. I cannot do too much. I think only of my headaches, not of the future or the past." Comrade Yen severely restricts her world. She withdraws from all but essential responsibilities. She cannot plan any outing "because of bad influences on my health: the weather, the noise, the crowds . . ."

Because of her feelings of inadequacy, failure, hopelessness, despair, she circumscribes her life to school and dormitory room. Only on occasional weekends does she visit her husband. Her daughter stays with her. They appear to be like two recluses, each grieving somewhat different losses. Comrade Yen's world is now that of pain: experiencing her hurt, waiting for it, fearing it, talking about it, and blaming her problems on it. It is the pain (and related complaints) that legitimizes her withdrawal at work and in family life, sanctions her isolation, her demoralization and depression. Her chronic pain is an unavailing expression of her multiple losses. Before we departed she sent us a letter:

> I feel always sad about being ill for such a long time. I feel headache, dizziness, don't like to talk, take no pleasure in things. My head and eyes feel swollen. My hair is falling out. My thinking has slowed down. Symptoms are worse when I am with others, better when I am alone. Whenever I do anything I have no confidence. I think because of the disease I have lost my youth and much time and everything. I grieve for my lost health. I must work a lot every day just like the others, but I have no hope in what lies ahead. I think there is nothing you can do.

I include this account to give additional emphasis to themes already discussed: the overdetermined basis of psychiatric disorder and psychological distress; the role of the Cultural Revolution as acute and chronic source of stress (especially key losses); the unavailing, even maladaptive, uses of somatization; and the value of biographical and ethnographic account to interpret what otherwise would be a superficial and narrow biomedical case. In the anthropological perspective on Comrade Yen's story, the Cultural Revolution is only one of a group of interrelated causes of distress and disease that include as well the other sources illustrated earlier in this chapter. Her case does illumine, however, a pattern of "learned helplessness" in a setting of persistent, inescapable frustration that Seligman (1975) has hypothesized is a shared psychological process underlying seemingly different origins of depression.

Case 12   Zheng Gueili is a thirty-five-year-old mother of two and head of a child care center. A plump, attractive, initially demure woman with a low voice, she becomes animated and insistent as she recounts her physical complaints. Zheng Gueili complains of a long list of bodily symptoms but pays special attention to her chronic headaches, insomnia, and poor memory. She also mentions that she fears making a mistake at work and being blamed for it. Although she volunteers no complaints of dysphoria while recounting her story, when specifically asked Zheng admits feeling depressed and answers affirmatively to the vegetative complaints of depression, with the exception of guilt and suicidal ideas. Though persistent since 1980, she hastens to add, her symptoms are now somewhat less severe. But periodically they become substantially worse.

The daughter of a retired head of a local factory and a head nurse in a nearby hospital, Zheng Gueili was sent to the countryside during senior middle school, as were many of her classmates. In the commune she met another student from her native city. They first became close friends and then married, years later at a time when it appeared both would remain their entire lives in their rice farming commune. "We gave up hope of returning to the city. We were very lonely. No family nearby, few friends. We were happier together." Zheng Gueili and her husband arranged the marriage through the local authorities.

One year after marrying Zheng's husband was given official permission to return to their home city (owing to political changes). He lived with his parents and rarely visited his in-laws, since they clearly disapproved of the marriage. They viewed the husband's work as a nonskilled laborer and his family's similar background as unsuitable. "They expected me to marry someone of higher status," she told us.[6]

From 1975 to 1979 Zheng Gueili did all she could to seek official permission to return home and join her husband. Finally, unable to succeed in her quest and despondent that she would live "forever" in the rural area she had come to abhor, Zheng Gueili illegally left the commune and joined her husband. Because his parents had no room in their small apartment for the married couple, they went to live with Zheng's parents, who made apparent their dislike for the husband and the living arrangement. From the first, daily life was filled with quarrels between Zheng's parents and her husband. She feared intervening because without an official residence permit she was totally dependent on her parents for food and lodging. But after a year she received official sanctioning to live in the city and thereafter was able to find employment. In fact her father arranged his retirement earlier than required so that she could obtain a job in his factory.

During this year Zheng felt herself becoming progressively more depressed and anxious. She began to doubt her competence in her job as a worker in the factory's day care center, fearing that she would make an error that would in some way result in injury to the small children she minded. She could no longer tolerate the squabbling at home, yet felt unable to change the situation. It was in this context that her headache, from which she had begun to suffer in the countryside, greatly worsened. Insidiously, the other symptoms slowly emerged and also worsened.

"This was a bad time. I could not adjust to work, and home life was tense and difficult. I had to do everything. I worked, cared for others' children, came home, took care of my own children, cooked, washed dishes, cleaned the house. Some mornings I began at 5:00 A.M. to go to the market for food. No one helped me. My husband was so angry at my parents and me he refused to help. My mother and father demanded that I be responsible for my family. They showed their unhappiness with my decision to marry by paying little attention to me and giving very little help. I cried to myself. I felt exhausted. But what could I do?"

As her symptoms worsened Zheng Gueili initiated a frequently repeated cycle of visiting different clinics (usually accompanied by her husband or her parents), trying many different medicines, altering her diet, drinking tonics, eating special foods, and avoiding "cold" foods because traditional Chinese medicine practitioners diagnosed her as constitutionally overly "cold".[7] For short periods her symptoms became so severe that she stayed in bed. During these times her parents did the housework and child care and also solicitously attended to their sick daughter. "My parents and my husband treated me very well. They were as frightened as I was that something was seriously wrong. When we learned the problem was neurasthenia then we realized my health was bad and easily upset. I would need help for a long time. The doctors told us this, as did our neighbors. I felt bad to be a burden, but there was nothing I could do. The headaches and insomnia were so bad. Nothing did any good."

But the home situation greatly improved. Her husband and parents regard Zheng Gueili's health as fragile and easily undermined. For this reason they have taken over many of the child care, cooking, and house-cleaning activities. They fear exhausting her and making her bodily complaints worse. Her husband confided to us that he even feared expressing anger at his wife because "her health cannot endure it."

Zheng Gueili's relationship to her factory physicians has not been good. She told us that they seem to discount the seriousness of her problem. She does not accept their diagnosis of psychosomatic disorder and referrals for psychiatric treatment. Zheng Gueili was indignant when she reported to us her disgust with the factory doctors. "My problem is not a psychological one. I have headaches, other pain, can't sleep well, and have trouble with my memory. Perhaps my neurasthenia has affected my brain. I am tired all the time. This is a serious sickness and perhaps there is no treatment for it."

There was no evidence to us at the time of mental illness. Even Zheng Gueili was aware that her symptoms greatly worsened because of work or family tension. But she adamantly rejected any connection between the two that suggested psychological problems contributed to her illness.

By the time our interview ended, Zheng Gueili became increasingly demanding and complaining. She manipulated her husband before our eyes. When he complained to us of the difficulty he had getting angry with his wife for fear he would worsen her symptoms, she grumbled about a headache, and he responded caringly and stopped talking about his discontent. We had the intuitive feeling that she was successful at controling her husband and parents, and also probably would succeed in returning to a less stressful job in the day care facility. We found ourselves growing impatient, however, with her whining tone of voice and querulous insistence that we provide her with a medical excuse from work so she could rest for several days. We also were impressed by the tolerance and concern her husband (and by report her parents too) continued to show for her physical condition.

A final case will end our accounts of psychological casualties of the Cultural Revolution.

Case 13   Yu Chunxia is a fifty-two-year-old cadre with a history of multiple vague gastrointestinal complaints of about two years' duration. After numerous medical workups her problem was diagnosed as neurasthenia, and she was referred to the psychiatry clinic. She has experienced abdominal pains, headaches, whole-body pain, periodic nausea and vomiting, and persistent constipation. Over the same two-year period Yu Chunxia has had insomnia with early morning waking, poor appetite, lack of energy, trouble concentrating, a marked slowing-down in speech, thinking, and bodily movements, an acute fear that she may have either an intestinal or a brain tumor, and strong feelings of guilt and low self-esteem. She appeared profoundly depressed, almost in a depressive stupor, but intially denied feelings of depression or sadness. She did admit to irritability, a vague unhappiness about which she refused to elaborate, joylessness, and pervasive hopelessness.

The onset of her symptoms coincided with the return of her husband to Changsha as a cadre in the civil administration, after twenty years of living in the countryside on different communes. Before 1958 Yu's husband had been an up-and-coming cadre, who in 1958 was labeled a rightist and subsequently was sent to the countryside to work as a peasant with infrequent visits home once each year or two for a brief time. During this period and especially during the Cultural Revolution her husband received a great deal of political criticism, and his wife had a very difficult time keeping the family going. She could not find work, had limited income, and was frequently criticized by her neighbors for her husband's problem. During the 1960s Yu's children could not attend senior middle school because of the family's political problem and instead had to accept menial jobs. During the Cultural Revolution two of her four children were sent to distant communes, and the family's situation, she reported, further worsened. In 1978 her husband was rehabilitated and returned home. Shortly after he returned home Yu Chun-xia's symptoms began.

After the psychiatric diagnostic assessment I asked Comrade Yu if her major depressive disorder could have resulted from marital incompatability and strain that only emerged once she and her husband were reunited. She disagreed with this formulation and offered an alternative one—a striking metaphor that I will now paraphrase. Suppose, she said, looking to the ground, you were climbing a mountain and this mountain was very steep and terribly difficult to climb. To the right and the left you could see people falling off the mountainside. Holding on to your neck and back were several family members, so that if you fell so would they. For twenty years you climbed this mountain with your eyes fixed on the handholds and footholds. You neither looked back or ahead. Finally you reached the top of the mountain. Perhaps this is the first time you have looked backward and seen how much you had endured, how difficult your life and your family's situation had been, how blighted your hopes. . . . She ended by asking me if this was not a good enough reason to become depressed.

Yu Chunxia's metaphor for the Cultural Revolution is revealing. Why, we may ask, was not this arduous ascent of a dangerous mountain experienced, once the climber and those clinging to her had reached safety at the top, with the joy of relief that a perilous course had been successfully negotiated and victory achieved? The answer, Yu suggests as a spokesman for many of the Cultural Revolution's psychological casualties, is that only at the end of the terrible ascent, as a survivor, can one afford to experience the pain of what one has been through: the losses, the fearsome threats to self and family, the undermining of social ideology, cultural tradition, and personal dreams, the bitter alienation and desperate sense of injustice, the hopelessness of it all.

This dejected state is clearly not the experience of all or even most survivors of the Cultural Revolution.[8] As noted before, the particular vulnerabilities in the depressed person's life place her or him at greater risk for the negative health consequences of major life events. But the Cultural Revolution cannot be regarded simply as just another life event—like marriage, divorce, loss of a job—although a more severe one. To begin with, it lasted for a decade and thus, at the very least, included a series of life events (uprooting, separation, losses, threats). Furthermore the Cultural Revolution pulled apart families and social networks, destroying social support. Even personal coping resources were exhausted by the extent and intensity of the threats (to body, self, family, job, friendships, political commitment) individuals experienced. Coping skills, moreover, for a large number of individuals, were systematically broken down in the crucible of community conflict. Withdrawal, denial, passive resignation, time off and away—these like many other coping processes were not tolerated. Hence vulnerable individuals were placed under great tension for long periods with little outside help and with great constraints on inner resources as well. Under such conditions it is remarkable that very many more did not break down.

In survival situations, where individuals and families feel that their very lives are at stake, it is only after the crisis abates that for some psychological effects take their heaviest toll; this seems to have been the case for Yu Chunxia.[9] For other of our patients, along with many of their fellow countrymen, there is abundant evidence that their psychological difficulties and medical problems began during the maelstrom itself.

Seven

★

Distress and Disease in Chinese Society

> For there is, I maintain, no such thing as the real world, no unique, ready
> made, absolute reality apart from and independent of all versions and
> visions. Rather, there are many right world-versions, some of them
> irreconcilable with others; and thus there are many worlds if any. A version
> is not so much made right by a world as a world is made by a right version.
> Obviously rightness has therefore to be determined otherwise than by
> matching a version with a world.
>
> Goodman (1984:285)

NEURASTHENIA AND SOMATIZATION

The cases I have described show how distinctive constellations of serious
work, family, personal, and political problems conduce, in the lived world
of everyday experience in China, to somatization. In certain cases personality
plays a central role, in others disordered physiology, in yet others cultural
value orientations and particular patterns of work or family difficulties. In
some instances a single factor emerges as most powerfully influential in
shaping the trajectory of somatic experience; in most the problems are constituted out of a tangle of factors that enhance each other. Certain of the
cases express the more or less unique configurations of the Chinese historical
and cultural setting; others are anchored in meanings and social structural
arrangements found worldwide that are shared sources of human misery.
Some of the problems are at least potentially remediable, many are not.
Somatic amplification is maladaptive in a number of cases, in several other
cases the reader may agree that somatization would seem to be adaptive.
In the discussion that follows I develop several explanatory accounts to make
sense of the issues these cases exemplify that relate them, on the one side,
to the results of the descriptive studies presented in the preceding chapters,

and on the other to a growing literature on the social sources and psycho-cultural significances of somatization.

Our empirical studies in their narrow sense address the relationship between neurasthenia, somatization and depression for patients in the psychiatry and primary care clinics where we worked in Hunan. But since I am not aware of a similar attempt to unravel this relationship elsewhere in China, I am tempted to generalize to the wider Chinese context so that a hypothesis is advanced that can be tested in future research in other local settings. If stated in general enough terms, such a hypothesis could be applied to those many areas of the world where neurasthenia may not be a common diagnosis but somatization, in other forms and names, is highly prevalent. Although I well recognize that the restricted nature of the samples, the preliminary quality of the investigations, and the danger of jumping from the scale of hundreds of cases to the scale of a billion people make generalization a risky undertaking, I believe that with appropriate restraint on my part and a good sense of skepticism on the part of the reader, such an exercise can be useful in thinking through the broad implications of our study for psychiatry and primary care in China and cross-culturally. After all, the purpose of comparative research must include the willingness, at the final stage, to translate from local context to the broader world, or else analysis is locked in an iron cage of incomparable localisms that fetter the very objectives of a science, even one as young and rough as this. It is in this exploratory spirit of theoretical inquiry that I offer the following analysis, one that seeks to integrate clinical and anthropological approaches to our findings in order to raise fundamental questions about the relationship of the social world to affect and illness as much as to suggest possible answers to the origins and nature of somatization.

A. Illness and Disease

Our best understanding of somatization is based on a now widely accepted distinction in medical anthropology between illness and disease. When we fall sick we first experience illness: that is, we perceive, label, communicate, interpret, and cope with symptoms, and we usually do this not alone but together with family members, friends, workmates, and other members of our social network. Within that network we *negotiate* the labels, the options, the trade-offs that result from and contribute to the lived experience of illness in the practical world of everyday life. Personal, interactional, and cultural norms guide this lived experience. That is to say, shared cultural beliefs (about the body, the self, specific symptoms, and illness generally), constraints in our concrete social situation, and aspects of the individual (personality, coping style, prior experience, and so forth) together with our explanatory model for the particular episode of illness orient us to how to act when ill, how to communicate distress, how to diagnose and treat, how to regard and manage the life problems illness creates, how to negotiate this social reality and interpret its meaning for ourself and for others.

Illness *means* in several senses. There is the taken-for-granted, ostensible, overt meaning of the symptom (for example, shortness of breath, toothache, immobility, fever) as pain, deformity, disfigurement, disability. These shared meanings, which are open to group communication and commentary, are more or less standardized in a local culture. As a result when we speak of hurt and limitation we are understood. Those understandings may be fairly subtle—in each social group there are a number of different ways to talk about, for example, headaches and those differences may make a difference in the way the sick person's circle responds to her or him.

A second sense of illness meanings has to do with the cultural significances certain disorders carry in particular societies. Leprosy and the plague in late medieval Europe, venereal disease in the Victorian era in Europe and America, mental illness in China throughout the millennia, cancer and AIDS in the presentday West—each holds unique significance and salience for the sufferer. Here cultural meanings inform perception and monitoring of bodily processes, as well as the very behaviors that constitute illness as a life experience. Culturally marked disorders can be said to *bring* these meanings to the patient and social network.

In a third sense illness is like a sponge that soaks up the peculiar meanings that differentiate each of our personal lives and interpersonal situations. Heart disease for the failed businessman in Western society can become embedded in a disintegrating marriage, alcohol abuse and related family violence, a demoralizing relationship with a boss, a midlife crisis in which change in body image and coming to terms with one's mortality assault a fragily constructed ego. Or for Chinese society, think of a thirty-year-old, deeply disaffiliated worker, a former Red Guard and rusticated youth, whose bitterness, cynicism, and mourning over multiple losses in the Cultural Revolution (of education, career mobility, family harmony, and so forth) are absorbed into the symptoms of a chronic illness so that treatment of the physical complaints needs to include response to the particular psychological and social distress that are likely sources of symptom amplification and worsening disability. Both Freudians (Balint 1958; Groddeck 1977) and phenomenologists (Buytendijk 1974; Plessner 1970) show how illness may crystallize deep inner meanings (threat, punishment, loss) that are moorings for the sense of self and bind these to moral and religious aspects of suffering. Regarding the latter, suffering in Buddhist theology and in traditional Christian eschatology is not a wholly disvalued experience but potential leverage for transcendence. Regarding the former, many traditional healing systems, like modern psychotherapy, encourage the search for personal illness metaphors in the biography of a life. Here narratization of one's life may make use of illness to create a story that conveys a special meaning to experience as much as illness draws on that life story for its significance.

As Plessner (1970) brilliantly shows, the essential feature of being human is the mediated nature of physical experience; bodily processes are mediated by our understanding (in an experiential and nonverbal more than discursive mode) of them as meaningful events and relations in our lives; that understanding (in a nondualistic interactionist manner) becomes part of the bodily process of illness itself. We simultaneously *have* a sick body (an "it" separate from the real me) and *are* the sick body (the sickness is me). Illness meanings so viewed are physiological as much as social. In the lived experience of social reality mediated by the body, this is the symbolic bridge, the sociosomatic reticulum that ties failure to headaches, anger to dizziness, loss and demoralization to fatigue.

The sick person as moral agency may be aware of such embodied illness meanings, though frequently he or she is not. Alternatively, the researcher or clinician interprets these meanings as the reflection of a particular problem experienced by a particular person environed in a particular social structure. Illness is often overdetermined and conveys several and frequently many meanings as it oscillates between agency and structure: not just this or that, but this and that . . . and that too. For example, a chronic illness like asthma may serve to authorize and sanction failure (in work, school, marriage, sexual relations), may marshall social support otherwise unavailable (for example, love and aid from an estranged spouse), may sanction the expression of anger that is otherwise illegitimate, may provide time out and away from terribly difficult circumstances that one feels she or he can no longer tolerate. Illness may empower the relatively powerless, such as the wife of a physically abusive husband whose symptoms authorize her otherwise unattended demands that her husband share in the burdensome round of routine daily household labor; but the same illness in the same person may also lead to greater powerlessness.

When the sick person visits medical professionals (or for that matter any healer), the channel for clinical communication is common sense understandings of illness meanings that patient and practitioner share as members of the same culture. Thus at the outset the talk of patients and practitioners is the language of illness.

But during the clinical transaction a radical change routinely occurs. The practitioner begins to construe the patient's problem as *disease*, that is, she perceives, labels, interprets, and treats it as a specific abnormality in her profession's nosological system. For the patient who complains of excessive thirst, urination, and hunger, the biomedically trained physician will seek out evidence to determine whether the patient is suffering from diabetes mellitus; for the patient with chest pain when jogging or walking up the stairs to his bedroom, the doctor will obtain data from treadmill tests and electro-cardiograms to test her hypothesis that the problem is coronary artery insufficiency. Through this process illness as lay experience becomes transformed into disease as biomedical explanation and a clinical entity materializes as a real thing: disordered pancreatic function, or narrowing of the arteries supplying the heart. The practitioner constructs a new social reality (albeit one dialectically constrained by physiology), the disease. The disease as interpreted by the practitioner and understood in the society will also come to influence how the patient thinks and lives his illness. (Think of what happens when the patient's weight loss is diagnosed by the physician as "cancer.") Indeed, in the biomedical viewpoint, the disease is an abnormality in biological structure or function that generates the symptoms of illness. (Helman (1985) demonstrates that the different physiologies of asthma and ulcerative colitis shape the distinctive explanatory models held by the sufferers of each disorder).

As Eisenberg (1977) has shown, however, the interplay between disease and illness aspects of a particular sickness can be and frequently is complex: in the course of a chronic disorder either aspect may become the major source of exacerbation and remission. Biomedical definitions of disease are especially significant because in most societies they acquire the cultural authority to determine bureaucratic definitions of disability. (Nandi [1983] shows that in the colonial situation such definitions from the Western cultural tradition are imposed on colonized societies as a powerful reality that changes how the colonized perceive and create their inner as much as outer world—a provocative image for understanding the cultural authority of professional definitions of disease.) These disease meanings are notably at odds with those attached to the experience of illness. It is this discrepancy in the cultural meanings of what is "real" that confers on disorder its innate ambiguity and tendency to polarize lay and professional viewpoints.

Let us apply this distinction, first, to somatization and, thereafter, to neurasthenia and depression. In my formulation of somatization we have cases either in which physical complaints are expressed but a corresponding organic lesion in biomedical terms cannot be detected, or in which such complaints are amplified so that symptomatology and perceived disability exceed what would be expected from a particular pathological lesion. As I have already shown, depression, anxiety, and other psychiatric disorders can produce either situation. Major depressive disorder in the course of heart disease can prolong recovery, exacerbate symptoms, and substantially worsen disability—all of which can be reversed by effectively treating the depression. Panic disorder in the absence of any other pathology can produce disabling physical symptoms that resemble those of cardiovascular disease, respiratory disease, epilepsy, and other medical disorders. When the panic disorder is alleviated, so are the physical complaints.

Alternatively, as the work of Mechanic (1980) illustrates, stress can so affect a susceptible individual that entirely normal bodily reactions are misinterpreted as symptoms of illness or, more likely, the psychophysiological correlates of affective arousal and personal distress are amplified and labeled as illness. When this happens psychological and somatic symptoms may not be differentiated, for personal and cultural reasons, and thus may not be expressed separately. (Indeed, where cultures and individuals monitor the body-self through nondualistic lenses, they are undifferentiable.) The individual complains instead of physical symptoms that are the embodied correlates of depressed, anxious, or angry affect. In the sick person's social group and in his own explanatory model there may be implicit understanding that these bodily complaints convey integrated psychological as well as physical meaning; nonetheless the dualistic framework and biological reductionism that biomedical professionals bring to the clinical encounter tend to press physicians to diagnose a physical disorder. Furthermore, many of the lay terms applied to such syndromes of personal distress also emphasize their physiological properties. Frequently psychosocial care for personal and family distress is provided indirectly as part of the "medical" treatment of the putative physical problem.

B. Social Uses of Somatization

I have described how somatization is created out of the illness experience associated with a medical or psychiatric disease, or out of the coping behavior associated with stress, or, when it is the practitioner who focuses on the somatic, out of a failure to recognize the biopsychosocial integration in these behaviors and a reductionistic tendency to label and treat them as disease entities. In the course of chronic disease, say a chronic pain syndrome associated with minor trauma to a limb, psychological and social factors such as an out-of-awareness desire to be dependent, or an all-too-aware desire to obtain financial compensation or time off from school, or a partially self-perceived wish to avoid an embarrassing situation or indirectly express resentment at a spouse may amplify the symptoms which, if the individual is further rewarded for displaying them, by financial compensation for persistent disability or by love and attention from an otherwise emotionally distant spouse, over time congeal into the chronic illness behavior of somatization.

This pattern has been extremely well documented in the clinical literature (cf. Katon et al. 1982; Ford 1983; Pennebaker 1982; Leventhal, Nerenz, Straus 1982). If it persists, such behavior often leads to inappropriate and excessive utilization of health care resources, unnecessary and dangerous tests, inappropriate and poor treatment, iatrogenesis, and enhanced personal and family suffering; it therefore becomes a major burden for the health care system and the society. Chronic pain syndrome, for example, is one of the major sources of disability in the United States. Early recognition and appropriate treatment, as in the case of previously undiagnosed depression causing chronic pain, can prevent acute and subacute somatization from becoming chronic somatization (Rosen et al. 1982). Once chronic somatization becomes well established as an illness career, it is difficult to reverse because the complex and powerful interplay between chronic disease and illness sustains a vicious cycle.

But this is only one kind of vicious cycle—albeit a type that conservative politicians like to wave before the public as an illustration of voluntaristic abuses of the disability system. Most vicious cycles are not voluntaristic. They are driven as much by significant physiological pathology as by dynamic ties with psychosocial processes. It is just as easy to tell the opposite story—that vicious cycles are driven principally by increased biomechanical distress and other physiological burdens of work- and class-related morbidity (back pain from strenuous jobs and work-related injuries, shortness of breath from black lung disease as the natural consequence of several decades in a mine, cancer from exposure to carcinogens in the workplace, and so forth). A number of our cases attest to vicious cycles driven by oppressive social structures and terrible work conditions. Type A personality is not so much a voluntaristic behavior as a product of a dialectic between personality and capitalist reward structures. It is characteristic of the complexities of life that many of us experience a mixture of vicious cycles, not a single, "pure" type.

Somatization is usually assumed to be maladaptive because it has been studied largely by physicians or by social scientists working within a disease epidemiology framework. Many psychiatrists seem to regard it as definitely pathological. Yet anthropologists have reported somatic idioms of distress as one of a series of cultural idioms that articulate distress in religious, kinship, moral, naturalistic, medical, and political terms in order to cope with it effectively. Nichter (1982), working with South Indian Havik women, presents examples of somatization as personally and socially adaptive coping in addition to illustrations of its maladaptive and pathological aspects. He shows that somatization may occur through distinctive cultural idioms of diet, bodily constitution, common complaints of women and children, the physiology of reproduction and child development, and commensality, sexuality, and other biological categories given salience in particular cultures (see also Lock n.d.; Finkler 1985; Ohnuki-Tierney 1984: 75–88). Parsons (1985) describes a kinship idiom for communicating symptoms and negotiating sickness episodes in Tonga. Taussig (1980b) and Commaroff (1985) describe examples of symptom idioms effectively expressing political opposition. I have also observed adaptive examples of somatization in my ethnographic research in Taiwan and in my clinical practice in the United States, and encountered some of the same as well as other somatic idioms. The data from our 1983 studies in Hunan indicate that a significant number of somatizing patients, especially in the primary care setting, cannot be diagnosed as suffering from a mental illness. Several of the case summaries suggest that a somatic idiom of distress may well have been adaptive for the affected person and, in at least one instance, for the entire family, although this cannot be said of most of the cases of neurasthenia I have described.

I anticipate that future ethnographies and surveys of communities will demonstrate that somatization can be expressed in a large but familiar number of lay conceptualizations of human biology and nonverbal communications. I suspect we will learn somatization is a ubiquitous coping pattern that is perhaps most often used adaptively, though it sometimes creates greater problems than those it seeks to resolve. Indeed, Pickering (1974) offers dramatic instances of somatization supporting rare creativity, such as Darwin's hypochondriasis and neurasthenia, which legitimized his social withdrawal while he single-mindedly worked through the enormous body of material that substantiated the idea of evolution in the *Origin of Species,* or Florence Nightingale's conversion symptoms, which gave her the sentimental authority of wheelchair and sickbed while she negotiated reform of the British hospital system and military with government leaders after the disastrous Crimean campaign. Few will have had such experiences, but many will recall various small benefits achieved from illness: permission to be passive or avoid difficult social situations, protection from criticism, attention and affection from family and close friends, needed time to bring important undertakings to fruition. And sometimes the benefits are not small. Sickness can reintegrate a family on the point of disintegration, or provide an escape hatch for a person no longer able to cope and feeling suicidal; it may legitimize personal failure that otherwise would be unbearable, or help in difficult negotiations over distribution of limited resources; it may teach us important moral lessons about how to better order our lives and, as many senior clinicians know, thereby help the chronically ill to live a more purposeful and productive life. The grim difficulties of living have many of us by the throat: to get through life we need all the friends we can get. This does not mean that we malinger or that we rationally choose to somatize.

There can be little question, though, that the sick role can at times be rewarding, and that once legitimated there may be unaccountable—though usually unconscious—delay in giving it up, for intimate personal and social reasons. Not the least of illness's properties is the medium of communication it affords to express distress, demoralization, unhappiness, and other difficult, dangerous, and otherwise unsanctioned feelings in terms that must be heard and may lead to change. Similarly, affection and support can be expressed through concern with others' health and care for their illnesses.

Now, suppose that somatization is positively sanctioned by cultural norms, as it appears to be in a number of societies, whereas psychologization is stigmatized, the case classically described in Chinese culture. There will then be pressure to selectively perceive and express the physiological components of the simultaneously psychophysiological symptoms of distress, and to deny and suppress the psychological ones. The former will be socially efficacious, the latter socially unacceptable and inefficacious, and indeed culturally repressed. One will have grown up a witness to the expert deployment of a somatic coping style, but will have had little experience of a psychological one. The somatic end of the perceptual and linguistic continuum will be especially marked; there may not even be any markings of the psychological end, which in that sense may be said not to exist. The cultural sources of social support will also be structured in terms of somatic patterns of help-seeking (medical facilities and treatments), but not psychological ones (psychotherapy); this includes the idioms used to nurture and help.

Somatization can be at times culturally authorized, socially useful, and personally availing. Since it appears to be historically and culturally prior to psychologization in most societies, there is no choice between somatic and psychic metaphors, which can—and often do—occur together. The very organization of experience is somatic (cf. Kirmayer 1984; Turner 1985).

No social system could sustain the cost of massive resort to this idiom of distress and coping stratagem. Health care resources, both familial and social, would be overwhelmed, and there would be immense suspicion of the motives of sick people. Perhaps this is what Parsons (1951) visualized when he described the American sick role as requiring that the occupant must want to get better and must seek out authorized help to do so. But this hardly applies to chronic illness where, despite the desire to be cured, the sick person will never fully cast off the sick role. Here, the meanings and uses of affliction are an integral part of the illness, which itself is inseparable from coping style and personality. Somatization, at least to a minor degree, is thus unavoidable in chronic illness and probably alternates, even in the same person, with its opposite—denial and minimization of symptoms. Social situations and the personal and cultural significance of symptoms, as much as personality and coping variables, modulate daily this swing from amplification to damping.

C. What is Neurasthenia?

If we understand major depressive disorder as disease, at least as construed in DSM-III, and somatization as illness, then where does neurasthenia fit in? I will contend that neurasthenia is both illness (a socially and culturally shaped type of somatization) and disease (a category in China's medical classificatory system and in WHO's ICD-9 as well). This double status provides neurasthenia with some of the peculiar qualities evident in our studies. Neurasthenic somatization, however, may at times be best interpreted as neither disease nor illness, but as a cultural idiom of distress and an interpersonal coping process. I did not study this aspect of neurasthenia in China, but I think it is an important subject for research on normal populations, family relations, the socialization process and child and adult development: the learned daily life pattern of communicating distress and seeking help.

The neurasthenic patients in our sample experienced symptoms which at one time or another they (and members of their family and wider social network) came to believe were those of "neurasthenia" or some related neurological disorder. Headaches, lack of energy, weakness, insomnia, dizziness, and a variety of other related complaints, when they cannot be diagnosed as due to a specific organic lesion, or do not respond to treatment, or especially when they become chronic and interfere with normal social activities, seem to be viewed (with more or less agreement) in lay culture as "neurasthenia." In the absence of formal ethnographies of the semantic networks of neurasthenia in various Chinese communities, this is about all that we can surmise from our clinical accounts. Neurasthenia in China is a popular sickness category that implies a common physical disorder (weakness or exhaustion of "the nerves"), but one that is understood to include social and psychological, as well as biological, antecedents and consequences.

This disorder is often suspected and diagnosed by the patient and other members of his family and friendship and work network even before it is confirmed by medical professionals. There are shared expectations of what being ill with "neurasthenia" is really like, expectations individuals have grown up with since childhood, have seen exemplified in family and friends, and perhaps have learned to confirm by monitoring their own bodies. These cultural expectations ostensibly emphasize physical complaints and causes, but personal, family, work, and other psychosocial problems are appreciated to be part of the syndrome too—even if they are regarded as of secondary importance. Neurasthenia thus fulfills the definitional criteria for illness set out above.

If our findings are valid, neurasthenia illness behavior includes typical meanings, uses, and social responses, including avoidance and rest from physically and psychosocially stressful situations; time off from wearying home and work commitments; excuse for poor performance in school, lack of success in career, and failure in key life tasks such as "enduring" stress; warranted expression of dissatisfaction, dejection, and demoralization; search for symptom relief and rehabilitation from official and nonofficial sources of care; aid from family, friends, and co-workers, including empathy for the sufferer and recognition that his disorder is an appropriate explanation for personal irritability, distress, and failure to perform his normal social obligations and for family dysfunction. Neurasthenia takes on the blame for misfortune and misery; it generally frees the sick person from responsibility for his actions—but there are ambiguities and limits. You can't get away with murder, or avoid the personal consequences of major political campaigns.

These shared cultural assumptions are held, to a greater or lesser degree of awareness, by laymen and health care workers alike. The patient's illness will therefore make similar sense to the patient, his family, the members of his unit, and to his medical care providers, who, however, eventually will reinterpret it as disease. All perhaps recognize that though the disorder frequently is of minor significance it can become a serious burden, may well have a long course and not respond to treatment, and can cause or complicate problems for each of them. For many the ambit of neurasthenia meanings may include a sense of uncertainty, lack of control, and frustration.

Chinese cultural orientations, traditional and contemporary, permeate the illness experience of neurasthenia. This may seem curious at first, since the term *neurasthenia* came from the West in modern times. Although the term is relatively recent the concept and, more importantly, the social function are ancient. The concept that weakness of vital essence causes disease is a core category in traditional Chinese medicine and can be traced back to the classical texts (see Porkert 1974). As already noted, a somatopsychic orientation and provision of a medical sick role for culture-bound syndromes that Western health professionals would diagnose as psychological problems also characterize traditional Chinese medicine. Hence there is every reason to suspect that neurasthenia replaced traditional medical categories which played the same role before the biomedical paradigm became dominant in China. This substitution would be an excellent subject for historical research on culture change.

Neurasthenia reflects other Chinese core cultural themes and psychocultural processes: for example, the emphasis on interpersonal relations over intrapsychic concerns; the view, guiding social communication, that intimate personal revelation outside the family is a shameful impropriety; the dominance of externalizing cognitive coping processes over internalizing ones; the practical situation-oriented cognitive style; the special family-based stigma of mental illness; and the strong concern with maintaining physical well-being through diet, exercise, abstinence, and taking medicine. Elsewhere I have offered a cultural analysis of neurasthenia as a symbolic form in Chinese culture based on my work and that of many others with overseas Chinese (Kleinman 1980), and I believe much the same could be said about the People's Republic. The thrust of these integrated cultural, social, and psychobiological determinants is to construct neurasthenia illness experience as one that is primarily somatic. The findings from our studies of symptom idiom, expressed versus elicited complaints, explanatory models of etiology and pathophysiology, and patterns of help-seeking abundantly affirm this point. Individuals do experience and have insight into psychosocial symptoms, but these are treated as marginal in the neurasthenia complex.

Lin Tsung-yi (1986) draws attention to the vicissitudes of neurasthenia as a cultural category in the People's Republic. Its meaning has not remained impervious to important social changes.

During the Great Leap, a large-scale national campaign against neurasthenia was organized, ostensibly to control what was alleged to be almost an epidemic among "mind workers" (intellectuals, including office workers, teachers, students) and, to a lesser extent, laborers (Editorial 1966). The campaign was a response to rates of the diagnosis neurasthenia, which had risen to 80–90 percent among outpatients in neurology and medical clinics, and to high rates of absenteeism in schools and factories. Even productivity was said to have been affected. Lin argues that these ideological claims may indeed have reflected a sharp increase in the actual incidence of neurasthenia. This increase and the political attention it attracted, he suggests, were the result of the intensification of social tension in China in the late 1950s owing to the end of the immediate post-revolution period of optimism and moral fervor; the harsh, demoralizing recognition of the immense economic and institutional barriers to modernization that had still not been significantly reduced by a decade of communism; and the excesses of the radical Maoist line of the Anti-Rightist Campaign and the Great Leap Forward. Perhaps under the extremely tight social controls of the Communist bureaucracy, neurasthenic somatization had indeed become one of the few available avenues of "escape" and symbols of alienation. It is difficult to imagine another reason for the prominence the anti-neurasthenia campaign was given during the Great Leap Forward.

The result was that eradicating neurasthenia became one of the three priority targets of the First Five Year Plan in Mental Health (1958–62). The Pavlovian view of the disorder was given national prominence, and for a time this diagnosis must have been a politically suspect and socially less acceptable one. It is a testament to the cultural significance neurasthenia has achieved in contemporary China that this interlude had little lasting effect on the meaning of neurasthenia in the People's Republic, though it may well have controlled, at least temporarily, its misuse and abuse.

After the anti-neurasthenia campaign, neurasthenia unavoidably became both a major concern in psychiatry and a subject freighted with potentially dangerous political significance for researchers in psychiatry and psychology. That the Intensive Comprehensive Group Treatment for neurasthenia initiated during the Great Leap Forward hardly survived the conclusion of the campaign in spite of claims of high (though probably very short-lived) rates of success for this sociotherapy (Lin et al. 1958; Kuang et al. 1960) perhaps indicates that the state has come to recognize that neurasthenia, for all its potential abuses, serves certain indirectly useful personal and social functions for Chinese society.

The work-disability system in China is a prepotent force encouraging neurasthenic somatization. Should our findings be replicated elsewhere in China, it would seem that chronic illness behavior offers workers some leverage, even if not a very great amount, over a system that otherwise does not contain many opportunities for changing jobs, getting out of very difficult work situations and stresses, resolving lengthy family separations due to different and distant work sites, and getting time off with compensation. Only field research in the workplace, something neither Chinese nor foreign researchers have undertaken, will adequately test this hypothesis. That many of the patients in our original sample continued to demonstrate illness behavior even when their symptoms had improved seems best explained by the fact that their work (and also family or school) situations had not changed for the better, and in a number of instances had actually worsened. That at time of three year follow-up only those patients who had retired, had changed to a job perceived as better, or had successfully altered a major family problem had significantly improved, is further evidence in favor of this hypothesis. Only a very few patients were purposefully using their illness behavior to openly manipulate the work system; the great majority were not consciously doing so. Nor were most of the former malingering; they were experiencing substantial somatic distress and had evidence of injuries and physiological dysfunction.

Illness behavior, once present for whatever reason, opens up options for dealing with the work system, and these come into play virtually automatically because of the cultural salience of illness among Chinese and the lack of significant alternatives in the work unit. Most work unit leaders and co-workers are probably genuinely concerned about a worker's health status and sensitive to the difficulties and dangers of working while sick. There is some recognition that certain work situations may create or exacerbate sickness. Where it is feasible to do so, the work unit's leaders probably attempt to better these conditions, especially for vulnerable individuals. This view is supported by Communist ideology. But the harsh reality of work in the People's Republic is that conditions are frequently bad. Factories are often poorly lighted and ineffectively ventilated and heated; and modern safeguards are few. Opportunities for advancement or for changing jobs are very limited. Even where they want to be helpful, the power hierarchy of the work unit is severely limited in what it can do for workers. In our 1980 sample one worker who operated a mining machine in a saltmine near Changsha reported that in midsummer the temperature at the machine site could get close to 50° C. He found the conditions extraordinarily difficult, but when he asked to change his job, he was told that though the leading cadres in the unit had great sympathy for his plight, someone had to do the work. If he changed jobs, someone else would have to work the machine. Other workers complained of intolerable levels of noise, dust, smoke, and fumes—all of which they attributed to either causing or worsening their neurasthenic symptoms. They had met with the same reply as the mining machine operator when they approached the cadres in their factories with requests for transfer to other jobs or improvement in working conditions.

China is a very poor country now undergoing rapid industrial development. It is not surprising that resources are unavailable to improve work conditions and that industrial hygiene, safety, and health concerns have been low on the list of priorities. Unemployment for urban youth is extensive; underemployment of high school and even university graduates is commonplace. One of our patients, a very bright high school graduate who had failed the university entrance exam, felt lucky to have secured a job with the national railroad system. But after six months he could barely tolerate his job anymore. He worked from late in the evening to the morning in an outlying building on a peripheral line. His job was to work several hand signals every few hours when trains passed. The rest of the time he was in an unlighted room with a flashlight that was only to be used for operating the signals and a telephone that rang periodically to check that he was up and alert. He had been told that he would have to remain in this job for several years before he would have a chance at something better. This worker cried when he reported what it was like to spend hours at his cold and lonely post, unable to do anything useful or—because of the lack of lighting and regulations as well—study. Of course his situation was much better than that of urban coolies or peasants before 1949: he had enough to eat and his work did not threaten his life. But to hear his bitter complaints, it was undeniable his work was seriously affecting his mental health.

Now that the hard years of famine and serious instability are past and illness as a work problem has become a legitimate problem, the barriers to assuming the sick role are fewer than in earlier years. In the aftermath of the Cultural Revolution, when nearly every family or social network included someone deeply hurt, there seems to be an additional concern to help those who were among its worst victims, as for example when they experience work difficulties created or worsened by illness. That this is not a subject for direct negotiation but one that is handled indirectly, in terms of a sanctioned illness—not work—idiom, is indicated by the finding that only two patients in 1980 had the temerity to openly suggest in their explanatory models that change of work might improve their illness, even though many regarded it as the result of work problems.

Nevertheless, the work-disability system in China cannot respond fully or immediately to illness needs without risk of enormous dislocations and widespread malingering. Like many other work-disability systems, including that of the United States, the impediments, difficulties, and length of time involved in trying to change work through illness must be sufficient to insure that this option is not exercised routinely. The patients in our study recognized that there were substantial obstacles and great uncertainty about the outcome. Most of those who had sought work relief had done so only after a long period of sickness involving substantial disability. Even so, many had still not succeeded in changing their work situations. This is similar to the situation chronic pain patients engaged in work-disability suits confront in the United States, though the specific deterrents and the levers for coping with the system obviously differ in these markedly different settings.

Chronic illness behavior in Chinese culture has historically had special uses. Confucian-style scholar-bureaucrats had a long tradition of claiming sickness to withdraw from dangerous political situations to a safer life of retirement. The practice was followed by not only a number of famous Confucian ministers of early Chinese governments, but—as the epigrams of chapter 4 suggest—by Mao himself on several occasions. Several of the patients I interviewed seemed to have used their illness behavior similarly during the Cultural Revolution. For a few cadres chronic neurasthenia distanced them from the fire of criticism that had threatened to consume them, but for most it seems to have had quite temporary and not very successful results. This topic deserves systematic study as an example of politically motivated illness idioms.

One flagrantly pragmatic use of chronic illness behavior is to sanction repeated failure on the national university entrance examination for former members of the urban Red Guards, who were sent to the countryside in the late 1960s and 70s and whose education was severely disrupted by the Cultural Revolution. This generation of young adults has been described as bitter and cynical because of what they lost during the Cultural Revolution (Frolic 1981). Those in our sample were children of well-educated professionals and cadres who had spent about a decade working in rural areas as peasant-farmers. They and their families had high expectations for their careers, expectations that had been shattered by the disruption of their middle school education and by repeated failures to pass the extremely competitive examinations for university, which only 4 percent of applicants pass. Their poor prospects are compounded by unemployment and underemployment in urban settings, and the fact that better jobs are going to those with higher levels of technical training and educational skills. This cohort of those most affected by the Cultural Revolution is unable to compete against the best students currently leaving senior middle school, students who have had much better academic preparation. They do not wish to live on rural communes where they feel they do not belong, yet cannot find suitable work in the cities where their families reside. For these members of a "lost generation" a medical excuse seems to be one of the only acceptable (face-saving) sanctions for seemingly intractable failure; resort to the sick role is perhaps a less dangerous means of coping with the personal bitterness such a profound sense of failure instills than is acting out through social or political deviance. (The stereotype of this cohort is that they possess poor work habits, lack moral commitment, are disaffected, and at times resort to illegal activities. Some of its members were imprisoned in the immediate post–Cultural Revolution period as political dissidents who advocated democratic reforms to protect individual rights.) A medical excuse also has the potential of achieving some practical benefits for individuals who often are desperate and without acceptable alternatives.

Neurasthenia also offers the disaffected and potential dissidents a safety valve. In a society where little if any disaffection or dissent is tolerated the neurasthenia label and the medical sick role it authorizes can provide a sanctioned way of being marginal, either as a drop-out or disguised critic. Several of our patients appear to have achieved this status. The public campaign against neurasthenia in the period of the Great Leap Forward probably makes this association of neurasthenia and disaffection at least latently understood, but it is not one that is raised by health professionals or in the media. Since the explicit ideological association of wrong political thinking with mental illness in the Cultural Revolution did not extend to neurasthenia—which is surprising in view of what happened during the Great Leap Forward—this latent meaning of neurasthenia is perhaps even more effective. That the authorities have not seen fit to resume their campaign against neurasthenia suggests that they themselves tolerate this social use of the diagnosis.

Neurasthenia as illness in China possesses social and cultural cachet. Intriguingly, the word *cachet* (an indication of approval connoting prestige or influence) at one time referred to the small case of gelatin enclosing a dose of medicine. The capsule became the distinguishing mark, the evidence of authenticity and efficacy of what was inside, namely the active ingredient. In the same way the culturally approved and socially legitimated illness behavior is the distinguishing mark of authenticity and efficacy of neurasthenia: a hard exoskeleton congealing key meanings in the popular culture. These meanings turn on a view of the affected individual as too weak or exhausted because

his or her neurological functioning (a physical disorder) is too diminished to
carry on normal family, school, political, or work activities. The neurasthenic,
furthermore, needs to rest and remove himself from sources of stress and
dis-ease. He is vulnerable to exacerbation and at risk for serious disability.
Because they cannot be unaware of its cultural significance and social power,
the members of sanctioning agencies (health professionals and work-disability
system authorities) must be cautious in authorizing this form of chronic somatization and must seek to prevent its abuse, which in turn creates difficult
negotiations between patients, health professionals, and work authorities—
several vivid examples of which I witnessed among our subjects. A 1982
article reporting the data from the 1980 research raised the following questions: How are the negotiations (formal and informal) actually conducted?
How effective is neurasthenia as a means of changing work and other social
responsibilities? How widespread is this? What are the typical problems it
creates for patients, families, work authorities, and health professionals? What
kinds of abuses does it give rise to, both among patients and health professionals? These and many related questions need to be investigated before
the functions of somatization in China can be understood (Kleinman
1982:178). Four years later the same questions seem just as central, and
there are still very few answers.[1]

From neurasthenia as illness we turn to consider neurasthenia a *disease*.
If the illness experience of neurasthenia is what the patient brings to the
initial clinical encounter with health professionals, and if this is what assures
patient and practitioner a common language for communication, the situation
soon changes radically as health professionals reinterpret the health problem
as a disease within their conceptual systems and apply "disease-specific"
treatment for it within their paradigms of practice. Physicians of traditional
Chinese medicine might diagnose kidney weakness or a *yin* or *yang* imbalance. Internists, psychiatrists, nurses, and barefoot doctors will refract neurasthenic illness through their particular theoretical lenses (not just a shared
biomedical model, but somewhat different models based on specialty, degree
of biomedical and psychosocial knowledge, amount of assimilation of traditional Chinese medicine theory, lay views, and so forth), and will come
up with the diagnosis of a *disease* and its treatment. They may diagnose the
cause of neurasthenic symptoms as migraine headaches, anemia, parasitosis,
cancer, thyroid disease, diabetes, depression, or some other disease. Once
the practitioner relabels neurasthenia as a biomedical disease the lay illness
category disappears for him, because he has constructed in its place an alternative social reality. Disease construction can be thought of as a form of

clinical reinterpretation that establishes two distinctive views of the same problem, the patient's and the practitioner's. This revisionist account removes the shared ground for clinical communication, setting up in its place the basis for future conflict. That conflict results from the discrepancies between the patient's and the family's orientation to the resolution of illness problems and the biomedical health professional's orientation to the much narrower and more technical disease problems.

This is exactly what happened in our study. We reinterpreted the patient's neurasthenia as major depressive disorder. Yet the outcome data show that few patients were converted to this psychiatric model, although many reported fewer symptoms on antidepressant treatment. The reasons for this phenomenon are complex, but they surely involve the culturally stigmatizing implication of psychiatric diagnosis, as well as the past association of "depression" with wrong political thinking and anathematized sociopolitical alienation. Most patients continued to prefer the diagnosis of neurasthenia as disease. (Perhaps the lack of an association with culturally stigmatized mental illness protected neurasthenia from the political interpretation given to depression during the Cultural Revolution.) But the follow-up finding three years later that a substantial number of patients had come to view their problem as psychological—and some even considered psychotherapy as a treatment—indicates that the psychiatric explanation over time did have some persuasive effect on patients' explanations.

The limited space devoted to neurasthenia in current Chinese textbooks of medicine and psychiatry, and the hesitancy with which medical academics and specialists explain its presumed pathology, disclose that neurasthenia's status as a biomedical disease is uncertain and undergoing change. Many of my Chinese psychiatric colleagues, who are experienced clinicians well read in the latest international psychiatric literature, continue to regard it to be a neuropsychiatric disorder with a neurological basis. But they recognize its relationship to stress and are sensitive to the skepticism with which neurasthenia is regarded by Western, particularly American, psychiatrists. Others regard it with great ambivalence, while a small but increasing group of younger psychiatric researchers seem almost ready to dispense with it entirely, replacing it with depression, panic disorder, obsessive-compulsive disorder, other anxiety disorders, post-traumatic stress disorder, and personality disorder diagnoses. Their general medical colleagues are also inconsistent; some think of it as a psychological disease, others as a physiological one, and still others as psychophysiological manifestations of several distinctive diseases. Nonetheless, neurasthenia is still widely used in general medical circles. Even my psychiatrist research assistants varied in their opinion as to whether the psychological or physiological component was dominant in a given case. Over time this uncertainty grew; by 1983 it became more likely they would entertain alternative diagnoses, and by 1985 this seemed even more to be the case.

Of course psychiatric assessment in Western society is similarly discordant: the persistent though unavailing attempt to distinguish endogenous (biologically-based) and reactive (psychologically-based) types of depression constitutes an obvious example, as do personality disorders that no longer appear on the axis of psychiatric diseases in DSM-III. Several of my Chinese colleagues, in pointing out the value of maintaining neurasthenia as a diagnostic category in China, expressed the personal view that there might be several subtypes of neurasthenia: depressed and nondepressed; primarily biological and primarily psychological. This might be viewed as an instance of syncretism between two opposing but not necessarily irreconcilable viewpoints. Chinese psychiatrists, as heirs to a long tradition of nationalistically motivated scientific modernizers who have attempted to create unique Chinese scientific institutions while under pressure from Western models and with deep concern to maintain some elements of the Chinese tradition, wish to construct a scientifically valid but culturally appropriate form of psychiatry—a Chinese psychiatry.[2] Neurasthenia opens the most revealing window on how this Chinese psychiatry is being constructed and how it differs from Anglo-American and European psychiatry.

The ultimate fate of neurasthenia in the new Chinese psychiatry is by no means certain. The great advantage of neurasthenia as a diagnostic category is its flexibility. Here its very ambiguity, which makes it scientifically suspect, is a clinical virtue. It is easy to use. As actually applied it has a range of meanings around a central somatopsychic core that extend all the way from a gloss for neurosis to brain pathology. These multiple, even contradictory meanings allow for the needed flexibility, slippage, and multiple reinterpretations essential in the day-to-day care of patients with a chronic disorder of greatly uncertain treatment response, course, and outcome. They are usually a more appropriate map of the variability and vagaries of this waxing and waning problem than the more precise psychiatric categories of DSM-III. Moreover, neurasthenia as currently applied in the People's Republic clearly maps a phenomenon in the world, sanctions a wide range of possible interventions for it, and is understood and accepted in the popular culture. It may be the best available way of dealing with somatization, which collapses biomedical categories and makes a hash of reductionism and mind-body dualism. In this portmanteau psychosocial and cultural issues can be (and routinely are) smuggled into medical practice; in the absence of a clinical axis for illness behavior neurasthenia's range of meanings seems to encompass both disease and illness, a decided advantage for making sense of the congeries of social, psychological, and biological interactions subsumed by this archaic name.

When I diagnosed major depressive disorder, panic disorder, somatization disorder, my Chinese colleagues might agree, or they might diagnose instead a neurasthenic syndrome or some other category in their local diagnostic system.[3] Their treatment practice may change to the extent that antidepressants, the new anxiolytic drugs, or biofeedback are found useful to treat particular patients. This does not necessarily mean the diagnostic use of neurasthenia will change, only that subpopulations of neurasthenic patients will be identified in ways that enable the use of these treatments. The neurasthenic syndrome does recognize the importance of key somatic symptoms in mental illness that are not incorporated in the American psychiatric diagnostic criteria; thus it is sensitive to an important element in the Chinese setting, one to which Western psychiatrists need to attend more closely. DSM-III's criteria of major depressive disorder need to be widened to include the common somatic symptomatology that research with psychiatric patients in primary care teaches us is central to the disorder. They also need to include the illness behavior problems included in neurasthenia's semantic network. Here Western psychiatrists can learn from their colleagues in China and other non-Western societies. They need to study the epidemiology, course, consequences (including suicide), and treatment response of somatized depression to see whether these data alter their understanding of depression generally. They must consider the possibility that somatized depression may have better outcome in certain ways and worse in others. The same can be said of the anxiety disorders. Western psychiatrists need to recast psychiatric categories to remove their implicit dualistic bias, so that psychological dimensions of illness are not viewed as more fundamental and representative of a necessarily higher level of personal maturation and cultural evolution. They need to consider whether somatic complaints in depression are best understood as idioms of expression, coping styles, interpretive schema, or somatic affects. And they need to take the crucial social aspects of depression, and of illness behavior, into account as much as the somatic and psychological ones.

Whereas much of biomedical nosology is similar in China and the United States, psychiatric nosology clearly is not. DSM-III, which replaced the prior official diagnostic system of the American Psychiatric Association only in 1980, represents a shift from a heavily psychoanalytically oriented nosology to that of a European-style descriptive (biologically-oriented) psychiatry. My Chinese psychiatric colleagues persistently pointed out the regrettable (to their minds) shift in American psychiatric fashions from neurasthenia to anxiety and personality disorders to, most recently, depression. As one remonstrated with me:

> How do we know how long DSM-III will last? Perhaps ten years from now what you call major depressive disorder may be regarded as something entirely different . . . perhaps phobic disorder or something as yet unheard of. Look at Briquet's syndrome: first hysteria, then Briquet's, finally somatization disorder. For us it has remained hysteria.

From the standpoint of many in American academic psychiatry, DSM-III is an advance over DSM-II because it is supported at least in part by empirical research and has been found valid and reliable in field testing in the United States. But it is quite mistaken to regard DSM-III as "atheoretical," as some of its creators assert. Major depressive disorder as a category is a good example of the influence of cultural and professional values. Inasmuch as dysphoria is the cardinal diagnostic criterion, it must be that psychologically minded Western patients in psychiatric settings have been the chief source of data. Both in cross-cultural and primary care perspectives, dysphoria is frequently experienced as a secondary complaint, as it was in our study, and thereby often denied and suppressed. This points up a serious bias in DSM-III created by a major bias in sample selection that excludes most cases of depression worldwide. The absence from DSM-III diagnostic criteria of the kinds of physical complaints the neurasthenic patients suffer, which again have been detected as common physical complaints in depression in primary care and non-Western psychiatric samples, is further evidence that DSM-III exhibits cultural and professional biases, as is the prominent place given to guilt and suicidal thoughts.

The classification of major depressive disorder, however, takes advantage of the therapeutic power of a revolutionary breakthrough in treatment—the antidepressant drugs—that makes this diagnosis an increasingly popular and practically useful one. Certainly the diagnostic category neurasthenia does not lead to an impressive therapeutic intervention. Yet therapeutic efficacy did not convince the neurasthenic patients whom we studied that they were suffering from depression. A few who rejected this diagnosis retorted that antidepressants might be effective against neurasthenia as well and therefore might be regarded as antineurasthenia medication. My Chinese psychiatric

colleagues raised a more telling objection. Although they were more impressed than our patients by the outcome findings, they did not regard response to antidepressant therapy as a conclusive reason to diagnose a patient
as a case of depressive disease. We reify a conceptual category—not explain
it—by labeling drugs that have profound and not fully understood effects on
the brain's neurotransmitters "antidepressants." These powerful agents quite
obviously exert a broad effect on biopsychological processes. The changes
they produce in limbic system and neuroendocrine functions are not simply
"antidepressive." They affect the psychobiology of demoralization, distress,
and misery. In this sense the objection of our Chinese colleagues is appropriate.

There is a substantial difference, then, between Chinese and American
psychiatric disease categories, which is best illumined by the neurasthenia/
clinical depression question. This is a difference, following Nelson Goodman's
provocative epigraph to this chapter, in distinctive cultural versions of the
same broad range of human behavior, versions that constitute and express
different cultural worlds. Such a conflict cannot be completely resolved by
empirical research alone, in spite of pretensions by research psychiatrists
that it is amenable to the latest techniques of data collection and analysis.
This is a question of the conceptual framework within which that research
is organized, its findings interpreted, and their validity established by tests
based on that framework (see Xu n.d. for an illustrative case). The exciting
opportunity for collaborative cross-cultural studies in this area is not one of
new research designs or instruments. Rather, investigators from different
societies are invited to reexamine their theoretical assumptions, to contribute
to the development of a more truly comparative psychiatry appropriate for
patients in both Western and non-Western societies. In taking up this extraordinarily difficult but potentially creative challenge, Western and non-
Western psychiatrists need to take an anthropological view of cultural influences on their own diagnostic categories and practices as much as a clinical
view of cross-cultural differences in the behavioral problems those categories
explain.

In summary, the findings from the Hunan studies support the contention
that neurasthenia can be most fruitfully conceptualized as *illness* experience—
a culturally salient form of chronic somatization that acts as a final common
behavioral pathway for several distinctive types of pathology,[4] of which major
depressive disorder is the principal *disease*. Typically, individuals suffer
several psychiatric diseases at the same time. Since none of the major systems
of classification in psychiatry, however, has a taxon or axis for illness behavior, a case can *and* should be made for retaining neurasthenia as a *disease*

category, especially in those societies like China where it is still popularly used by health professionals. In keeping neurasthenia as a category no assumptions should be made about its contested biological basis, which is probably unfounded. It is worthy of a place in diagnostic systems for the points raised above, as much by my Chinese colleagues as by me. An ironic outcome of this research, then, is that I have changed at least one of my ideas about neurasthenia in spite of data that could be taken to confirm my original hypothesis, whereas a number of Western and even Chinese psychiatrists have used those findings to challenge China's system of psychiatric diagnosis to rid itself of neurasthenia. Perhaps the two greatest virtues of an anthropological framework are that it opens our eyes to alternative models (after five years of research I have come to accept, at least in part, an argument made by my Chinese colleagues from the beginning and one I strongly differed with when I began these studies) and makes us self-critical of the cultural bias in our own model.

That so many of the symptoms of neurasthenia in China in the 1980s are the same as Beard listed for neurasthenia in America in the 1880s is evidence of biological shaping of neurasthenic illness behavior. Cultural shaping of the phenomenology of neurasthenic illness is clearly seen in the salience and frequency (or infrequency) of certain symptoms, such as headache, guilt, suicidal thoughts, and especially the culture-specific complaints of our Chinese patients; it is more importantly evidenced in lay medical beliefs, help-seeking choices, treatment evaluations, and certain special meanings and uses of this form of somatization in contemporary China. There are also certain strong cultural resemblances between neurasthenia in contemporary China, neurasthenia as it was conceived and handled in the nineteenth-century West, and contemporary forms of somatization such as chronic pain syndrome in the United States and other societies.[5] This indicates that there are universal commonalities as well as particular uniqueness in social and cultural processes. We have also seen that distinctive lay and professional (Chinese and American psychiatrists') construals of neurasthenia give rise to distinctive social realities such that the same phenomenon is perceived, conceptualized, and treated differently. Neurasthenia and major depressive disorder are cultural constructions which illustrate the powerful effect of meanings and legitimacies on sickness and health care. What we have charted is a particular instance of the dialectic between biology and culture that is fundamental to the experience and the understanding of sickness and to the therapeutic process. It is an impoverished science and clinical practice that takes a unidimensional, reductionist view of this innately multidimensional, interactive, dialectical reality.

THE SOCIAL CAUSES OF DEPRESSION

The cultural construction of depressive illness only tells half the story. The other half is a tale of the social sources of depressive disease. The Chinese patients we studied had experienced severe political, financial, and social (work and family) distress. Chapters 4 and 5 enumerated the nature and magnitude of distress, the prevalence of depressive and anxiety disorders, and the uses (and abuses) of a somatic idiom for expressing that distress. What we learn from the case vignettes, however, is that the epidemiological and clinical statistics fail to explain the problems our patients suffered in sufficient ethnographic depth to enable the reader to interpret their significance in the Chinese context of particular meanings, norms, and power. The quantitative data, important in other respects, create a thin, medicocentric, in places almost lifeless, reduction of richly plangent, socially complex findings. The case descriptions and their interpretations, on the other hand, make it hard to see the forest for the trees: how does one generalize and reliably assign weights to the different components of cases? Here quantification is essential.[6] Can we use one source of data as a foil against which to rework the other? If so, perhaps we will receive a clearer image of the dynamic dialectic linking culture and social world to depression and symptoms in our patient sample.

What can we say of the social origins of depression? How is depression sociophysiologically produced? Our data would fit well into the causal model of depression articulated by Brown and Harris (1978) in their masterly *The Social Origins of Depression,* which is perhaps the single best account of the social sources of a disorder. Why the particular patients we studied developed clinical depression, whereas others who went through the same experiences did not, may reflect in part underlying genetic and psychological vulnerability, and in part the meaning of the precipitating stressors for them and the social resources available to them to buffer the effects of severely stressful life events. But there are larger determinants of depressive disease: the social sources of human misery that generate hopelessness, demoralization, and self-defeating conceptions of self and situation (Moore 1970: 40–77; 1978: 49–109). These social sources of affliction give rise to situations that undermine self-esteem, block alternative behavioral options, further limit access to already limited resources, create untenable interpersonal tensions, delegitimate established roles, and lead to outcomes which are simply intolerable. Here we have the micro depressogenic system, and its macro origins; but this is the same system that leads to demoralization, despair, and distress generally. And it is the same set of problems that fosters vicious cycles that sustain somatization. The social sources of human distress are local human contexts of power that distribute resources unequally, that transmit the effects of large-scale sociopolitical, economic, and ecological forces unjustly, and that place particular categories of persons under greatest social pressure. The micro context may be a wretched marital relationship in which a wife's self-esteem is systematically undermined by the conjugal communication system established by cultural rules as much as by idiosyncratic discord, or it may be an oppressive relationship with a supervisor that plays out as much a hierarchical structural dialectic of authority and subordination as conflict among particular individuals, or it may be a conflicted school or alienating community situation that assaults the embodied self. Sometimes macro origins exert a small effect on local context; at other times, as in the Cultural Revolution, they may be determinative.

The local context itself is a nested hierarchy of family, network, work, and community settings. This local cultural system systematically relates person (agency) to social structure, bridging physiological processes and social relations. The symbolic medium (the dialectical connection) mediating sociophysiological processes is cultural meanings that connect affect and cognition (here understood as overlapping and interpenetrating biological-psychological relations) and self and body concept as a person-centered system with social relationships as a small group system to ethnoepistemological and moral and political components of the macro system. The systematic interactions within this local system might be thought of as generating pathological processes, as well as health promoting and therapeutic ones (Hahn and Kleinman 1983); risk for illness onset and psychological distress is in large measure the result of one's place, and particularly one's *relationships,* in local cultural systems. The effects can be primarily on biological processes (injured back, industrial sources of asthma, radiation-induced cancer, malnutrition-based hormonal changes), or on psychological ones (demoralization, anger, giving up). However the cycle begins, eventually it links bodily changes, transformations of the self, and the local social world into a social system.

It seems most plausible, then, to regard the core psychobiology of depression as the outcome of the interaction between personal vulnerability (psychological-physiological state), major stressful life events, coping processes, and the social support *within* these local contexts of power that influence how risk, stress, and resources are configured and systematically interrelate. For example, what in one local system may be a source of support in another may be a stressor, and this is likely as true of a particular network within a local system as of an entire system. These local contexts, which are left out of most epidemiological studies but central to anthropological analysis, give stress and support vector and cachet as lines of tension linking person to social structure. Serious stressors and inadequate support are not reified entities in this formulation, as they often are in stress research, but rather are construed as systematic relationships among meanings, legitimacies, and structural arrangements of power in local cultural systems that taken together conduce to distress (Young 1980). How these interactive (interpersonal) systems contribute to the social production of disease should be a central focus of what might be called anthropological epidemiology (or in the case of the social production of depression, anthropological psychiatry).

But this is not the way our patients regarded depression, which few acknowledged as suffering. Even for the few who admitted its presence, depression, in their somatopsychic cultural view of self and body, was the result, not the cause, of pain, a medical not a social psychological problem. This somatizing view was shared by many of their practitioners (somatization, after all, is a transactional process). As we have demonstrated elsewhere (Kleinman 1980, 1982), it is supported by the universe of symbolic meanings that comprises the Chinese cultural tradition. The core principles of this cultural worldview center on the harmonizing of interpersonal relations, the sociocentric orientation of the self, and for these reasons the constitution of affect as moral positions in a social field of reciprocal behavior. Denial of dysphoria is also of course a neutral and safe position to hold in an ideological context in which depression signifies potentially dangerous political implications: disaffiliation, alienation, potential opposition. Here, as a complementary process to disease causation, we have the process we previously analyzed as the cultural construction of illness.

It is worth analyzing the interdigitation between the social production and cultural construction of clinical depression in our Hunanese sample in somewhat more detail. We can posit that genetic vulnerability and childhood and adolescent experiences with depressed mothers and difficult family situations may contribute to the development of a self-concept in which self-esteem is fragile or already in doubt and in which Beck's negative cognitive schemata (view of self as socially ineffective and of world as generally frustrating) are reinforced (Beck et al. 1979). But our patients appear to have been at higher risk also because of their place in local Chinese contexts of power and the sociopolitical and historical changes those contexts had undergone. A number of our patients came from highly stigmatized families that carried the "black" labels of rightist or landlord background. Growing up in that setting, our future patients had faced systematic discrimination and blocked access to resources (senior middle school, university, desirable jobs, Communist Party affiliation, membership in the People's Liberation Army). Many had internalized a spoiled identity, one that was dramatically reaffirmed in large national campaigns (Anti-Rightist, Cultural Revolution) in which techniques for enhancing feelings of shame and guilt (self-criticism sessions, criticism of and by family members and family friends) were regularly employed, and in which their traditional Chinese moral universe was quite literally stood on its head. The children of "stinking intellectuals" learned to criticize themselves and their families, for example, for the very intellectual values so central to China's millennial culture that were an active socializing force in their own families.

More practically, they were sent to the "distant" (read most impoverished) countryside to live with peasants, where they often were greeted with hostility and suspicion in the peasant world of limited goods. The open mouths and empty stomachs of rusticated youth were seen as more of a threat than their usually unimpressive muscles were seen as a gain to the local economy. There many literally "wasted their years" without completing schooling. Separated from other family members, often by great distances that blocked communication, they were without access to resources to sustain their intellectual development and urban interests, and they frequently failed to achieve full acceptance in their impoverished rural communities either. They became increasingly critical, and many cynical, about the ideological shifts from the radically equalitarian rural-oriented rhetoric of their youth to the pragmatic, materialist, urban-centered policies of their majority. When they finally returned (those who could leave the countryside—many still cannot), they found themselves literally "lost." They had no jobs, no chance to successfully compete in university entrance exams against a new generation of well-prepared students whose scientific and technological education was up to date, not woefully behind the times. Often they lacked even the official residence permit required to live in the city and thus were totally dependent on family and the "hidden economy." This was the trajectory of vulnerability among one group of our patients. Others had various but often equally disconfirming experiences in which severe threats to the self and serious multiple losses were normative.

But other things besides these societal-wide threats to the integrity of the self happened to those who developed depression. Some experienced such overwhelmingly destructive personal tragedies that they developed major personality changes: a few became so deeply embittered that every aspect of their lives radiated anger and hatred and alienation; others withdrew with fear and hurt into the inner privacy of the isolated self, diminishing performance to match greatly reduced expectations, to protect against further losses. Yet others organized their lives around their repeated and multiple losses as prolonged or even continuous grief reactions.[7]

The inadequate or ineffective resources and responses to meet these assaults on self-esteem and uncontrollable losses disclose a few social psychological sources of distress that are perhaps unique to China, along with others that are widely present in the West and in other non-Western societies. The latter include severe marital disharmony that in several cases established sociolinguistic dialogues with spouse or in-laws that further undermined confidence and reinforced the negative cognitive schemata. Other patients participated in tension-ridden, disconfirming relations with work supervisors or unit leaders in which their aspirations were blocked and they saw themselves sentenced to a lifetime of numbing drudgery and bitter chronic stress. Each of these situations of high social risk and personal vulnerability in an intimate behavioral field comprised of inadequate coping and social support resources and desperate local power relationships seems to have followed the same final common pathway charted by Brown and Harris (1978) as the social production of clinical depression. Greatly diminished self-esteem and hopelessness "specific" to particular losses and other stressful life events, in vulnerable individuals, became generalized into a pervasive hopelessness attributed to most aspects of their lives; finally, there developed the psychophysiological symptoms of depression and illness careers. Depressive disorder, thereafter, seems to have conduced to the development of chronic somatization in most of our cases, though anxiety disorders contributed to many of these cases as well.[8] The primary point is that the origin, organization, and consequences of this pathophysiology are a dialectic between social world and person, cultural values and physiology.

Chinese culture affected this process of disease production in the creation of particular kinds of stressors (self-criticism sessions, being sent to the countryside, and so forth), the valuation of certain types of stressors as most stressful (those that broke up family system or undermined the sociocentric moral underpinnings of the Chinese self), and the labeling of the psychophysiological reactions these stressors produced as "neurasthenia," to which the tendency to amplify the somatic component and dampen the psychological component of the stress response contributed. Chinese culture also affected the pattern of excessive medical help-seeking, the use of particular styles of illness behavior to communicate social and personal distress, and the special ways by which these idioms opened up behavioral options in tightly organized family and work systems.

Chinese cultural norms come into play in the very perception of a life event as a loss or threat (real or symbolic) so that the percept is as much cultural construct as neurological sensory input (cf. Pennebaker 1982; Leventhal, Nerenz, Straus 1982). Further scanning and monitoring of the psychophysiological state of arousal (reaction to the loss or threat) incorporate structuring principles based on cultural norms and meanings, which combine with personal significance to organize that arousal into a particular pattern of dysphoria that can now be more accurately regarded as a psychocultural process. The symbolic significance of the loss (both for the individual and as part of the collective representations of the group) will contribute to organize its psychobiology and social construction as "stress," "grief," "depressive affect," and so forth. In this structurally dynamic dialectic between meaning and biology, social relations are also tied to psychophysiology (who is lost; what are the nature, quality, and intensity of the loss; what are the setting and relationships within which the loss is experienced and communicated; what support is available and how is it regarded and mobilized) as are norms (for example, the cultural rules governing how loss should be responded to). Hence the cultural construction (categorization) of depressive disorder contributes to its social production (etiology), while the latter initiates the former. The result is a sociosomatic system in which neuroendocrine dysregulation might be thought of as a component of disrupted social relations, and disconfirming personal meanings might be regarded as both contributing to and expressing the malfunctioning of the brain's neurotransmitters (Hofer 1984). This *system* should be the focus of studies of how to prevent and treat distress.

FROM CHRONIC DEPRESSION TO THE SOMATIZATION OF DISABILITY AND DESPAIR

The social sources of clinical depression, as noted, are also the sources of demoralization, despair, and distress. An analogous sociosomatic system for these problems creates and maintains chronic somatization. Physical complaints, based on psychobiological processes of serious disease (for example, diabetes, heart disease, depression), persistent mild illness behavior, or chronic stress, may be instigated by a culture's behavioral norms, rules of propriety and social etiquette, and even by language usage. Disability, as has been well documented and is apparent from the findings in our Hunan studies, can be (and often is) supported or even worsened by financial reward and advantages resulting from enhanced personal efficacy and desired change in interpersonal relations with spouse, children, parents, in-laws, friends, work supervisors, co-workers, teachers, health professionals, and others. These altered social relationships and economic benefits reinforce psycho-biological processes and maintain illness behavior in the ways we and others have described (see Barsky and Klerman 1983; Cacioppa et al. 1983; Cheung and Lau 1982; Ford 1983; Katon et al. 1982; Kleinman 1983; Mechanic 1972, 1980; Pennebaker and Skelton 1978; Tessler and Mechanic 1978). But in the terms of our dialectical model these social sides of illness must be viewed as an integral part of the whole of illness, not as discrete factors that are less vital and therefore "secondary"—a term frequently applied to them. I also wish to reemphasize the point that these social factors are linked to actual physiological change (functional and structural), often of a serious kind, which itself (like work injury to the lumbosacral spine, inhalation of toxic chemicals leading to neurological and systemic pathology, work-related respiratory disorders like asbestosis, work-stress-induced peptic ulcers, or hypertension and heart disease in executives and professionals) may be a direct physiological effect of the social environment.

In anthropological perspective somatization includes interpretive schema for making sense of life problems (school and business failure, an unsuccessful marriage, loss of a child) (Nichter 1981), rhetorical devices for controlling local relationships by persuading others (spouse, parents, employers) to pro-vide greater access to scarce resources and empower the somatizer (Beeman 1985; Csordas 1983; McGuire 1983), and symbolic forms that constitute and express salient modes of life in particular cultures (abusive marital relations with alcoholic husbands in rural Mexico; conflicts over the use of contra-ceptives in rural Iran) (Finkler 1985; Good 1977). The ethnography of chronic somatization seeks to explore the way somatization is organized in local cultural systems through these and related communicative processes acting upon the psychobiological and sociosomatic reticulum described.

As a result disability may be amplified or dampened in complex and varied ways that represent the interaction between the parts and the whole of local cultural systems and vicious cycles fomenting illness behavior. Where desired change occurs in local relationships of power, psychophysiological ampli-fication may be reversed if it is no longer needed to maintain change, or it may persist where it is needed. Damping as a sociosomatic and psychosomatic process may occur where the personal despair and demoralization associated with powerlessness and its mediating affect—depression—are altered so that there is an enhanced sense of self-efficacy even if there is little or no change in the local situation. Damping may also occur if other means are employed to alter local power relations, and the language of bodily distress no longer has major strategic significance in these relationships. Amplification may persist even where desired change has been achieved if it has become a fixed coping style, or if the somatizer is no longer able to effectively communicate through other channels. (Therapy, then, can be seen as achieving damping through its influence on local power negotiations or through remoralizing the demoralized powerless [Frank 1974], or as a form of cultural rhetoric in which the therapist's adroit reconceptualization of the situation alters the channel of communicating distress and persuasively enhances self-esteem and thereby removes depressive dysphoria [see Beeman 1985; Csordas 1984]). Maladaptive somatization may be said to be present either when persistent amplification fails to achieve personally desired change, or when change has been achieved at too great a cost to the person, the family, or the medical care and work disability systems.

Psychiatrists and psychologists emphasize the study of somatization as maladaptive coping style or expression of depression and other forms of psychopathology. They view somatization as a means of coping with emotional problems (discharging anger in a sanctioned way, fulfilling dependency needs, sanctioning perceived failure). Most have not considered its normative and adaptive aspects, nor have they detailed its function as discourse strategies to open up behavioral options (time off from work, change of jobs, marital separation), to control interpersonal transactions (except where family therapists have focused on its pathological role within the family), to gain greater access over scarce resources (for example, disability payments), to empower the relatively powerless (in gender-related family, work, and political settings). These are precisely the problems that require an interpretive approach, be it ethnographic, historical, or integrated with quantitative analysis (cf. Figlio 1982; Good and Good 1981; Yelin et al. 1980; Rosen et al. 1982; Nichter 1981; Good 1977; Stein 1982; Lewis 1971; Pickering 1974).

From the perspective advanced here, we hypothesize that persons who are at greatest risk for powerlessness and blocked access to local resources are most likely to somatize (Katon et al. 1982; Nathanson 1977). There is already some evidence to support this hypothesis, since in North American society working-class patients comprise a disproportionately high percentage of patients attending pain clinics for chronic low back pain (though this also has something to do with biomechanical stress in certain types of physical labor), while women appear to be overrepresented among chronic pain patients in the middle class. Our Chinese patient samples are predominantly individuals from stigmatized class background, in vulnerable positions, who are powerless to alter work, family, school, or political situations. Ethnic and refugee populations, under the constraints of uprooting, acculturation, and modernization, also have been reported to somatize extensively (Katon et al. 1982; Lin et al. 1985). But local relationships of power, as our case vignettes attest, are complex and vary so greatly even within class, gender, and ethnic categories that the focus of analysis must be more precise. In distinctive sociopolitical settings, the effects of somatization on distributive politics may well influence its utilization (Stone 1979a, 1979b). When powerlessness produces demoralization and despair, as has been shown to occur to lower-class women in Great Britain who become depressed (Brown and Harris 1978), and as happened to a number of the patients described in chapter 6, it is more likely that somatization may be socially ineffective and personally maladaptive. As a result, in a given case there may be no simple and direct relationship between somatic amplification and social and psychological outcomes.

One point repeatedly made by researchers of this subject is worth remembering. Somatization is only uncommonly due to "malingering"; it is often out of the patient's awareness. Among our Chinese subjects this was almost always the case. This does not mean, however, that it is always or even routinely "unconscious," in the strict sense. Patients, families, and practitioners differ substantially in their skill not only in articulating and negotiating distress discourses (Plough 1981; Stewart and Sullivan 1982), where those who are depressed may be least successful, but also with respect to their insight into the sociodynamics and psychodynamics of these processes, where depression may also block insight. Even where there is insight, it cannot readily be expressed in an open fashion since this removes the social sanctioning of the illness discourse and labels the patient a malingerer (Figlio 1982). But clearly there is at least partial personal recognition of the significance of the somatization discourse and the fact that it is multilevel: overt response to symptoms, covert negotiation of relationships and resources— although this recognition cannot for the above reason be publicly expressed.

CULTURE AND DEPRESSIVE EMOTION

Thus far, most emphasis has been placed on the relationship between social sources of distress and the physiology of demoralization and despair, which is proper given the general inattention to this sociosomatic dialectic in medicine and social science. But psychological experience—demoralization, frustration, bitterness—clearly is also central to this relationship. Psychological experience serves as a mediator of sociosomatic interactions. Psychological processes come to be shaped and organized in this dialectic between social world and inner bodily states. In fact, psychological experience is itself a product of that dialectic. Furthermore, just as either social problems or biological abnormalities may, in a particular case, exert a predominant effect on symptom amplification, so too can the psychology of the individual act as the prime determinant of the somatization of distress. For the patient with a lifetime personality pattern of chronic anxiety, hypochondriacal preoccupation, and morbid introspectiveness, serious somatic amplification may occur even in the absence of significant stressors and in the presence of substantial social support.

Just as social relationships and physiological reactions are shaped by culture, so too are psychological processes. I have tended to emphasize cognitive processes (perception, labeling, interpretation), which we have seen link cultural meanings and norms to distress and symptoms. Now I wish to examine affect, and show how it is constituted and expressed by the same bridging dialectic between local social system and inner experience. As a pertinent example, let us examine depressive affect (sadness, hopelessness, demoralization, loss of interest in the world).

Affect (feeling, emotion) is integral to human nature. But even though we may all "feel" the same psychobiologically produced patterns of autonomic arousal and neuroendocrine dysregulation (though this is by no means certain), our unique biography and interpersonal context and the particular orientations of our culture lead to divergent social genesis and cultural construal of specific affects. Even when each of us feels depressed, the perception, interpretation, and labeling (the construction) of the experience are distinctive, and in that sense what we actually "feel" is different. But emotions can be distinctive in the very quality, intensity, and pattern of the emotion itself. There may well be an obdurately human core to the psychobiological and social experience of loss and of lowered self-esteem which is universal. Nonetheless, to experience depression principally as headaches or as existential despair is not to experience the same feeling, even if "headaches" radiate symbolic meanings of frustation and unhappiness, and if despair causes headaches.

Depression and other affects can also be viewed as particular moral sentiments. Feelings are judgments in an ideologically constructed behavioral field (Myers 1979). There is a long Chinese tradition of paradigmatic exemplars of moral behavior whose ethical choices are simultaneously conveyed as emotion and as political statement (cf. Metzger 1981). Perhaps it is this tradition that makes depression so potentially dangerous an affect in China; it points to the social sources of human misery that have not been altered by Communist revolution and the building of a new socialist state.[9] Much the same can be said of our own society, though we are socialized to view affect as a natural ("gut") component of the self, not as an interpersonal response or manipulation or a moral act with political connotation. In our society, however, the commercialization of human feeling ("the managed heart" of television, movies, sports, and politics) is a visible sign of the capitalist construction of affect (cf. Lasch 1979; Hochshild 1983), which has its surface (and probably equally superficial) counterparts in the socialist construction of enthusiasm, selflessness, and the other "red" emotions. Intriguingly, during the Gilded Age of late-nineteenth-century America when Beard was popularizing the term, neurasthenia sounded a note of moral criticism against an age of "wear and tear" in which the body's supplies could not keep up with society's demands, and when to be neurasthenic was to withdraw from the frenetic race for material success and to replace competition with rest, contemplation, and the sensitivities of an earlier age (cf. Sicherman 1977). The cross-cultural parallels are striking: to feel is to value or disvalue, to connect with or stand apart, to act in resistance to or to be paralyzed by our embodied social circumstances and our socially projected bodily experiences.

But affect as moral position in a social field of behavior is not affect as private experience. To make either pole of this dialectic, as relativists and materialists do, stand for affect *en tout* is to mistake its thoroughly interactionist nature (Averill 1980; Eckman 1980). The outward movement from private feeling to public meaning that transforms affect in one direction has as its reciprocal the opposite inward cultural transformation that organizes meaning into feeling as personal experience.

We can regard universal psychobiological and social (loss, powerlessness, failure) processes as providing the substrate with which cultural norms react to create affect as a public and private form of experience. This cultural reaction is constrained both by the universal substrate and the culturally and personally particular reagent. The product—meaningful affective experience—is constituted out of both, but each has been changed. It is as unavailing to interpret only collective representation and personal significance in depression or headaches as it is to explain them away either by neurophysiological processes or by social universals of the human condition. A

disembodied affect is as artifactual as an affectless body. If psychiatric anthropology and anthropological psychiatry are to advance the cross-cultural
study of depression and other emotions, they must study both sides of the
reaction: the sources, consequences, and intervening processes in the symbolic dialectic between person and life world, symptoms, and society.

Depression as an affect in China, the United States, and other societies
for which we possess adequate clinical ethnographies appears to have something to do with loss of crucial social relationships, withdrawal from established social structural positions, and undermining of the cultural norms
guiding the self, with concomitant changes in mood (hopelessness, helplessness, sadness, experience of self as useless and the world as frustrating
and no longer of interest.) It is an emotion that poses a threat to social arrangements and symbolic meanings, and not just when, as part of a serious
depressive illness, it leads to suicide. Demoralization, despondency, hopelessness, withdrawal, and loss of interest in the social environment are asocial.
They call basic norms and relations and institutions into question, undoing
the ties of the symbolic reticulum that connects person to society; thus,
these asocial emotions underline with poignancy the problems of bafflement,
suffering, and social order that Weber (1978) saw as fundamental to the social
enterprise. In ego-centric societies such as our own, this affect is perhaps
not nearly as threatening as it would be in socio-centric societies such as
China. Indeed, the expression of personal alienation and existential despair
is intrinsic to the ego-centric community as a liminal state that discloses the
limits of the possible and establishes the border for solipsism and narcissism.
But in socio-centric China, it would be both more threatening to cultural
norms and less useful for social control to sanction ego-centric depression
as a liminal state. Rather somatized affect—feeling as physical pain and bodily, not psychic, suffering—is perhaps the appropriate liminal state.

Here pain, communicated as a symptom but experienced as a feeling, is
an opportunity to reintegrate the sick person into the social support group
and to reaffirm (in the Durkheimian sense) the norms of solidarity and social
control (cf. Turner 1967). Depressive affect is socially and culturally unsanctioned and therefore suppressed. Somatization is sanctioned and expressed, and it carries both cultural cachet and social efficacy. Depressive
affect is unacceptable in China because it *means* stigmatized mental illness
and the breakdown of social harmony—in modern terms political alienation,
in traditional terms display of excessively negative feeling harmful to health.
It does not signify what it *means* in middle-class white American society:
the heroic romance of the lonely individual testing his existential condition

by being obdurately solitary, the equity of each independent person naked before his just god (see Berton's *Anatomy of Melancholy*), the immortality of the personal soul, the narcissistic conception of man's ultimate, ego-centric rights, the bitter disillusionment with sentimentality at not "making it" in the marketplace. But somatized depression or anger is as authentic a feeling as feeling sad or enraged. It is not simply that individuals communicate in a somatic idiom; emotion is also experienced somatically. Anxiety is *felt* in breathing, sadness in the chest and face. The feeling is part of the bodily process and of its communication to others.

Culture enters into this picture as the *systematized relations* between physiology, feeling, self-concept, body image, interpersonal communication, practical action, ideology, and relationships of power. These systematized relations are distinctive in different societies. This makes for a difference in more than content, but in the very structure of the links between affect, self, body, and social reality that are produced and reproduced distinctively in different social worlds. Culture always particularizes. The cross-cultural continuities in emotion—and there are many—come from the constraining influences of the separate elements in the cultural system: shared psycho-biological processes, universal aspects of social relations, the limited variations of the politics of power.

The social production of depression tells us as much about universal *and* particular features of social structure as about emotion and cognition, while the cultural construction of depressive affect tells us about meaning systems and norms as much as it does about physiology. Had I traced biological themes, we would have arrived at the same place for that academic discourse. How we choose to interpret depression—or any emotion or disorder—clinically, poetically, in the societal-wide terms of social science, or in the intimate interiority of psychodynamic psychology—is inseparable from its construction. This poses a vexing problem for interdisciplinary work on emotions, somatization, and depressive disorder. Our divergent disciplinary "interests" help shape our subject; they take apart the symbolic bridge and dissect the sociosomatic dialectic so that we are left with one end or the other, now no longer integrated. This constitutes an immense barrier to the study of emotions and emotional disorders. One of the central concerns of the academic colloquy on depression, neurasthenia, and somatization must therefore be how to go about building an interdisciplinary discourse about a unified subject that always seems to hold a mirror up to both disciplines and become as fragmented as they are. Our Chinese findings hold up such a mirror, for both psychiatry and anthropology.

Epilogue

There now is barley,—Let it be sown and covered up; the ground being the same, and the time of sowing likewise the same, it grows rapidly up, and, when the full time is come, it is all found to be ripe. Although there may be inequalities *of produce,* that is owing to the *difference of the* soil, as rich or poor, to the *unequal* nourishment afforded by the rains and dews, and to the different ways in which man has performed his business *in reference to it.*

Thus all things which are the same in kind are like to one another;—why should we doubt in regard to man, as if he were a solitary exception to this? The sage and we are the same in kind.

Mencius VIA 7.2-3
James Legge, trans.

The first part of this chapter ties up loose ends; the second addresses broader themes that emerge from comparative analysis.

What would be the appropriate therapeutic response to the neurasthenia-depression-somatization tangle of problems in the PRC? The antidepressants reduce symptoms but have relatively little impact on illness. To the extent that the illness behavior of somatizing patients results from a set of environmental conditions (context-specific and universal) that are harsh and difficult to modify, what is it Chinese psychiatrists can do for their patients? By extension, what is it mental health and medical professionals in any society can do? If psychiatrists or any physicians address the political, economic, and social structural sources of human misery, how can they avoid medicalizing—and thereby trivializing and disguising—problems that are best addressed in the wider community as political and moral questions? In highly centralized, tightly controlled societies like China, what can health professionals do for their patients (or social scientists do for social problems) and still stay out of major political difficulties like those that brought psychiatry (and social science) to a halt in the Cultural Revolution? Why should the

Chinese bureaucracy encourage studies that raise potentially troubling political questions?

INTERVENTIONS AT MACROSOCIAL AND LOCAL LEVELS

There is no longer any doubt that the major gains in the health of communities are primarily the result of macrosocial changes which yield three types of improvements: in nutrition, housing, family economics, water supply, sewage disposal, and education; in great inequalities in the distribution of resources within populations and relative deprivation across groups and statuses (gender, class, caste, age group, and so forth); and in provision of and access to public health and health care programs. Health status is a function of these aspects of social development. We do not require a single additional study to be able to say with confidence that where social conditions are altered so as to remedy these interconnected problems health improves. The history of Europe since the mid-nineteenth century, of Asia in this century, and of China since 1949 offer all the evidence needed to sustain this assertion. We now have in hand the equally persuasive findings that mental health problems—suicide, substance abuse, violence, admission rates to mental health facilities, depression and certain other psychiatric disorders, family pathology—also worsen under conditions of social disorder, economic deprivation, unemployment, forced uprooting, and migration. Like general health problems, mental illness and social pathology have their highest prevalence among those in the lowest social statuses in society. Stressful life event changes and social supports are not randomly distributed in society. Where individuals are the most deprived, in the lowest socioeconomic statuses, in situations of powerlessness and exploitation, there stressors are more numerous and social support, like other resources, is most inadequate.

There can be little doubt that the health consequences of human misery are most effectively improved by significantly altering the macrosocial sources of misery. But the argument of this book is that local systems mediate the effects of macrosocial forces on groups and individuals, such that in settings of deprivation not all groups and individuals suffer to the same extent. Certain social statuses (the poorest, the least powerful, the stigmatized, those experiencing systematic discrimination) place individuals at greater risk for human misery and its health consequences. Unskilled laborers experience disability from chronic back pain more than do white-collar workers because they are subject to more injuries and greater biomechanical strain on the spine, as well as greater stress, less social support, greater job insecurity, more difficult working conditions, and greater work dissatisfaction. But in local systems, as we have seen, it is not all unskilled laborers (or the unemployed, or young married lower-class women with small children in the house) who are at highest risk for disability and demoralization; some are for social, psychological, and biological reasons at enhanced risk. Local systems (communities, families, work units) help determine who is at highest risk for health problems and other forms of misery.

Of the range of social problems contributing to symptoms and disability that health and mental health professionals meet in society, many require change on the macro level outside the narrow confines of the practitioner-patient relationship. Here public health interventions need to focus on political, economic, and social structural change. Where such changes are effected, however, local interventions are also necessary to alter the relationships of oppression, powerlessness, deprivation, and despair that place particular social categories of persons and particular individuals under the worst health conditions, the greatest social pressure, and the most risk for life troubles.

Thus, among the range of social problems that psychiatrists and other health professionals meet in China (or in any other society) many are in practice corrigible at the level of local interventions, while others are corrigible only at the macrosocial level. Mental health services in certain societies have expanded to respond to such problems in local social systems: for example, intervening to treat or prevent the worsening of family conflict, school problems, and, more recently, even work or community-wide difficulties. They have also begun to play a role, as have health professions in general, in articulating health policy issues that may lead to focused macrosocial change. Even without altering the macrosocial sources of misery, it is still possible to intervene to disrupt vicious cycles that undermine self-esteem and social support, generalize hopelessness, and lead to health and mental health problems. Even small changes in the always highly personal equation of despair can prevent individual breakdown and the failure of interpersonal bonds, and dampen the intensity of symptoms and limit disability. Those at greatest risk for illness onset or amplification can be identified, helped to cope, protected. The biological and psychological sources of misery that afflict particular persons can be diagnosed at an earlier time and more effectively remedied.

A much wider range of psychosocial interventions could be made available by Chinese psychiatrists: behavioral, marital, family, work, combinations of traditional and modern, even perhaps psychotherapeutic. Psychiatric social workers and other categories of mental health and social welfare professionals could be trained and added to local health teams with responsibility for community and individual health. In the past some of this has been done by other social agencies in China, but in the mental health field it needs to be systematized.[1] To do so, mental health services in China must be given a broader mandate and greater resources. While treatment intervention is important, preventive intervention is of special significance.

Preventive intervention requires programs in schools, in the work unit, in neighborhoods and communities with serious problems, with individuals and families at high risk. As with psychosocial treatments, particular psychiatry programs in China have made significant advances in prevention under the constraints of limited manpower, inadequate funding, and narrowly authorized scope of programs. What is needed is a wider mandate, greater support, and the permission (indeed encouragement) to address at least the most widespread and disruptive mental health problems and to integrate other—often fragmented—community resources into local mental health programs. Thus far psychiatrists in China possess neither this mandate nor the authorization to gather the necessary national data on such sensitive topics as suicide, family pathology, work-related mental health problems, and the social antecedents and consequents of disability. Given the necessary health priorities of an overpopulated, poor society with very limited resources difficult to spare, it is understandable that the problems identified have had less cachet than chronic psychiatric disorders. But, I would argue, the time has now come to empower psychiatrists and community mental health workers to deal with a much broader range of troubles. Working with local community leaders under the authorization of the community (and thereby held accountable to it) mental health professionals should be legitimated and given the resources to intervene in local systems to respond to more severe problems.

To do this the Chinese government must be willing to acknowledge that these problems do in fact exist and can (and should) be dealt with. The current leadership of China has been more open than its predecessors about poverty and hunger among the more than 1.1 billion Chinese. It is now time to put aside a vulgar Marxism that would spuriously claim that social problems have disappeared with liberation and the creation of a socialist state, because they are the resultant of capitalist forces. The Chinese government must be willing to acknowledge that certain of the more stubborn of social problems are pan-human, while others may have been intensified or even specially created by China's chaotic recent history and current local conditions. Articulation of such a vision, which rightly should emphasize the great advances that China has made in the health and mental health field since 1949, would empower psychiatrists, other mental health professionals, and social scientists to respond to forms of misery that are not strictly disease-based and that require the critical assessment of local conditions that give rise, as in all societies, to vicious cycles of relative powerlessness, oppression, and desperation. The Communist Party of China needs to legitimate the fact that thousands, perhaps millions, of Chinese are demoralized and even alienated; that the Marxist state has not done away with these pan-human problems and may even at times have contributed to their prevalence and intensification; that there are corrigible social origins of mental health problems at both macrosocial and local levels—attention to which does not threaten the cultural legitimacy of the state.

It is now apparent that the anti-neurasthenia campaign during the Great Leap Forward and the cultural authority given to neurasthenia and its treatment in recent years have been indirect, disguised attempts to define, legitimate, and respond to such problems. Our findings and those of others suggest that this indirect approach has not been wholly successful because it has inappropriately and ineffectively medicalized psychosocial problems as disease (in an overly narrow biomedical construal that leaves out their illness aspects) and thereby centered attention on their somatic manifestations, not their human sources in relationships, roles, norms, and labels. Moreover, haphazardly organized interventions by untrained community members have often been ineffective and actually worked against the systematic identification and treatment of local problems. A major advance would be to sanction and train practitioners (and others) to redefine such problems and either provide appropriate treatment and preventive interventions or refer patients to those who can (social workers, other mental health professionals, trained members of local neighborhood and community groups).

Dealing with corrigible social problems is the best that can be expected at this time. After all, these problems have a worldwide prevalence and have become the concern of societies in both East and West. The Chinese are no more likely to focus on the deeper, structural, culturohistorical sources of human misery than other socialist or capitalist societies. These presently must be viewed as incorrigible problems, some of which pose a threat to the legitimacy of the state and as such cannot be openly acknowledged and dealt with. It is utopian to pin one's hopes on the resolution of these problems. A realistic goal is to see a number of problems, previously regarded as incorrigible and thereby politically threatening, recast as corrigible ones appropriate for both macrosocial and local mental health intervention. Whatever its sources, once initiated a self-defeating cycle of demoralization and depression is, in principle, potentially remediable. But antidepressants, as our data show, are unlikely by themselves to break the vicious cycle, though they may well reduce its effects. To do the former means to create, propagate, and legitimate a national array of psychosocial interventions appropriate to the Chinese context but presently unavailable. (Such arrays of interventions, to be fair, are available in few societies, fewer still that are poor; and even where available in economically and technologically developed societies, they have only begun to work effectively and in a much narrower way than I have suggested here).

The consequences for individuals and families of large-scale social structural forces are mediated by local systems of relationships, norms, and meanings.[2] Even where it is infeasible to deal with macrosocietal forces, influencing these local systems of power can be crucial. Indeed, even where macrosocietal forces are addressed, inattention to local contexts of distress is likely to perpetuate vicious cycles of misery; only now the victims are different. It is precisely at this level that one has the right to expect psychiatrists with a broader mental health mandate, and other mental health and social welfare professionals oriented to social systems, to exert an effect. In practical, on-the-ground terms, this means that practitioners must be trained and authorized to assess illness problems side by side with disease problems, to take health as seriously as sickness, to see prevention as central a task as treatment, to provide intervention and referral for family, school, and work-related problems, to monitor high risk groups and intervene at the community level. This is a type of practice which presently does not exist in any substantial sense in China, but with governmental encouragement it could become a part of the Chinese health care system over the next decade.

What will this do for the members of China's "lost generation"? The thrust of this analysis is to affirm that benefit might well accrue to many of this large group and their families if their shared problems are given legitimacy and appropriately responded to; but our analysis suggests that no treatment or prevention is likely to be successful on a larger and more fundamental scale when a problem emerges from the very structure of society and its vicissitudes. Change must also occur at the macrosocial level. Here history (both Chinese and Western) teaches that these incorrigible problems for the health system will respond only to political, economic, and social structural change. It is not comforting, however, to read history for evidence that such change resolves widespread individual dilemmas, though at times it has done so (for example, immediately after 1949 in China). Instead one is tempted to regard major social change as potentially disruptive of the fragile home-ostasis of individual and family life: modernization and other social trans-formations have human costs in serious health and psychosocial troubles. The question is how to control macrosocial change in such a way as to right current wrongs without producing new ones, without protecting one group from high risk while placing another in that vulnerable position. Anyone whose focus of analysis is the individual in his local world must be pessimistic about this macrosocial level of analysis. Effective change when it occurs treads on local ground. This is a further reason for linking large-scale social change to the particular conditions in local settings both to plan desired change more precisely and to monitor and modify its effects.

I do not mean to underestimate the importance of macrosocietal change. Such change has greatly improved the local life worlds of ethnic minorities in the United States since the beginning of this century; and it has vastly improved the health of peasants and workers in China, the Soviet Union, Cuba, and Western Europe. In the absence of macrosocial change, the con-ditions of blacks in South Africa, Indians in Guatemala, and ethnic minorities in Burma have not substantially improved. Local change in the microcontexts in which individuals live is needed to modulate large-scale effects and assure that they yield desirable local outcomes (intended and unintended). Forced collectivization of peasants in the Soviet Union and China, the Khmer Rouge's murderous rustification of the urban population in Cambodia, the Brazilian government's ruthless development policies for Amazonian Indi-ans—all graphically illustrate that macrosocial change in and of itself can have disastrous local effects. And many public health interventions at the societal level have had unintended negative consequences. And there are also examples of local transformations that have worsened the lot of the community or particular groups.

The appropriate evaluation of societal change, nonetheless, is at the local level in the inveterate and delicately balanced life worlds of particular in-dividuals, families, and communities. Focus on world-systems, nation-states, and even regions—the concern of most experts studying social development (Wolf 1983; Worsley 1984)—draws attention to macrosocial indicators which mask local life worlds. (Even the data large-scale planning projects generate make little sense unless interpreted locally, and that is surely true of their effects.) What is needed is community change that alters local systems of oppression. But this level of intervention is also not without serious problems: Whose interests do local change agents serve? How can they alter structural sources of powerlessness and alienation? Effective social development must link change at both levels.

Opposing dangers of the type of study undertaken here are either to place too great a burden of responsibility on current Chinese society for problems that occur worldwide in radically different social structures, or to throw up one's hands in the face of desperately limited chances for major change in local systems in China and thereby exonerate both the society and its health professionals from doing anything fundamental about human distress. The former is a common anthropological failing, the latter a frequent psychiatric one. A book whose objective is to create a combined anthropological and psychiatric framework for analysis and comparison could conjure no greater irony than to commit both failings. The individual cases we have described provide all the moral argument we need to appeal that something be done to relieve the suffering of real people.

TO MEDICALIZE OR NOT TO MEDICALIZE

The approach advocated may be criticized as yet another instance of medicalization, that is, labeling social problems as medical and psychiatric ones in order to provide health interventions (cf. De Vries, et al. 1982). Much attention has focused in recent years on the dangers of medicalization, such as policing families, further strengthening and more widely diffusing social control over individuals, and disguising the need for social change. And while much of this discourse is overstated, and some of it rather exclusively oriented to ethnocentric, Western libertarian concerns with protecting individual rights (with far too little attention to their reciprocal relationship to social responsibilities), there is no question that medicalization can be a dangerous social process (in the case of the abuse of psychiatry in the Soviet Union to oppress political dissidents, or when medicalization weakens the family's functioning to the benefit of professional and commercial interests in the family therapy movement in North American society). Labeling human misery with a medical label (depression, anxiety disorder, antisocial personality) does have the potential to trivialize social problems, distract attention from resolving them, and reify a single aspect of complex difficulties to argue that they can only be treated by particular kinds of experts.

But medicalization can also have (and indeed has had) positive effects. Some mental disorders can be effectively treated; they require early identification to make that treatment available. The high rate of suicide attempts among depressed patients makes depression a mortal disease, and there is effective treatment for most clinical depression. Transforming alcoholism from a moral problem into a medical one has indeed led to effective prevention and intervention programs that significantly advance the community's and the individual's health. Medicalizing smoking may have the single greatest impact on mortality and morbidity from cancer, heart disease, and chronic respiratory disease. Professionalization, including medicalization as one of its components, is a central part of modernization worldwide. The question is not really whether to medicalize or not, but how to modify professionalization in the Chinese setting so that the problems raised here will be most effectively addressed.

There is something to be said for transforming certain social problems into health problems. In most societies (including the United States and China), it is only through medicalization that effective interventions will be brought to bear on problems which, when articulated socially, are too threatening to the political system to allow them to be addressed directly. (This is especially true for totalitarian societies.) Making a social problem into a health problem can be a means of addressing it socially, on both macro and local levels, and authorizing significant social change that otherwise is deemed unacceptable. Somatization in modern China and elsewhere suggests that medicalization occurs on the individual level everywhere, and that laymen contribute to it as much as professionals. The history of neurasthenia in China and the West suggests that such ad hoc medicalization is not a recent phenomenon. But these examples also indicate that unless medicalization leads to combined macro and local change it merely diagnoses social sources of misery without encouraging any systematic approach to alter them. Conceiving of somatization in broad biopsychosocial terms does hold out the possibility that appropriate public health and mental health programs can be developed to address the combined biological, psychological, and social sources of at least some forms of human misery. If medicalization includes recognition and authorized responses to psychosocial as well as biomedical factors, it can have beneficial effects for certain psychosocial problems often regarded as structural and therefore incorrigible.

I am not unaware of the potential problems, however. In the United States, for instance, a political administration that has attacked the system of social welfare programs is also inclined to label the disabled malingerers and take away their deserved disability benefits. With the best of intentions the worst of results could occur if somatization were viewed as an excuse to strip away sick role and disability support under the guise of distinguishing pseudohealth problems from "real" ones. But this will surely happen as part of demedicalizing health problems. Advancing the dialectical model central to this book—that social and biological processes overlap and are interrelated in illness—in principle would be a means of avoiding this abuse.

Obviously the kind of process that I have in mind must be linked to community control over the labeling, treatment, and prevention of health problems. The role of the practitioner would be seen, then, as that of a community change agent responsible not only for the health of individuals but for advising and working with communities on the health of families, subgroups, and the entire community. This is a particularly important role for health professionals in rural areas in underdeveloped countries. Primary care practitioners in many societies increasingly view their role in community perspective and see the work of caring as empowering individuals and communities. This is not the place to resolve this problem. I only wish the reader to think about medicalization in a new way based on the interpretive schema brought to the analysis of the materials reviewed in the preceding chapters. My own field research experiences have made me personally skeptical that societal changes will be crafted to address the structural sources of human misery. While I also have doubts about how practically effective the health and mental health system can be, who will determine if a problem is corrigible or not, and how the potential dangers of medicalization of societal problems can be controlled, I do think that if properly planned and monitored, and run on a community level, this is a potentially useful direction that can do some good. I would see a role for the medical anthropologist in the planning, ongoing monitoring, and outcome assessment of the utility of such local systems' interventions.

QUESTIONS FOR FURTHER RESEARCH

Before any interventions can be planned, however, it is essential that research be conducted to determine the frequency of different types of social problems. The research presented in this volume, it cannot be strongly enough insisted, merely points up the kinds of issues that must be studied more systematically and in many different settings, if the required information is to be made available without which health and mental health policy formulation and program planning is unlikely to be useful. Heretofore large-scale, systematic health and mental health studies in China have paid scant attention to social indicators of work, family, school, and other community problems. Nor have they assessed mental health in any broad sense of the term, beyond documentation of major mental illness. Alternatively, China's fledgling social sciences have not regarded health and mental health problems as appropriate subjects for study.

Whether we label somatization as neurasthenia or depression, the point is to gather information on its social origins and outcomes. This kind of medical social science research is new to China. If the only model guiding mental health studies is the narrow epidemiological one that now dominates psychiatry in the West, it is very unlikely that the requisite social data will be collected. Furthermore, those aggregate national data that will be assembled will mean little if they are not interpreted in local contexts, because the differences within and among local systems are great. Professional passions are being expended on the cultural constructionist question of whether neurasthenia is depression, or vice versa; our work suggests that a more profitable task is understanding the social production of misfortune and misery. This calls for a new kind of social or anthropological epidemiology. I believe this is the only approach that can analyze somatization and provide the basis for effective therapeutic, prevention, and social change programs.

Is it in fact the case that rates of somatization are higher both where social control is tighter and where highly controlled social systems pass through rapid transitions that exacerbate institutionalized stress, undercut social structural supports, and tolerate somatic idioms of distress and not others that raise politically threatening questions? This would seem to be a most appropriate moment to gather systematic, long-term information to affirm or refute this hypothesis, since we are witnessing a "red reformation" in China that is not only delegitimating much of the traditional Communist ideology but loosening social control and changing the nature of stress and support while authorizing alternative idioms of distress (social, religious, artistic). If our hypothesis about vicious cycles is correct, then Chinese women are at especially high risk for mental health problems since they are now exposed to chronic sources of stress in work while still shouldering most of the burden of domestic care. Again we find a researchable question that holds important health and public health consequences. Is the situation any different from that in other societies undergoing rapid social transformation, our own included? While one can speculate at length on the answer, there is virtually no comparative research to provide empirical grounding to such speculation. We have not gathered nearly enough systematic information on the untoward effects and negative consequences of modernization for individuals and families. This can also be said of many of the other questions raised in this book: for example, do patients with the neurasthenia-depression-somatization group of problems stay in the sick role longer in China? Does somatized depression have a different outcome in China and the West than depression experienced as existential despair? Does somatic amplification, when studied in the general population, actually occur at a higher rate in China than in other societies? Does bodily awareness differ cross-culturally, and when does bodily awareness as a culturally constituted style of perception and communication pass over into somatization? Can we distinguish somatization as perception and experience from somatization as discourse? How frequently is somatic amplification adaptive for the individual and family but maladaptive for work-disability and health care systems? Can behavioral techniques be successfully used to teach patients to dampen symptoms in the absence of substantial local social change? Can community programs be practically organized to produce such change in workplace and family so as to reduce the burden of somatization? These are key questions for the next generation of comparative studies, which need to go beyond bicultural investigations to be truly comparative. Comparing the situation in China to that in India and other rapidly modernizing, large-scale, non-Western societies would make for a sharper analysis of the questions we have raised.

SUMMARY

Recent issues of North American or Western European newspapers will show that the magnitude of social problems in China is substantially less than in the West. Take, for instance, the March 17, 1985 issue of the *Manchester Guardian Weekly*. It contains articles on major forms of social pathology in the United States that read like Lamson's 1935 account of social pathology in China prior to Liberation. We read about Chicago's street gangs, whose impoverished black and Hispanic youth are literally trapped in the very buildings and blocks where they have been raised in a world of deadly violence. There are few options open to them to escape from their inner-city hells. Their individual powerlessness and vulnerability to local oppression virtually assures that they will seek refuge in gangs which will lead them to drug abuse, street crime, and violence. Some will end up dead, many in prison, most so deeply influenced by the local lifestyle that their normative personality will fit the American Psychiatric Association's antisocial category. In the same newspaper issue we read about the Eisenhower Foundation's report that the epidemic of street crimes in North America is a form of "slow rioting," that inner cities have become "places of terror" for all, that the middle and upper classes live in "fortified cells." Alcohol-related violence— meaning homicides, suicides, and accidents—the report goes on to show, has become one of the leading causes of death in American society. Other newspapers' issues chronicle on a daily basis for North America the enormity of social problems resulting from chaotic and disruptive change associated with cynicism, alienation, and brutality.

In comparison, Chinese society, for all the problems reviewed here, is better ordered, less chaotic, much less violent. There is a very low rate of alcoholism in China, and hardly any drug abuse. Street crime and violent deaths are unusual. Divorce and family breakdown still are uncommon. The elderly are more highly valued and, for the most part, more humanely cared for by the family. The major social problems of Chinese society take origin from a very tight and widely diffused system of social control that severely restricts individual rights and places each person in an iron cage of authoritarian restrictions. The social origins of demoralization in China spring from this oppressively relentless control over individual choice (a traditional problem in Chinese society), from the chaos of major social movements organized by the hierarchy of power, from a gathering crisis of cultural delegitimation of core socialist values barely covered over by new prosperity, and from an immense population mired in poverty.

These are not the same social sources of misery and misfortune as in the West. It is local systems of power which place individuals in both societies, however, in human dilemmas that must strike even the most stubborn of relativists as awfully similar. The gravamen of this book is that it is these local contexts which mediate the effects of social structural forces on the psychobiology of the person, and that it is also within these contexts that cultural norms and personal orientations are negotiated in the experience of misfortune and disorder.[3] For this reason, what is pan-human in depression and neurasthenia is the resultant not only of a shared psychobiology, but equally importantly of a shared social process which, despite great cultural variation in the particular meanings of events and relations, constitutes and expresses a limited number of ways of being human (experiencing loss, threat, anger, and alienation). Also for this reason, to be successful clinical and public health intervention programs, as well as programs of social change, need to intervene in these local contexts, which are indeed the visible vicious cycles that are the dynamic source of distress. In China, in America, and cross-culturally, these local contexts and their relationship to macrosocial forces constitute the appropriate focus (an anthropological one) for those engaged in clinical care, public health work, and social development.

Two larger themes loom behind our analysis of the neurasthenia-depression-somatization complex: the question of how we interpret the body's relationship to society and the question of how that interpretation informs our understanding of the interaction between culture and self. Before closing this account, it is useful to address these broader themes within which our analysis has lodged, and indicate several of the problems they project for the next level of inquiry. Not the least reason for addressing these questions is the recognition that behind the specific empirical questions in the last section lurks a conceptual and methodological conundrum. How can we study the symbolic bridge between symptoms and society without destroying the very dialectic that is most central to it, as is routinely done in disciplinary studies which focus on one end of the bridge or the other? How can we construct an interdisciplinary methodology appropriate for the complex, dynamic interactions inherent in our subject matter?

THE INTERPRETATION OF THE BODY

Anthropological studies indicate that the body is a powerful source of symbols to make sense of society, and that society stamps the body with meaning (Douglas 1966, 1970; Blacking 1977; Comaroff 1985; Turner 1985). The Western division between body and mind is anomalous in cross-cultural perspective. Most non-Western societies conceive the body as mindful, the mind as embodied. Moreover, the body may be construed as a social, not a personal domain. In traditional Confucian thinking the body is part of the immortal vehicle of descent linking ancestors to future generations of family members, and for this reason it is not to be abused by the person, who is a transient occupant. The body is also the microcosmic pole of the continuum of symbolic harmonies resonating from the planetary and terrestrial macrocosm. The flow of *qi* (vital energy) in the body resonates with its flow in the earth, and it is concentrated and radiated from ancestors to the living members of the family line, affecting bodily constitution, self, and health. The organization of the body, in traditional Chinese medical theory, was often analogized to the social organization of the state, and vice versa. Hence the body carries moral meaning.

While we have learned a great deal about how the body is conceptualized in Chinese and other societies, we know very little about cross-cultural differences and similarities in the way the body is experienced. Yet much of human attention is taken up in bodily experiences. The *experience* of normal bodily processes (growth and aging, rest, activity, pregnancy, bereavement, daily bodily functions) and abnormal bodily processes (symptoms) has only recently become a subject in psychology and anthropology, and these are both appropriate questions for cross-cultural comparisons. Such comparisons would inform us if physiological states are monitored (perceived and interpreted) in distinctive ways cross-culturally, if symptoms are not merely labeled differently but actually felt in different ways, and how bodily awareness is culturally shaped and amplified to become somatization. Just as we have examined the cultural construal and social production of illness and emotion, we can study the social production of the body as well as its interpretation. That is to imply that the cultural understanding of psychobiological processes (respiration, digestion, excretion, sexual functioning) alters those processes, and that the symbolic reticulum linking body to society both produces real bodily effects (changes in respiration, blood pressure, intestinal motility, sweating) and reproduces distinctive sociosomatic patterns (levels of autonomic nervous system arousal, biorhythmic profiles of hormonal secretion and immunological responsivity, patterns of relationships among neurotransmitters).

The study of somatization suggests that the body can be a vehicle for experiencing, interpreting, and communicating about emotion and social issues, that the person's experience, interpretation, and expression of bodily functions is negotiated in interpersonal relations. Somatic idioms of distress also indicate that in some nontrivial sense the body feels and expresses social problems.

Little research heretofore has examined how these things happen, how the body comes to mean, not simply personally but in terms of the cultural system and interpersonal transactions, and how those bodily meanings become an intimate, sociophysiological part of bodily processes.

How would we go about determining if the Chinese experience of the body differs from the Western experience, and if that experience has changed with modernization? Perhaps what we first need are phenomenologies of bodily modes of experience in an array of societies and across divergent social statuses (gender, age, education, religion, ethnicity, health and sickness). Since chronic medical disorders are the norm in old age, bodily experience in this age group cannot be separated from the experience of disorder and senescence. Heretofore few ethnographic or cross-cultural clinical accounts have attempted to explain how the body is experienced, or the way we are socialized to experience our body. Yet it is unlikely that we will significantly advance our understanding of cultural differences and cross-cultural universals until we achieve a more discriminating understanding of this subject.

The paradigm for such research is the study of local cultural ethnotheories and categories of bodily processes, followed by phenomenological ethnographies of actual bodily modes of experience and cross-cultural comparisons. This is precisely the background required to deepen our understanding of somatization; but understanding the bodily concomitants of affect, affective disorder, and culturally marked behaviors would also emerge from this line of investigation. In Chinese culture, for example, we possess extensive historical data on categorization of bodily states (*yin, yang;* hot, cold; the Five elemental phases *wu xing;* and so forth) against which studies of current conceptualization would be enriched. But the real focus needs to be how Chinese across particular social statuses and communities learn to experience bodily processes: perceive, feel, label, live with, communicate, and negotiate them. Such studies should start with how Chinese talk about these processes, but should not end there. We need to penetrate to the experience qua experience, say, of pain. This requires a kind of clinical or experiential ethnography that hardly exists at present.

This phenomenology of bodily experiences is also a basic requirement for understanding the self. Brian Turner (1984) in a recent work, *The Body and Society,* asks us to conceive of social reality as *embodied* such that desire (gastronomic, sexual, financial), for example, is a social category that comes to be part of physiological experience and private life. To view the social world from the vantage of the body is to gain purchase on the powerful processes that shape the lives of individuals and groups—to see, in Foucault's (1978) terms, how the social forces that organize our life world come to dwell within (and oppress) our most private experience. The argument advanced here is that the body mediates social structure and cultural meanings, making them a part of our physiology. This book offers much support for this thesis, but it does not take us very far in the interpretation of how the symbolic reticulum between body and society is created and their processes interconnected. That has not been our chief concern here. But it should become a central question in medical anthropology and cross-cultural psychiatry in future, if these disciplines are to penetrate one of the great interdisciplinary conceptual issues of our period. Quite obviously this inquiry must proceed along dialectical lines that are biologically, as well as sociologically, sophisticated.

The interpretation of the body brings us to a new stage in the study of social order since the body is socially ordered, indeed might be regarded as the most fundamental form of social control, and its experience of disorder is the source of primary deviance. Government extends into the body and its functions and practices, as Turner (1985), following Foucault, Lasch and others, convincingly demonstrates. Armstrong (1983) discloses that the body is both seen and experienced as a representation of politically dominant cultural models. In the Durkheimian sense social relationships and cultural categories are experienced in the body. But these powerful social insights are only now being translated into empirical investigations, and it is quite uncertain what research methods are most appropriate for this investigation. Nonetheless the door is open and the subject is now with us.

TOWARD A THEORY OF THE SELF IN CULTURE

A fundamental contribution of anthropological studies to the understanding of the self is the strong emphasis they give to indigenous categories and ethnotheories (cf. White 1982; Shweder and Borne 1982; Lutz 1985). The argument advanced is that these local categories and theories not only tell us about how the self is *construed* in a particular cultural context, but disclose how the self is *created* as a locally shaped experience (Rosaldo 1980). Anthropologists, working in small-scale preliterate societies, have shown the complexity, contradictions, and subtlety in interpreting even these seemingly homogeneous cultural conceptions of the self, its components, competencies, and scope of involvement with the social world. When examining large-scale, pluralistic, civilizational societies like China, India, Islamic societies, Western Europe, or the United States, the danger to be avoided is reification of simplistic dichotomies that implicitly divide experience into crude oppositions (for example, independent/dependent, ego-centered/group-centered) and that present a monolithic account even where it is obvious to most that gender, class, ethnic minority status, religious affiliation, education, professional training, and many other modes of experience conduce to fairly distinctive definitions of the self and its tasks.

For example, interpretation of the self in Chinese cultural settings clearly must be attentive to the following residual sources of distinctive modes of experience and models of the person: the Confucian tradition of organizing family, work, community, and political relationships in terms of paradigmatic moral exemplars of behavior; the classical medical and Taoist traditions of conceiving the person in terms of ideal typical harmonies (symbolic correspondences) among *yin/yang,* hot/cold, other dialectical (or complementary) oppositions, and the Five Elemental Phases resonating between macrocosmic environment and microcosmic bodily processes, including their correlative psychic states (the seven emotions); the folk religious tradition's idiom of influence of gods, ghosts, and ancestors on the self perception of efficacy; the priority given to capitalist, Marxist-Leninist, and Christian models of man in different Chinese sociopolitical settings; and expected differences across rural/urban, male/female, traditional/Western, and stage in the life-cycle divisions. This is a more complex and complicating residuum of value orientations than Munro (1977) outlines in his contrastive poles of liberal democratic, communist, and indigenous Chinese conceptions of man. But Munro's analysis of the way the self is configured, nonetheless, offers a useful paradigm. It is intuitively appealing to think of the Chinese experience of the self as shaped by value orientations that contrast with Western visions of privacy (see also B. Moore 1984), personal rights, ego-centricity, and in-trapsychic needs. In the Chinese vision the person draws his or her signif-icance from a hierarchical, organic vision based on socio-centricity, family and community obligations, interpersonal harmony, and a public moral model of personal virtues. Yet there is also a countertradition, emphasizing the individual's unique talents and contributions, that must be accounted for as well, along with the peculiarities that result from differences in personality and negotiations of self-definition in particular families and networks.

There are few empirical findings on the concept of the person in local Chinese communities. On the level of interpretation, scholars have been troubled for some time by the clear anachronism and ethnocentrism of using Freudian categories to chart Chinese psychodynamics, but this subject still is virtually unexplored. Using the same line of argument that led me to suggest that psychological-mindedness and even the Western understanding of the interiority of the person might best be regarded as fairly recent creations in Western history, I would suggest that the notion in Western psychological theories that sexuality is the core of selfhood implies a type and intensification of sexual preoccupation which, while perhaps discernible among Chinese, seems less central in the Chinese case. Perhaps, as Hsu (1971) and Lin (1982) suggest, a more adequate account of Chinese psychodynamics would turn on the modulation of the self in interpersonal transactions by means of an internal dynamic of familism, moral harmony, and somatopsychic holism. Or, extrapolating from Errington's (1984) analysis of the person in Minang-kabau society, we might regard Chinese culture as resting on such funda-mental agreement on the moral premises guiding behavior that surface inter-pretations of conventional signs of a unified self are more valid than the Western style of deep interpretations of a rootless, divided self. This is to suggest that the Chinese self, to some extent, is culturally distinctive and should be understood in that society's dominant value orientations and sys-tems of meaning.

These issues are largely empirical questions. The chief reason that we cannot presently limn an adequate account of the self in Chinese culture is that our knowledge base (both from field research and from historical studies) is too poor. Doubtless contributing to this impoverished knowledge base is the systematic inattention to psychological questions by China scholars encouraged by the Chinese tradition itself, which articulates these questions as moral, political, and somatopsychic medical inquiries (cf. Metzger 1982; Kleinman and Lin 1982). But anthropologists and cross-cultural psychiatrists and psychologists have also avoided confronting how the self differs in different societies. Since the self as a system is the basic unit of integration in society—the unit of analysis that shows how social structure and cultural meanings organize social life—it is unlikely inquiries that fail to assess the self can carry us very far in understanding how individuals come to reproduce social experience. Without such inquiries social studies create oversocialized, stereotypical, and thereby false models of the person that are inadequate for understanding the oscillations between agency and structure that are central to human action. For example, absence of a sophisticated understanding of the self in society leads either to a simplistic, wrongheaded, voluntaristic view of somatization that readily is distorted into the erroneous equation that somatization equals malingering, or to the equally tendentious notion that somatization is purely a cultural model of communication that can be separated from individual experience.

The line of inquiry required to provide a more discriminating theory of the self begins with recognition of the production and construction of the self in society. That is, as Keyes (1985) avers in his anthropological formulation of the self: the sense of self is a changing process of making events and experiences meaningful in resistance to the lived world. That processual elaboration of the self in action is informed by life texts, including cultural orientations and personal significance, that respond to shared life realities—birth, aging, sickness, misfortune, death—that are negotiated in local webs of relationships. As with illness and affect and the body, so with the self: there is a social production of the self, a negotiated reproduction of the self in paradigmatic interpersonal situations, and a cultural construction of the experience of the self as much as the discourse about it. While psychological anthropologists have begun to interpret these processes in small-scale, preliterate societies (cf. Rosaldo 1980; Schieffelin 1985; Lutz 1985), we possess hardly any relevant research for China. Indeed, though not extensive, the data-base for India and Japan is richer. What we need are empirical studies in different local cultural systems of Chinese conceptions of the self, methods of socializing self-competencies, discrepant (major and minor) versions of the self in transaction, the psychodynamics of Chinese selfhood compared across age, gender, class, and sociopolitical lines, and analysis of discourses on such things as self-confidence, self-efficacy, and the tasks and pathologies of the self. Since much of the limited knowledge we now possess comes from the study of illness, it is especially important to generate studies of normal behavior. But while such studies doubtless will alter significantly our current understanding and will lead to broad theoretical elaboration, they will need to incorporate our findings on neurasthenia, depression, and somatization to provide an adequate account of the self in Chinese society. For in the face of distress crucial tasks of the self include ordering inner experience, relating collective and individual poles of that experience, creating a life story that oscillates between those poles, and integrating life story, aspirations, norms, and feelings to act in the social world.

One especially significant point from our research is that the construction of the self involves a dialectic between universal biological and social aspects of human nature, on the one side, and the process, outlined above, of creating meaning in particular social interactions based on shared cultural models and value orientations, on the other. Here again we advert to experience as embodied: the self is inseparable from its body, which is in fact, counter to standard Western thinking, both a part of the self and of the social world. Thus *the self is a system* interrelating different levels of reality and modes of experience, a systematic relationship among feeling, cognition, interpersonal relations, and cultural expectations about judgement and action.

The upshot of more extensive and sophisticated empirical data should be theory-building. The purpose of such cross-cultural research is not only to test hypotheses generated from existing theories of the self, but more importantly to create alternative theories. The dominant theories of the self are almost wholly derived from the Western cultural tradition's ethnopsychological models; studies of non-Western populations, including Chinese, have sought to incorporate findings into these dominant Western ethnotheories (psychoanalytic, behavioral, cognitive, and so forth). These theories tend to see the self as unchanging, emerging progressively from childhood experience and strongly anchored in it, separable from its sociodynamic interactions, and consisting of a deeply private, authentic, stable interiority at odds with changing surface impressions. This Western bias contrasts with the anthropological vision of the self as a work of culture in particular social interactions that changes with changes in those transactions, the life texts (meanings, values) that inform them, and with taking on a particular, embodied perspective (illness, religious, intellectual) toward the world (Riesman 1983; Beeman 1985; Keyes 1985). It is high time we created alternative dialectical theories of the self, based on studies with Chinese and other non-Western populations.

At the end we are left with some of the more provocative questions in anthropology or psychiatry. Cross-cultural studies, such as the one reported in this book, will, I predict, come to occupy a more central place in the building of theory in both disciplines. These new theories, I have tried to convince the reader, should lead to a rethinking of what is the appropriate subject matter of medicine, public health, and the social sciences.

Appendix of Tables

Tables 1–34 are modified from Kleinman (1982); and tables 35–47 are reprinted from Kleinman and Kleinman (1985).

Table 1

Demography of Psychiatry Outpatient Clinic, Hunan Medical College
N = 361 Consecutive Patients[a]

Sex
Males 184, Females 177

Occupation	
Peasant – farmers	22%
Cadres	17%
Workers	42%
Students	11%
Professionals	0%
Housewife or retired	8%

Age Structure	
15 and under	7%
15–25	25%
26–45	50%
46–60	17%
over 60	2%

---

[a] These were all the patients seen in one week of 10 half-day clinic sessions.

Table 2
Diagnoses of 361 Consecutive Patients, Psychiatry Clinic, Hunan Medical College[a]

	% of Cases[c]
Schizophrenia	31
Other psychosis (including organic mental disorder)	4
Neurasthenia	19
Neurasthenia syndromes	12
Neurasthenia (all forms)	31
Neurosis[b]	15
Hysteria	4
Depression	1
Neurological disorders	11
No diagnosis	4

[a] Diagnoses made by psychiatrists in the Department of Psychiatry, Hunan Medical College, using their own diagnostic system.
[b] Including neurological headaches, vascular headaches, anxiety states, phobias, obsessive-compulsive disorders.
[c] Percentages add to more than 100% owing to rounding.

Table 3

100 Neurasthenia Patients
Males 52, Females 48

Accompanied 28, Unaccompanied 72
Referred by doctors 48, Self referred (or by family or friends) 52

Occupation
Peasant-farmers	2	
Cadres	16	(13 political, 3 technical)
Workers	48	(45 laborers, 2 office workers, 1 retired, 1 unemployed)*
Teachers	18	(6 primary, 6 junior middle school, 6 senior middle school)
Professionals	10	(3 engineers, 3 nurses, 2 doctors, 2 senior technicians)
Students	6	(4 college, 2 senior middle school)

Age Structure
18–25   16%
26–45   66%
46–56   18%
Mean Age 36, Males 33, Females 38

* Unemployed worker is listed as one of the 45 laborers.

Table 4
Diagnoses[a] of 100 Neurasthenia Patients

	Number of Cases
Major Depressive Disorder	87
Manic Depressive Disorder (Depressed)	3
Dysthymic Disorder (Depressive Neurosis)	2
Cyclothymic Disorder (Depressed)	1
Depression (all forms)	93
Panic Disorder	35
Generalized Anxiety Disorder	13
Phobic Disorder	20
Anxiety States (all forms)	69
Somatization Disorder (Briquet's Syndrome)	15
Conversion Disorder	10
Somatoform Disorders (Hysteria, all forms)	25
Shen kui Syndrome ('kidney weakness')	11
Frigophobia (*pa leng*, fear of 'cold')	3
Culture-Bound Disorders	14
Obessive-Compulsive Disorder	2
Alcoholism	1
Drug Abuse (intoxication and addiction)	1
Chronic Pain Syndrome	44

[a] More than one diagnosis per patient (mean 2.5).

Table 5

Diagnoses of Somatization Cases in Taiwan N = 51[a]

	Number of Cases	%
Major Depressive Disorder	22	43
Dysthymic Disorder	2	4
Atypical Affective Disorder, Pathological Grief	1	2
Depression (all forms)	25	49
Panic Disorder	5	10
Generalized Anxiety Disorder	14	27
Phobic Disorder	0	0
Anxiety (all forms)	19	37
Somatization Disorder (Briquet's Syndrome)	2	4
Conversion Disorder	4	8
Hysteria (all forms)	6	12
Chronic Pain Disorder	15	29
Obsessive Compulsive Disorder	3	6
Chronic Personality Disorder	3	6
Schizophrenia	2	4
No Mental Illness	1	2
Culture-Bound Disorder	1	2
Alcoholism and Drug Abuse	0	0

[a] Note: 58 cases of somatization were included in the "Taiwan Comparison of Western and Traditional Healing", but full psychiatric assessment data were available for only 51 of these cases. Almost all of these cases had been diagnosed at one time or another by Western-style or Chinese-style doctors or shamans as neurasthenia, or had self-diagnosed themselves or been diagnosed by family members with this label.

Table 6

Neurasthenia Patients

		Hunan	Taiwan
Major Depressive Disorder	Yes	87 (87%)	22 (43%)
	No	13 (13%)	29 (57%)
	Total	100	51

Chi-square (ld.F.) is significant. (Chi-square = 30.2; P < 0.005)

Table 7
Major Depressive Disorder (N = 87)

	Number of Cases	%
With Melancholia	26	30
Acute	35	40
Chronic	32	60
Recurrent (both Acute and Chronic)	18	21

Table 8
DSM-III Symptoms, Major Depressive Disorder N = 87

Mean number of symptoms per case	5.9
Number of cases with 4 symptoms	9 (10%)
Number of cases with 6 or more symptoms	54 (62%)
Number of cases with all 8 symptoms	11 (13%)
Number of cases with dysphoria[a]	84 (97%)
Number of cases with anhedonia	53 (61%)

[a] Depressed mood, hopelessness, irritability. (Note: most of these complaints were not spontaneously expressed, but elicited in response to specific questions about them.) This definition of dysphoria follows DSM-III (see Note 4).

Table 9
Pain Complaints and Depression in Neurasthenia Patients (N = 100)

	Chronic Pain Syndrome	Pain Complaints without Chronic Pain Syndrome	Total (Pain all forms)
With Major Depressive Disorder	37 (84%)	41 (89%)	78 (87%)[a]
With other forms of Depression	2 (5%)	3 (7%)	5 (6%)[a]
Without Depression	5 (11%)	2 (4%)	7 (8%)[a]
Total	44	46	90

Note: Ninety percent of patients with Major Depressive Disorder and 90% of the entire sample of neurasthenia patients have pain complaints, while 43% of the former and 44% of the latter have Chronic Pain Syndrome.

[a] Percentages add to more than 100% owing to rounding.

Table 10
Breakdown of Patients with Pain, N = 90

| Complaints | Types of Pain | | |
	Chronic Pain Syndrome	Pain complaints (without CPS)	Pain (all forms)
Headache (primary)	38 (86%)	40 (87%)	78 (87%)
Headache (secondary)	3 (20%)	3 (13%)	6 (15%)
Other pain[c] (primary)	6 (14%)	6 (13%)	12 (13%)
Other pain (secondary)	12 (80%)	21 (88%)	33 (85%)
	44[a] (15)[b]	46[a] (24)[b]	90[a] (39)[b]

[a] Primary complaints.
[b] Secondary complaints.
[c] Back pain, chest pain, neck pain, limb pain, abdominal pain, whole body pain, etc.

Table 11
Major Categories of Presenting Complaints of Neurasthenia Patients N = 100

Mean number of complaints per patient	7
Mean number of somatic complaints per patient	5
Mean number of psychological complaints per patient	1.8
Mean number of affective complaints per patient (but 39 had none)	1
Mean number of cognitive complaints per patient (but 38 had none)	0.8
Mean length of time of chief presenting complaints 7.8 years (range 6 months – 30 years)	

Table 12
Illness Idioms[a] in Major Depressive Disorder N = 87

	Number of Cases	%
Somatic: entirely somatic complaints	26	30
Somatopsychic: somatic and psychological complaints, but somatic viewed as most important	61	70
Psychological or psychosomatic: entirely or mostly psychological	0	0

[a] Forms of expressing complaints.

Table 13
Chief Presenting Complaints[a] in all Depressive Cases (N = 93)

	Number of Cases	% of Cases
Headaches (primary and secondary	84	90
Insomnia	70	78
Dizziness	68	73
Pain (other than headaches; primary and secondary)	45	48
Loss of or poor memory	40	43
Anxiety	36	39
Weakness	33	35
Loss of energy	28	30
Feeling of swelling or fullness in head, neck or brain	27	29
Irritability	21	23
Disturbing dreams	20	22
Palpitations	17	18
Poor appetite	17	18
Stomach complaints	15	16
Tingling of head	12	13
Poor concentration	11	12
Non-specified dysphoria (displeasure or unhappiness)	11	12
Fear or panic	10	11
Coldness in limbs, head, rest of body	9	10
Restlessness	9	10
Depression	8	9
Heaviness (or pressure) in head	8	9
Heaviness (or pressure) in chest	8	9
Ringing in ears	7	8
Sweating	6	7
Paresthesias (numbness)	5	5
Feeling of shaking, ringing, picking in brain	4	4
Hotness of body or head	4	4
Trembling or jumping in hands or feet	4	4
Hair falling out	4	4
Speech unclear	3	3

[a] Spontaneously expressed by patients when asked to describe their chief problems.

[b] Percentages add to greater than 100% since there were more than one complaint per case.

Table 14

Comparison of Presenting Affective and Cognitive Complaints[a] in All Depressive Cases
N = 93

	Number	%
Cognitive Complaints	*74*	
loss of or poor memory	40	43
dreams	20	22
Poor concentration	11	12
speech unclear	3	3
Affective Complaints	*95*[b]	
Specific, Differentiated	*44*	
anxiety	36	39
depression	8	9
Nonspecific, Poorly Differentiated or Undifferentiated	*51*	
irritability (general, vague)	21	23
displeasure-unhappiness	11	12
fear or panic (general, vague)	10	11
restlessness	9	10
Total Affective and Cognitive Complaints	169[b]	

[a] Spontaneously expressed by patients when asked to describe their chief problems.
[b] Note: These numbers add to more than 93 since certain cases had more than one affective and one cognitive complaint.

Table 15
Elicited Psychological Symptoms[a] for All Depressive Disorder Patients N = 93

	Number of Cases	% of Cases
Dysphoria[b] (depression, sadness, displeasure, unhappiness, irritability)	93	100
Anhedonia	57	61
Hopelessness	46	50
Helplessness	39	42
Low self-esteem, worthlessness	56	60
Guilt	8	9
Poor memory	37	40
Mind slowed down	58	62
Trouble concentrating or making decisions or difficulty in thinking	78	84
Hypochondriacal preoccupation (including fear or brain tumor in 13 cases and fear of going 'crazy' in 17 cases)	47	51
Diurnal mood variation, mornings worse	21	23
Suicidal thoughts	8	9
Suicidal plans	1	1
Suicide attempts	1	1

a Obtained during clinical diagnostic interview in response to specific questions regarding each symptom.
b This definition of dysphoria is different from that in DSM-III and includes such undifferentiated complaints as displeasure and unhappiness, but does not include hopelessness.

Table 16
Culture-Bound Complaints[a] in Neurasthenia

	Number of Complaints
Men as 'heaviness or pressure depressing into head or chest'	16
Fear of excessive loss of semen with diminished vital energy (*shen kui*)	11
Huoqi da (excess of hot inner energy)	7
Fear of cold (*pa leng*) in body (frigophobia)	3
Fear of ghosts	2
Suan ('sourness' in heart and body)	1
'Cold fire' in body	1
Total	41

a Most of these were not spontaneously expressed, but offered in response to specific questions about them.

Table 17
Explanatory Models (EMs) of Neurasthenia Patients N = 100

1. *Nature of Problem*

Wholly or partially organic	Organic problem 44% Mixed organic and psychological problems 34% (somatopsychic > psychosomatic EM)	78%
Psychological problem		22%

2. *Name of Problem*[a]

Neurasthenia	44%[b]
Neurological disorder (e.g., neurological pain, brain tumor, etc.)	27%
Minor psychological problem (general, vague)	18%
Psychosis	10%
Other	7%
Don't know	4%

3. *Perceived Cause*[c]

Work problems	61%
Political problems	25%
Separation	25%
Marital/Family Problems	20%
Exam and school stress	16%
Another illness	13%
Economic problems	12%
Grief (loss of close relative)	12%
Emotional tension or stress	12%
Nutritional	9%
Genetic	5%

4. *Expected Course*

Acute (will quickly end)	4%
Chronic stable	57%
Progressive worsening	31%
Improving	2%
Don't know	6%

[a] No traditional Chinese medicine or folk illness categories spontaneously expressed by patients in answer to question: What is the name of your problem?

[b] Percentages add to more than 100% since a small number of patients gave more than one name of problem.

[c] Percentages add to more than 100% since more than one cause was expressed by patients.

Table 18
Desired Treatment[a] of Neurasthenia Patients

Choice of treatment is up to the doctor	40%
Traditional Chinese medicine	16%
Drugs of Any Kind	12%
Western medicine	7%
Electroencephalogram to rule out brain tumor	6%
Other diagnostic tests of brain	6%
Hospitalization	3%
Psychotherapy	3%
Rest and change work	2%
Don't know	5%

a Patients were asked: What treatment do you wish to receive?

Table 19
Help Seeking of Neurasthenia Patients N = 100

	% of Cases
Self treatment (total)	85
Self treatment (first used before any other treatment)	34
Sacred folk (religious) treatment	23
Resort to shamans, sorcerers, other religious experts	14

Table 20
Self (Family) Treatment

	% of Cases
Special foods, diet, tonic	76
Traditional Chinese medicines	51
Western medicines	18
Western exercise	38
Traditional Chinese exercise	14

Table 21
Illness Behavior of Neurasthenia Patients

Mean visits to doctors 1.9 per month (range 0.5–8 per month).
Perceived percentage of time sick past year: 75% (mean).
Percentage of cases who viewed themselves as sick 100% of time past year: 33%.
Percentage of cases perceiving self as at least moderately socially impaired[a] in past year: 52%.
Percentage of cases perceiveing self as seriously socially impaired[b]: 15%.

[a] Moderately socially impaired: Illness interferes with work, school, personal and/or other relationships and prevents normal social performance.
[b] Seriously socially impaired: because of illness unable to work, attend school, or carry out relationships or activities in unit or family.

Table 22
Prior Medical Treatment Received

	% of Cases
Western physicians	98
Traditional Chinese doctors	84
Mostly saw Western physicians	76
Mostly saw Chinese doctors	24
Sedatives (all types) in past year	58
Benzodiazepines in past year	47
Received mostly traditional Chinese medicine past year	60

Table 23
Family History of Neurasthenia Patients

	% of Cases
Family history of neurasthenia[a]	36
Family history of chronic pain	25
Family history of chronic illness	57
Family history of mental illness[b]	24
Family history of significant psychological problems	64
Family hisotry of significant family problems	35
Family history of members working in health field	28
Family history of "step parents" (remarriage)	12

a Mothers of patients made up 70% of these.
b Mothers of patients made up 54% of these, and depression accounted for 62% of all mental illnesses in families.

Table 24
Types of Major Stressors Experienced by Neurasthenia Patients
Number of major stressors per patient in 6 months prior to onset of illness, mean 3.3
(range 0–6)

	% of Cases
Work	75
Separation[a]	57
Financial	45
Political	31
Death of spouse or other family member	29
School (including exams)[b]	26
Family	19

a Owing to different work sites and involving a mean time of 6.2 years (range 4 months to 20 years).
b Either experienced by patients directly or vis-à-vis their children.

APPENDIX OF TABLES

Table 25
Illness Problems of Neurasthenia Patients

Number of illness problems per patient, mean 3.4 (range 1–6).
Percentage of cases with maladaptive coping with illness: 96%.
Percentage of cases in which illness was used to change job, or to try to change job, or to
    return from separation due to different work sites, or to try to do so, or to go on sick
    leave to avoid or reduce work: 74%.

Table 26
Types of Illness Problems of Neurasthenia Patients N = 100

	% of Cases
Work	90
Family	80
School	56
Marital[a]	52
Financial	45
Doctor-Patient Conflict	15
Other[b]	23

[a] Also includes problems with girlfriends or boyfriends.
[b] Includes excessive anxiety about illness and its effect on life style, personality and social
relations.

Table 27
Significance (Meaning) of Illness N = 98[a]

	% of Cases[b]
Communicate personal or interpersonal distress or unhappiness	93
Manipulate interpersonal relations	74
Time off from work or other social obligations	72
Receive love and care from family and friends	66
Personal threat	55
Personal loss	46
Avoid unpleasant situation	39
Receive medical attention	33
Keep together family or marriage	26
Sanction failure	22
Receive financial compensation	9
Avoid intrapsychic conflict	5
Break up family or marriage	4

[a] Two of the 100 neurasthenia cases were not assessed for significance of illness.

[b] % is greater than 100% since more than one significance was assigned for most cases.

Table 28
Patient Self-Assessment of Symptom Outcome of Major Depressive Disorder[a] N−71[b]

	Number of Cases	%[c]
Improved (1−4)	58	82
Substantially improved (1−3)	46	65
(1) Completely (no current problems)	1	1
(2) Greatly (only minor current problems)	30	42
(3) Partially (still has some problems but substantially less than before)	15	21
(4) Slightly (still has significant current problem)	12	17
No Improvement	6	9
Worse	7	10

[a] All patients treated with tricyclic antidepressants.

[b] Major Depressive Disorder patients who returned for follow-up 71/87 = 82%.

[c] Percentages of 4 improved subcategories, no improvement, and worse categories add to more than 100% owing to rounding. Percentages of 1−4 and 1−3 add to less than 82 and 65, respectively, owing to rounding.

Table 29
Physician Assessment of Symptom Outcome of Major Depressive Disorder Patients[a]
N = 71[b]

	Number of Cases	%
Improved (1–4)	62	87
Substantially improved (1–3)	50	70
(1) Completely (no current problems)	3	4
(2) Greatly (only minor current problems)	29	41
(3) Partially (still has some problems but substantially less than before)	18	25
(4) Slightly (still has significant current problems)	12	17
No Improvement	3	4
Worse	6	9

[a] All patients treated with tricyclic antidepressants.
[b] Major Depressive Disorder patients who returned for complete follow-up 71/87 = 82%.

Table 30
Major Depressive Disorder Patient Self-Assessment of Change in Social Impairment[a]
N = 71

	Number of Cases	%[b]
Less socially impaired[c]	26	37
No change in social impairment	24	34
More socially impaired	21	30

[a] Assessment made by patients, and by family or co-workers who accompanied them at time of follow-up interview.
[b] Percentages add to greater than 100% owing to rounding.
[c] Patients were asked at first and follow-up interview to assess the degree to which they were socially impaired on a 5 point scale of none, minimal, moderate, serious, extreme social impairment, and concrete examples were provided to operationally define each degree of impairment.

Table 31
Change in Help Seeking of Neurasthenia Patient[a] N = 76[b]

		Number of Cases	%
(A)	No further help seeking[c]	48	63
	Further help seeking	28	37
	Visit to Chinese-style doctor	11	15, 39[d]
	Visit to Western-style doctor	4	5, 14[d]
	Self or family treatment	14	18, 50[d]
		Number	
(B)	Total visits to clinics	34	

a This assessment was made at time of follow-up interview.
b Neurasthenia patients who returned for follow-up interview, whose help seeking was assessed, 76%.
c Since first interview, approximately 5 weeks before.
d Percentage of those who sought further help. Percentages add to greater than 100% since more than one form of help seeking was chosen by certain patients.

Table 32
Outcome of Patient Illness Problems[a] N = 76

	No Problem[e]	Improved	Same	Worse
Family problems[b]	12%	45%	31%	12%
Marital problems	38%	33%	12%	17%
Work problems	4%	41%	35%	20%
School problems[c]	19%	32%	29%	20%
Financial problems[d]	44%	25%	15%	15%
Maladaptive coping with illness	0	37%	54%	9%
Doctor (or staff) -- patient conflict	87%	13%	0	0

a Assessed in initial interview and at time of follow-up (see Katon and Kleinman 1981; and Kleinman 1978). N is neurasthenia patients who returned for follow-up, 76%.
b Family problems include problems with in-laws, parents, children, and various relatives except for spouse.
c School problems refers both to problems experienced by patients and by children of patients.
d Percentage adds to less than 100% owing to rounding.
e No problem at time of first visit and at follow-up.

Table 33

Compliance as a Function of Symptom Outcome of Patients with Major Depressive
Disorder[a] N = 71

	Number of Cases	%	Compliance[b] (Mean Score)
Substantial improvement	25	35	3.4
Overall improvement (at least slight)	37	52	3.1
Same (no change) or worse	9	13	1.8

[a] Outcome and compliance assessed by psychiatrists at time of outcome.
[b] Compliance Scores: 1 = None   0
                        2 = Partial   (<50%)
                        3 = Mostly Complies (>50%)
                        4 = Complies   (100%)

Table 34

Depressed (all forms) Patients' Name of Their Disorder at Time of Follow-Up[a] N = 73[b]

	Number of Cases	% of Cases[c]
Neurasthenia	50	69
Depression	8	11
Other	15	21
Change of EM from Neurasthenia (1st visit) to Depression (Follow-up)	5	7

[a] All patients in this group had been told at time of initial visit their problem was depression, had been given a biomedical EM of depression, and had been treated with antidepressants (in more than 70% of 71 cases evaluated at follow-up by psychiatrists with substantial improvement).
[b] Number of depressed patients for whom a follow-up EM could be obtained; in two via correspondence.
[c] Percentages add to more than 100% owing to rounding.

Table 35
1983 Follow-Up Study: Demographics: (N = 21)

Age:	
Mean 39, range 25–59	
Mean for men 34	
Mean for women 42	
Sex:	
Men 7 (33%)	
Women 14 (67%)	
Occupations:	
Workers	10 (48%)
Teachers	9 (43%)
Cadre	1 (5%)
Technician	1 (5%)

Table 36
1983 Follow-Up Study: Psychiatric Diagnoses[a]

Depressive Disorders	
Major Depressive Disorder	7 (33%)
Dysthymic Disorder	5 (24%)
	12 (57%)
Anxiety Disorders	
Panic Disorder	6 (29%)
Phobic Disorder (Simple 4, Agoraphobia 1)	5 (24%)
Generalized Anxiety Disroder	0 (0%)
Obsessive-Compulsive Disorder	1 (5%)
	12 (58%)
Somatoform Disorders	
Conversion Disorder	2 (10%)
Somatization Disorder	1 (5%)
	3 (15%)
Personality Disorder	5 (24%)
Hypochondriasis	6 (29%)
Suicidal Ideation	1 (5%)
No Mental Illness	4 (19%)

[a]Percentages add to more than 100% as there was more than one diagnosis made per case.

Table 37
1983 Follow-Up Study: Pain Complaints

Completely improved (cured)	1 (5%)
Greatly improved (75% improved)	3 (14%)
Somewhat improved (50% improved)	10 (48%)
No change (Pain same as before)	7 (33%)

Table 38
1983 Follow-Up Study: Social and Work-Related Change[a]

Social Change	2 (10%)
Married	1 (5%)
Mother left home	1 (5%)
Obtained degree	1 (5%)
Wants divorce	1 (5%)
Wants to retire	1 (5%)
Daughter left home	1 (5%)
Work-Related Change	
Illness affects work	12 (57%)
Dislikes work	9 (43%)
Wants to change work	7 (33%)
Retired	3 (14%)
Reunited from work separation	4 (19%)
Changed work since 1980	8 (38%)
Total changed work	10 (48%)

[a]25 matched neurotic non-neurasthenia psychiatry OPD patients, 0 = number changed work in past three years

Table 39
1983 Follow-Up Study: Symptom Change among
Those Who Changed Work or Retired

Changed Work (N = 10)	
Better	6 (60%)
Worse	2[a] (20%)
Same	2 (20%)
Retired (N = 3)	
Better	3
Worse	0
Same	0

[a]Both involved change to more stressful job

Table 40
1983 Follow-Up Study: Symptom Change among Those with Positive
Negative, and Neutral Work Change

Positive (N = 5)	
Better	4 (80%)
Worse	0 (0%)
Same	1 (20%)
Negative (N = 2)	
Better	0 (0%)
Worse	2 (100%)
Same	0 (0%)
Neutral[a] (N = 3)	
Better	2 (67%)
Worse	0 (0%)
Same	1 (33%)

[a]New job perceived as neither better nor worse than previous job

Table 41
1983 Follow-Up-Study: Change in Symptoms among Those Who Resolved
Problems in Family Situations (N = 6)

Better	4 (67%)
Worse	0 (0%)
Same	2 (33%)

Table 42
1983 Follow-Up Study: Chief Presenting Complaints

Sources of Pain (N = 21)	
Headache	19 (90%)
Backache	1 (5%)
Other Pain	8 (38%)
Other Symptoms (95%)	
Weakness, Tiredness	20 (86%)
Insomnia	18 (86%)
Dizziness	15 (71%)
Bad Memory	13 (62%)
Poor Appetite	7 (33%)

Table 43
1983 Follow-Up Study: Significance of Symptoms

Sanction Failure	4 (19%)
Symbolize Distress Due to Cultural Revolution	5 (24%)
Desire to Change Work	6 (28%)
Wish to Reunite from Separation	2 (10%)
Control Family Members	10 (48%)
Sanction Expression of Anger	4 (19%)
Express Frustration over Unresolved Family, Work, or Political Problems	6 (28%)
Time off and away from Stressful Life Situation	4 (19%)
Bereavement Response	4 (19%)
Other Loss	2 (10%)

Table 44
Chronic Pain in Primary Care Study, Demographics (N = 26)

Age:
Mean 36, range 20–59
Mean for men, 39
Mean for women, 34

Sex:
Men 9 (35%)
Women 17 (65%)

Marital Status:
Married 22 (85%)
Single 3 (12%)
Divorced 1 (4%)

Occupation:	
Workers	12 (46%)
Peasants	1 (4%)
Cadres	6 (23%)
Teachers	3 (12%)
Professionals	4 (15%)

Table 45
Chronic Pain in Primary Care Study, Psychiatric Diagnosis (N = 26)

Depressive Disorders	
Major Depressive Disorder	14 (54%)
Dysthymic Disorder	6 (23%)
Double Depression	2 (8%)
	22 (85%)
Anxiety Disorders	
Generalized Anxiety Disorder	1 (4%)
Panic Disorder	3 (12%)
Phobia Disorder (Simple 2, Agoraphobia 3)	9 (19%)
	9 (35%)
Personality Disorder	2 (8%)
Hypochondria	5 (19%)
No Mental Disorder	7 (27%)

Table 46
Chronic Pain in Primary Care Study, Social Problems

Work	14 (54%)
Separation	5 (19%)
Family	8 (31%)
Economic	10 (38%)
Political	9 (35%)
School	1 (4%)
Loss	1 (4%)

Table 47
Chronic Pain in Primary Care Study, Significance of Illness

Affects Work	6 (23%)
Can't Work	6 (23%)
Can't Do Housework	4 (15%)
Wants to Change Work	10 (38%)
Time off and out	4 (15%)
Better Support at Work	3 (12%)
Spouse Better to Patient	2 (8%)
Wants Divorce	2 (8%)
Cry for Help	1 (4%)
Sanction Failure	1 (4%)

Notes

PROLOGUE

1 The first two sections of the *Prologue* are adapted from Kleinman and Kleinman (1985).

2 By *illness* I mean the way individuals and the members of their social network perceive symptoms, categorize and label those symptoms, experience them, and articulate that illness experience through idioms of distress and pathways of help seeking.

3 By *disease* I mean the way the illness experience is reinterpreted by practitioners in the terms of their theoretical models and through clinical work. When I speak of disease etiology in general, such as in the social production of disease, I am referring to biomedical refor-mulations of disease as malfunctioning, maladaptation, or structural abnormalities in biological systems.

4 In spite of Lyman's success in *postgraduate* training of psychiatrists at PUMC, that most elite of China's medical schools (whose few hundred graduates have continued to play a major role in the development of medicine in China, out of all keeping with their numbers) produced only one graduate who went into neurology and psychiatry out of its first 116 graduates from 1924 to 1933 (Bullock 1980:126). This is yet another indicator of the relatively low status psychiatry has occupied in China. An ironic twist to this tale of psychiatry at PUMC is that the old PUMC buildings now house a new medical school and hospital, the Capital Medical School and Hospital. This institution, in keeping with its heritage, is a high-technology biomedical research setting whose aim is to train the next generation of China's physician-scientists in classes smaller than those at the elitist PUMC. This very high-status medical school, the pinnacle of China's system of medical education, has no department of psychiatry! A further twist: recently this school was renamed PUMC.

5 The widely publicized political criticism of the psychiatrists at the Nanjing Psychiatric Hospital turned on their alleged adherence to Freudian psychodynamic concepts. The political criticism of Freudianism as a reflection of capitalist morality continues in a fairly heavy-handed fashion (cf. Zhao 1983): it is labeled an "idealist ideological set-up" whose sexual orientation reflects the perverted values of capitalism's ruling class and is an extremely powerful corruptive agent in society. The interest in wedding Freudian with Marxist perspectives is denounced as "a capitalist class hotch-potch of falsehoods." These two schools of thought are held to be opposing and irreconcilable even today. Although China has semi-officially proclaimed the literal application of Marxism an insufficient guide in the modern world, this partial volte-face is unlikely to be accompanied soon by a warmer official reception for Freudian thinking, albeit a few psychiatrists express an interest.

6 Pavlovian concepts came to dominate Chinese psychiatric and psychological theory during this period and have exerted a strong influence up until the end of the Cultural Revolution (T.Y. Lin 1986).

7 Much the same feeling radiates from Anne Thurston's (1985) interviews with victims of the Cultural Revolution. Thurston seems to want to attribute this effect, at least in part, to the possibility that her subjects were suffering from post-traumatic stress syndrome, and indeed

that many maimed by the Cultural Revolution may have developed this (DSM-III) disorder as a long-term psychophysiological consequence of the trauma they suffered. None of our patients, as the reader will discover in chapters 4 and 5, could be considered clinically to make the research diagnostic criteria for post-traumatic stress syndrome. But several exhibited a few of the characteristic symptoms, even though they suffered from some other (usually affective) disorder or had no mental illness (see case 13 in chapter 6). Hence it may well be that there are many forms of post-traumatic stress of which the full blown disorder is only one outcome. The concrete reenactment of traumatic experience and the powerful need to narratize it in a compelling fashion to others may be a general, not necessarily pathological (even perhaps at times therapeutic) tendency of those who have undergone severe personal trauma, especially when that experience is shared by so many others that it has taken on culture-wide meaning.

CHAPTER 1

1 Some of the material on the historical background of neurasthenia that appears in this chapter, first appeared in Kleinman (1982).

2 Although it has not attracted much attention from historians, Beard's initial description (perhaps invention is more apt) of neurasthenia barely beat out an apparently independent formulation by Van Deusen (1869) that coined the same name. But clearly the idea if not the term had been gathering momentum among medical men since at least the eighteenth century. Mora (1971) cites the eighteenth-century English practitioner, John Brown (1735–88), as the originator of the theory of neurological stimulus and counterstimulus that provided the conceptual tradition that Beard codified and popularized.

3 As the historian of psychiatry, Bynum (1983), notes even the term *neurosis*, in its original usage by William Cullen in 1783, implied a neurological (physical disease) basis to the disorders to which it was applied, where structural pathology could not be seen. Fischer-Homberger (1983) argues that before neurasthenia gained popularity, hypochondriasis carried the same meaning of somatic amplification, but in the age of neurasthenia it was displaced and came to signify only nosophobia. Even by the end of the eighteenth century, however, hypochondriasis had taken on a pejorative patina of the "maladie imaginaire."

4 For example, neurasthenic symptoms of fatigue, weakness, and the like have been reported by Wang et al. (1984) as the result of occupational lead exposure among workers in a battery factory in Shanghai. But lead toxicity and other specific biological sources of neurasthenic symptoms are uncommon; the vast majority of cases of neurasthenia have no toxic or other biological source.

5 Neurasthenia seems to have held an important place in Russian neuropsychiatry in the past, where it was underpinned by the theories of Pavlov and neurophysiologically oriented psychiatrists, who were widely translated into the Chinese psychiatry literature, and still is a component of contemporary Soviet psychiatry. For example, the dissident psychiatrist Semyon Gluzman, in a recent paper written from his internal exile in Siberia, has mentioned "simple conflict reactions (situational neuroses), characterized by affective instability, irritability, nervousness, tension, low moods, low productivity, and sometimes depression (all these symptoms fall into the so-called neurasthenia complex described by Soviet authors)" (Gluzman 1982:60). One of my Chinese colleagues attributed the idea of cortical asthenia directly to Pavlov (Young Derson personal communication). And in his writings Pavlov does relate neurasthenia and hysteria to cortical weakness and inhibition; but fascinatingly, Pavlov recognized, at least in the case of hysteria, that the neurophysiological mechanism resulting from "numerous life shocks, such as the loss of close relations or friends, unfaithful love and other deceptions encountered, the loss of property, collapse of convictions and beliefs, etc., and in general

difficult conditions of life—unhappy marriage, poverty, violation of self-respect, and so forth—all these factors produce in a weak individual, at once or eventually, violent reactions accompanied by different abnormal somatic symptoms" (Pavlov 1962:45). Pavlov also noted that "in a weak subject, an invalid in life, unable to win by positive qualities respect, attention and favour of other people, the latter motive acts most and contributes to the prolongation and fixation of the morbid symptoms. Hence, one of the most striking features of hysteria is the desire to be ill, to take refuge in illness." (Pavlov 1962: 46). Thus even Pavlov's strict neurological psychology includes an awareness of the social uses of illness, a point no doubt not lost on his Chinese psychiatric readers.

Chatel and Peele (1971) remark that the Russian literature divides neurasthenia into two stages: a hyperasthenia stage of irritability, insomnia, and psychophysiological symptoms, and a hypoasthenia stage of fatigue, depression, and work inefficiency. "The Russian literature manifests an interesting and recurrent concern with inefficiency, decrease in productivity, malingering, and "low work curve" as symptoms of neurasthenia and other psychiatric illnesses" (p. 39).

6 "Study," *xuexi*, has a very special significance in the Chinese tradition and in present-day China. Besides actual study in the classroom, this term connotes emulation of other's virtues and overcoming one's own limitations, following paradigmatic moral exemplars of proper behavior, self-study, and preparing one's self for opportunities and challenges. During the Cultural Revolution people studied Mao's writings, whereas today they study technical subjects in order to prepare themselves for advancement. All educated Chinese are expected to engage in *xuexi* at work and at home in order to develop themselves and (as the ideology puts it) so that they can contribute to the development of the country. This Confucian concept is a powerful moral term that symbolizes what the Chinese themselves take to be a genius of their culture: hard work at the intellectual level that leads to mastery of technical skills. Even workers employ the term to refer either directly to formal education as a major avenue of social mobility and career development or indirectly to continuing adult education that is viewed as a symbolic as well as an instrumental good.

A cultural history of *xuexi* discloses continuity of a core cultural concern punctuated by the special emphasis of particular periods. The term appears as one of the first words of the *Lunyu* (I.1), the sayings of Confucius compiled by his disciples: "Is it not a pleasure to *learn* and *constantly apply* it" (italics are mine). In the twelfth century A.D. Zhu xi, a Sung Dynasty scholar who led the greatly influential Neo-Confucian movement, said that "to study" is to be taught by words; "to practice" is the bird flapping its wings in flight; to study *continuously* is like the bird in flight (italics are mine). For Mao Zedong, *xue* is the process whereby knowledge is acquired from books; *xi* the process of putting knowledge into practice, that is, praxis (Cihai 1969:869c). The latter is more important in Mao's thought. *Xuexi's* current meaning emphasizes both the acquisition of theoretical knowledge and the practical mastery of a skill or detailed techniques. *Xuexi* clearly is central to the Chinese understanding of self. Being unable to study is a double entendre signifying problems of the self and its competencies as much as educational problems.

7 Neurasthenia was listed as one of the three priority targets in the First Five Year Plan in Mental Health (1958–62). During the Great Leap Forward, neurasthenia was reported as a rampant problem affecting all members of the society, especially "mind workers," leading to absenteeism from school and work and reduced work productivity. It was discussed as a national problem and received wide public attention. T.Y. Lin (1986:21–22) relates the intensification of concern with neurasthenia to reverses in the productivity and optimism that characterized the early years of the Communist state and the consequent disaffection and alienation, especially of intellectuals, which was symbolized in the ideology by the alleged epidemic of a disorder that in the dominant political theory was associated with capitalism,

not socialism. That "neurasthenia" emerged from this campaign without significant stigma is an impressive instance of the cultural authority it had achieved in Chinese society.

CHAPTER 2

1 Depression has been used variously to mean a common mood, a pathological affect, and a disorder. This ambiguity compromised earlier accounts as much as did different diagnostic criteria used to make the diagnosis of depressive disease. The term *clinical depression* is used to refer to a disorder. In the Diagnostic and Statistical Manual Number III (DSM-III) of the American Psychiatric Association, depression (like Caesar's Gaul) is divided into three parts: (1) bipolar disorder, formerly called manic-depressive disorder, a disease involving both depression and mania, which in a mild form may be called cyclothymic disorder, (2) dysthymic disorder (formerly depressive neurosis), a chronic disturbance of mood that is not of sufficient severity and duration to meet the criteria for (3) major depressive disorder. The diagnostic criteria for major depressive disorder are:

(a) Dysphoric mood or loss of interest or pleasure in all or almost all usual activities and pastimes. The dysphoric mood is characterized by symptoms such as the following: depressed, sad, blue, hopeless, low, down in the dumps, irritable. The mood disturbance must be prominent and relatively persistent, but not necessarily the most dominant symptom, and does not include momentary shifts from one dysphoric mood to another dysphoric mood, e.g., anxiety to depression to anger, such as are seen in states of acute psychotic turmoil.
(b) At least four of the following symptoms have each been present nearly every day for a period of at least two weeks:
    1. poor appetite or significant weight loss (when not dieting) or increased appetite or significant weight gain,
    2. insomnia or hypersomnia,
    3. psychomotor agitation or retardation,
    4. loss of interest or pleasure in social activities, or decrease in sexual drive,
    5. loss of energy, fatigue,
    6. feelings of worthlessness, self-reproach, or excessive or inappropriate guilt,
    7. complaints or evidence of diminished ability to think or concentrate, such as slowed thinking, or indecisiveness not associated with marked loosening of association or incorecurrent thoughts of death,
    8. suicidal ideation, wishes to be dead, or suicide attempt.

Furthermore, the clinical picture cannot be dominated by bizarre behavior or preoccupation with a mood-incongruent delusion or hallucination when the affective syndrome is absent, and the depression cannot be superimposed on schizophrenia, schizophreniform disorder, or a paranoid disorder, or due to any organic mental disorder (for example, dementia, tumor, infection, alcohol or drug intoxication or withdrawal) or uncomplicated bereavement. Major depressive disorder may be in remission or present with psychotic features (that is, when there apparently is gross impairment in reality testing, or when there are delusions or hallucinations, or depressive stupor (the indidivual is mute and unresponsive). It is said to occur with melancholia, if there is loss of pleasure in all or almost all activities, lack of reacting to usually pleasurable stimuli (doesn't feel much better, even temporarily, when something good happens), and at least three of the following:

(a) distinct quality of depressed mood, i.e., the depressed mood is perceived as distinctly different from the kind of feeling experienced following the death of a loved one.

(b) the depression is regularly worse in the morning,

(c) early morning awakening (at least two hours before usual time of awakening),

(d) marked psychomotor retardation or agitation,

(e) significant anorexia or weight loss,

(f) excessive or inappropriate guilt. (DSM-III, American Psychiatric Association, [1980:213–15])

2 In order to meet the DSM-III diagnostic criteria for major depressive disorder, the symptoms must have been severe and disturbing enough to affect the patient's life (disability) and/or led to help seeking (visit to physician, therapist, clergyman).

3 Beginning in 1983 the Chinese began to report higher rates of depressive disorder diagnosed in clinical samples, although the rates are still below those in American psychiatric clinics.

Since lower rates of depression have been reported from clinics in Taiwan and Hong Kong, though these rates are still higher than those reported from China, it may be that there is less depression in China than in the United States. The important community-based epidemiological studies of T.Y. Lin and his collaborators (1969) in Taiwan in the late 1940s and early 1960s indicate that depressive rates (lumped together with other psychoneurotic disorders in their analysis) are lower in Taiwan than in the West. But these rates were increasing over the fifteen years of Taiwan's rapid industrialization and urbanization. Nonetheless, the epidemiological studies are only now being conducted to answer the question of whether, using culturally valid criteria for depression, the rate in Chinese populations is low. A recent, but still unpublished, population-based study in Shanghai, using research diagnostic criteria and a standarized instrument based on the National Institute of Mental Health's diagnostic interview schedule is said by its principal investigator to demonstrate a low rate of depression, at least for an urban sample (William Liu, personal communication). But since this study applies an American research instrument, the diagnostic interview schedule, directly to a Chinese sample, without taking into account Chinese cultural categories and idioms of distress, finding that depression so measured has a lower prevalence rate in Shanghai may not be a valid assessment. The conceptual and methodological problems that confound cross-cultural psychiatric epidemiologies are discussed later in this chapter (see also Marsella et al. [1985] and Good and Kleinman [1985]).

4 Women have higher rates of depression (and of most, but not all, mental illnesses) worldwide. This has been shown in population studies not to be an artifact either of help-seeking or willingness to overtly express complaints (Weissman and Klerman 1977). Higher rates for women have also been demonstrated among Chinese in Hong Kong (Lee 1982). This subject has not yet received detailed investigation in the People's Republic.

5 Melancholia has been used in medical circles up to the present; it receives an official designation in DSM-III. Depression as a term only came into use in the nineteenth century (Starobinski 1983:42–44).

6 The Chinese have not set out official research diagnostic criteria for depression; those set out by Xu Youxin and Zhong Youbin (1983) are the most formal criteria published in China to date. The reader can compare these with the DSM-III criteria (see note 1 above). Xu and Zhong state that the diagnosis of depressive neurosis must comport with the following four conditions:

I. Symptom Criteria: the principal symptom is morbid mood manifested as dejection, low spirits, distress. Besides the general experience of low mood, there are at least three of the following symptoms: (1) a clear loss of interest. . . ; (2) the feeling that life has no meaning; (3) low self-esteem; (4) getting no pleasure from praise or reward; (5) persistently dwelling upon unhappy past or bitter experiences; (6) considering one's self to be careless or lazy, and unable to exert self for long periods of time—feeling tired and without energy, thinking of difficulties, or remembering personal experiences of feeling inferior, often the patient is experiencing physical discomfort; (7) social withdrawal, no initiative to communicate with others, but patient is good at communicating when contacted by others; (8) often cries or sighs mournfully; (9) frequent thoughts of death, having grave contradictions about this in his heart so that patient cannot make a decision.

II. Duration Criteria: symptoms persist for at least one year. While the afflicted patient is depressed for at least two or three days at a time, he can have periods of normal mood, but not for more than two months at the most each time.

III. Severity Criteria: Owing to symptoms effectiveness at work, study, in daily household chores is clearly reduced.

IV. Exclusion Criteria: no past history of mania or depression. This episode has no symptoms of mania and does not correspond to other diagnostic criteria. If one of the following symptoms exists, the possibility of an endogenous depressive psychosis must be considered: (1) sluggish mental functioning; (2) early awakening and symptoms more severe in the morning compared with afternoon; (3) if body weight has clearly dropped and it is not due to a somatic disease; (4) if internal organ function is reduced; (5) self-guilt; (6) if there is serious suicidal behavior; (7) if there are any delusions or hallucination; and (8) if patient cannot manage on his own.

These criteria disclose the strong influence of DSM-III and particularly British diagnostic criteria which label severe depression "psychotic." Few psychiatrists in China are likely to use precisely these criteria, but many others are hard at work constructing diagnostic criteria that similarly put DSM-III, ICD-9, and other Western diagnostic criteria in a peculiarly Chinese arrangement. Using these criteria, together with those he developed for neurasthenia (see chapter 1), Xu (n.d.) diagnosed seven of forty-two neurotic patients as suffering from depression, and twenty-five as suffering from neurasthenia. Thus, he claims to demonstrate that there is more depression than has previously been diagnosed in China, though not nearly as much as in the West or as Westerners think there is in China, and that depression and neurasthenia can be distinguished. In another study in the PRC, Zhong Youbin (1985) diagnosed 6 percent of 142 neurasthenic cases as endogenous depression.

7 The cross-cultural material in this section is revised and adapted from the introductory chapter in Kleinman and Good (1985).

8 Shweder's critique can be leveled against attempts by European phenomenologists to write phenomenological accounts of symptoms and illness. See, for example, Buytendijk (1960, 1974), who describes pain and other physiological conditions in terms strongly influenced by Christian values and Western thought that are unlikely to be generalizable cross-culturally.

9 The Swiss psychiatrist Angst (1973:270) suggests that on balance cultural differences may significantly outweigh shared dimensions of the depressive experience. His summary is worth quoting in full:

The results of research undertaken to date on the culture-dependence of the symptomatology indicate, in fact, not only that severely psychotic depressive states suggestive of endogenous depression are very rare, but also that culture-dependent influences affect such symptoms as suicidal tendencies, apathy, inhibition, retardation, agitation, and the facial expression worn by the depressed patient (as exemplified, for instance, by the occurrence of so-called "smiling" depression in Thailand). Further symptoms subject to such influences include: feelings of guilt which—though certainly encountered in Christians, and to some extent also in the Moslem and Japanese societies—are hardly ever met with in other cultures; hypochondriasis; all forms of delusions. . . and, finally, also hallucinations. A wide variety of depressive symptoms are thus culture-dependent.

CHAPTER 3

1 As defined here, somatization must not be confused with somatization disorder in DSM-III. The latter is a gloss for hysteria: a chronic disorder commencing in late adolescence or early adulthood associated with a large number of physical complaints affecting many of the body's organ systems for which pathological lesions usually cannot be found.

2 Bloom's (1981) linguistic analysis of cognitive schemas in Chinese culture that support concrete reality-centered discourse over theoretical discourse offers an analogy of how a related culturally constituted perceptual style and cognitive schema may underpin the discourse of somatic amplification.

3 Kirmayer (1984), in an exhaustive review of somatization, argues that too much attention has been placed on the cognitive basis of somatization and not enough on genesis of bodily idioms and metaphors out of the direct effect of interpersonal interaction on bodily experience. Such interaction, including nonverbal ones, he reasons, may form the mediating processes between cultural values and bodily experience. This suggestive line of analysis is quite in keeping with discussion in this book of the mediating effect of local systems of power relationships linking macrosocial forces to somatization (see this chapter and chapter 6). This mediating function clearly has cognitive *and* noncognitive aspects. Unfortunately Kirmayer's review appeared after this chapter and most of this book were written, and hence I am unable to comment in detail on its many interesting points. But students of somatization are well advised to read Kirmayer's essay, which includes an excellent bibliography and critical commentary on the major contributions to this quickly expanding subject.

4 These two examples were given me by my former colleagues Professors Charles Keyes and E. Valentine Daniel, respectively.

5 Ironically, in an edited volume entitled *Masked Depression,* thereby connoting dualism, the Swiss psychiatrist Angst (1973), has made a similar anti-dualistic point, arguing that what we see as central in depression in the West (psychological complaints) are an artifact, and that what is in fact central is the basic bodily experience of which the psychological complaints are a particular, embodied part. For a non-Cartesian view of the phenomenology of embodied experience of emotions and illness, see also Buytendijk (1974).

CHAPTER 4

1 The data presented in this chapter are adapted from Kleinman (1982).

2 Because I regard hypochondriasis as a symptom constellation, a common form of somatizing that is either part of a primary psychiatric disorder (for example, major depressive disorder, panic disorder, somatization disorder) or of socially learned illness behavior (for example, chronic pain syndrome, cf. Pilowsky 1978 on pain as abnormal illness behavior) and not a disorder on its own, I did not specifically diagnose patients as suffering from this problem. Hence the diagnosis does not appear in table 4 with other DSM-III diagnoses. But as table 15 discloses, 51 percent of the ninety-three cases with all forms of depression had hypochondriacal preoccupation, including disease fears and bodily preoccupation. Since virtually all these patients also had somatization and persistent pursuit of medical care, they would make the DSM-III criteria for hypochondriasis. However, it seems more availing to me to view disease fears as a specific mode of somatizing, since just about every somatizer has the other characteristics attributed by DSM-III's authors to hypochondriasis. In this respect one might regard such cases as a particular style of phobic (or hypochondriacal) somatization associated with depression, or as a hypochondriacal form of acute, subacute, or chronic somatization (Rosen et al. 1982). A point in favor of the first view is that many of the patients

in our sample with hypochondriacal fears experienced decrease in these fears as part of their general symptom improvement after treatment with tricyclic antidepressants, suggesting that the hypochondriasis was secondary to their major depressive disorder.

Although we did not initially assess patients for post-traumatic stress disorder, retrospectively when we analyzed patient's symptom histories using the DSM-III diagnosis for this disorder none of our patients made the criteria for PTSD as a primary diagnosis, though twelve had various of the core symptoms. I do not report a figure here for PTSD because these were post hoc judgments, and hence invalid. We may well have underestimated symptoms in our initial evaluation.

3 This structure is being replaced by a six-floor modern building scheduled to be built beginning in October 1985, which will be a significant symbolic as well as an instrumental improvement for psychiatry. It will house the department of psychiatry as well as a Center for Psychiatric Research that includes both biological psychiatry and behavioral medicine research groups, and the clinics, among which is a special clinic for affective disorders!

4 See DSM-III diagnostic criteria for melancholia in chap. 2, note 1.

5 See note 1 above.

6 Two-thirds of patients achieved daily doses of 150 mg of Amitriptyline, Imipramine, or Doxepin, while the rest were roughly evenly split between patients who took more and those who took less than this amount.

CHAPTER 5

1 The data presented in this chapter were first published in Kleinman and Kleinman (1985).

2 It is unclear what our patients meant by psychotherapy, since we did not explore this concept with them. The kind of psychotherapy Chinese psychiatrists mean when they use the term to refer to their practices in the PRC is a very brief, highly directed, supportive therapy that emphasizes suggestion, moral exhortation, and heart-to-heart talks *(tanxin)*. *Xuexi* (study), as we have noted, conveys the Confucian idea of perfecting one's character, reforming one's thoughts, developing self-control, and undergoing self-criticism to improve one's attitude and conduct. *Tanxin* and *xuexi* are what Chinese psychiatrists usually mean when they use the term *psychotherapy*. As T. Y. Lin (1986) notes, they expect such interventions to illuminate the origin and nature of the patient's problem, to develop the patient's social conscience and motivation to improve himself, and to reintegrate the patient into society as a member of a group (family and *danwei*). A very different notion than the ideas of individuation and personal exploration that characterize most psychotherapies in the West, but one wholly in keeping with China's millennial sociocentric value orientation.

3 This survey was completed with the help of Dr. Shi Zuorong and his colleagues in the department of internal medicine, Second Affiliated Hospital, Hunan Medical College.

4 The study was conducted by Jennifer Haas, a Harvard medical student, working in Chinese, under our supervision with Dr. Huang Nangda, lecturer, department of psychiatry; Dr. Liu Shixie, instructor, department of psychiatry; and Dr. Chen Xuechin, assistant director, department of internal medicine, Second Affiliated Hospital, Hunan Medical College. Although the research design called for selection of consecutive cases, whose informed consent was solicited, from the medical outpatient clinic, Jennifer Haas noted that a few patients with chronic pain appeared to self-select to participate, thus confounding sample selection.

5 Women in many societies seem to be at greater risk for somatization (cf. for Taiwan, Kleinman 1980; for Hong Kong, Lee 1981; for Japan, Lock n.d.; for Mexico, Finkler 1985; for India, Nichter 1981; for Saudi Arabia, Racy 1980; for Qatar, El-Islam 1985; for the United States, Leventhal et al. 1982). While a number of explanations of this finding have been advanced (greater willingness to openly express distress, higher rates of depression and certain other

psychiatric disorders, greater resort to medical treatment settings), these seem to vary some-what for different societies. What does not seem to vary very much is the situation of relative powerlessness that women find themselves in cross-culturally. We advert to this explanation in chapter 7 to interpret the findings from our Hunan studies.

CHAPTER 6

1 Cases 1–3 and 13 are revised and, in several instances, expanded accounts of patients whose case histories originally appeared in Kleinman (1982). Cases 4 and 9–12 are adapted from Kleinman and Kleinman (1985).

2 Because of the difficulties which youth experience finding employment in China, as a result of an extremely tight job market and the large number of those finishing school each year, work units allow senior workers to take early retirement and transfer their jobs to their children. The employment situation is such that few have an opportunity to change type of work or even take up different jobs in the same work setting. The job a person starts off with is likely to be the one from which he or she will retire. There is serious unemployment and under-employment for adolescents and young adults.

3 Class background in the People's Republic, which in the past strongly influenced one's life chances, is inherited from a child's father, while rural or urban residence is inherited from the mother. When the father is dead, the class background of the person providing financial support for the child determines the class of the child (Potter 1983). Since the end of the Cultural Revolution the government of China has decreed that class background no longer can be used in assessing a person's suitability for entering university, or the party, or a particular job.

4 During the Cultural Revolution millions of Chinese adolescents left their urban middle schools and were rusticated in rural communes, often remote and poor ones, where they were expected to engage in agricultural labor and learn from the peasants. Adjustment to conditions of rural life was difficult for urban adolescents, who lacked experience or often even appreciation of the drudgingly difficult routine of rural life. Alternatively, adjustment of rural peasants to urban students was also difficult, especially when these students were seen as a drain on the limited and already oversubscribed resources of the commune. The stage was set for a culture-wide crisis that has captured the imagination of creative writers in China (cf. Chen 1978; Link 1983; Barme and Lee 1979) and occupied central stage in the biographies of Chinese expatriates (Frolic 1981; Liang and Shapiro 1983).

5 From a biomedical perspective it is hardly likely that the congenital abnormality resulted from Comrade Yen's actions during the pregnancy. But her guilt over her desire to terminate the pregnancy is fed as well by traditional Chinese ethnomedical beliefs that the thoughts, moods, and behaviors of the mother during pregnancy can symbolically impress themselves on the growing fetus.

6 Class differences, or perhaps more accurately social stratification and inequality, remained in China after Liberation. Political and military cadres became an elite class. But with the exception of the Cultural Revolution, intellectuals have also viewed themselves (and been viewed by others) as higher status than workers and peasants. The hierarchy of social status has become more visible in the past few years, as great emphasis has been placed on the role of technical experts in China's modernization. A related force at present is the increasing differential in wealth in the countryside and cities, among all segments of the population, as some families (the so-called 10,000 Yuan families) prosper much more than others, so that stratification by income and material goods becomes more conspicious.

7 In traditional Chinese medical theory the individual's constitution is prone to imbalances in the body's harmony between symbolically "hot" and "cold" constituents. Imbalances can

affect personality, behavior, and health. Illnesses, then, may be the result of an excess of hot or cold constituents. Treatment involves righting the balance by changing diet and by ingesting tonics and medicines to increase the constituents of the opposite polarity. Hot/cold humoral theories of disease have been shown by anthropologists to be present in the popular beliefs of Asia, South America, and Europe.

8 It also could be that the hopelessness central to the depressive experience distorted patients' memories of the Cultural Revolution, so that they exaggerated how bad it was. Interviews with patients who were no longer depressed and with many Chinese who were not patients about their experiences during the Cultural Revolution convince me that this is not a confounding factor.

9 See notes on post-traumatic stress syndrome, chap. 4.

CHAPTER 7

1 We learned of several cases in China outside of our samples where patients bribed physicians for authorizing leave-taking or changing jobs. In our samples, out of more than 150 subjects, only in five cases (3 percent) were we able to establish that patients participated in such a medical "back door." But given the persistent problem of the "back door" in China, and the difficulty patients might have felt openly discussing this illegal practice with a foreigner in a medical setting, this may be a serious underestimate of the problem. In several of our cases a kind of bartering took place for short periods of sick leave, in one case two weeks for a pair of shoes and in another the same time for various items of food.

2 In a remarkable and quite comprehensive article on the philosophy of medicine in China from 1930 to 1980, Qiu Renzong (1982), a philosopher at the Chinese Academy of Social Sciences in Beijing, shows that among medical philosophers and theoreticians the discourse on disease and mind/body relations is a great deal more complex and discriminating than what I have described as the views of practitioners and patients. Qiu notes that the ascendancy of Pavlov's ideas in the 1950s reflected both the importance of Russian influence at that time as well as the ideological association of Pavlovian theory with the legitimated dialectic materialism that had become the basis of medical philosophy in China. He shows as well that the converse of this influence was the criticism of Virchow's cellular pathology, Freud's psychology, Mendel and Morgan's genetics, and Galton's eugenics as "bourgeois idealism." This article demonstrates that formal metamedical theory in China has moved well beyond vulgar Marxism, but it makes one wonder how far the views of patients and practitioners have changed. Qiu discusses his own views "that psychological activity is not only dependent upon matter on the levels of organism, organ and molecule, but also itself [sic] a form of matter movement. Thus we can change human psychological state and behavior by material means."

I believe this notion of the material basis of psychological processes, illness, and treatment is shared by a number of Chinese psychiatrists who follow dialectic materialist philosophy. But whereas Qiu Renzong goes on to argue that the identity theory of psychology and physiology is incorrect, since it fails to recognize the effect of mind on physiology and of the social world on mind, and therefore interactionism is a preferable philosophical position, I am not at all sure that psychiatrists in China share this view. Rather they may find their materialist, somatopsychic position more acceptable because it is supported by the shared physicalist value orientation of biomedical, traditional Chinese medical and popular Marxist paradigms. This is an important topic for ethnographic research on the practical functioning epistemology of China's psychiatrists. This culturally constituted common sense clinical epistemology is more influential, I believe, than formal medical philosophy in determining the theoretical foundation of Chinese psychiatry. The same is true of American psychiatry.

3 Somatization of psychiatric disorders like major depressive disorder or anxiety disorders may

not be given a psychiatric diagnosis in China for another reason as well. The threshold for symptom recognition as depression or anxiety may be higher, and therefore mild and perhaps even some moderate cases will go undiagnosed. I do not believe that this explains why most cases are not diagnosed, but I do think it may be a contributing factor. Indeed, the cultural tendency to differentially attend to and amplify somatic symptoms, which I regard as operating in lay and professional circles, doubtless results in a tendency only to recognize marked expressions of psychopathology.

4 Carr (1978) develops the concept of culturally constructed and socially legitimated final common behavioral pathways in his analysis of culture-bound illnesses, and I would extend his analysis to all illness experience.

5 El-Islam (1975) describes a pattern of somatization among women in an Arabian Gulf society that has certain resemblances to the neurasthenia I have described in Hunan, both in symptomatology and in social uses, though he too describes core cultural meanings of the syndrome that are particularly salient in the Qatari community where he practiced. Cross-cultural comparisons of similarities and differences in neurasthenia-like forms of somatization would be of great interest.

6 As already noted, the small sample size makes us cautious generalizing to the situation in China as a whole, though prior research by us and by others (Kleinman and Mechanic 1981; and studies reviewed in Lin, Kleinman, Lin 1981), lends support to the limited quantitative findings from the study reported in this paper. The fact that the control group of twenty-five non-neurasthenic neurotic patients in the psychiatry clinic experienced few job changes in a three-year period, however, makes us hesitant to extend all of our conclusions to non-neurasthenic somatization patients in China, though we think some are probably valid.

7 The China scholar Anne Thurston (1985), following the psychiatrist Robert Lifton, regards some of the experiences of those psychically hurt in the Cultural Revolution as instances of post-traumatic stress syndrome (PTSS). Although we did not employ this diagnosis during our field study, several of our patients showed a few of the classic symptoms: recurrent and intrusive recollections of the traumatic event, recurrent dreams about it, feeling as if it were reoccuring, numbing of responsiveness to the external world, estrangement, constricted affect, avoidance, and survivor's guilt. But most did not, and none made the diagnostic criteria for the disorder. It may be that PTSS is more common in the general population, as a relatively minor form of psychopathology outside of psychiatric and medical clinics, but it will require a population-based epidemiological survey to determine this. What we can say is that some of our patients experienced chronic grief reactions or recurrence of grief of a disabling kind as a result of experience in the Cultural Revolution. At times a double grieving occurred in which a present loss generated bereavement for earlier losses in the Cultural Revolution that could not be fully grieved then.

Other sources paint in less technical and more personal terms the same portrait of traumatic human suffering during the Cultural Revolution: see Liang Heng and Judy Shapiro (1983) who provide a moving Hunanese case, and Frolic (1979).

David Mechanic (personal communication) suggests that the Cultural Revolution may not have actually created an increased prevalence of depression. He argues that it may have become widely used in the 1980s because it is a publicly acceptable explanation. In the absence of pre- and post-Cultural Revolution incidence data on depression, we cannot know whether this is true. Our hunch is that the Cultural Revolution may have increased the incidence of major depression, post-traumatic stress disorder, and other mental disorders with a strong psychosocial causal component. But we concur with Mechanic that use of the Cultural Revolution as a causal attribution has occurred for the reason he mentions. Brown and Harris (1978: 78) make the same point under the rubric "reworking the past." This process of retrospective rationalization has also been discussed by Amerisingham (1980) for a non-Western society. She refers to it as narratization of illness events. Retrospective narratization to make sense of illness experience in terms of life course and circumstances is a common occurence worldwide and a major source of illness meanings (Kleinman, in press).

8 It was not feasible to determine whether major depressive disorder or anxiety disorders were a more important source of somatization in particular cases (cf. Good and Kleinman, 1985). It is plausible to assume that their relative contribution as the template for somatic amplification varied for different types of somatization (Beiser 1985). This is a topic that deserves careful assessment in future field research. Since our samples are treated samples and do not come from a population survey, it is reasonable to suspect that depression and anxiety are less important in the generation of somatic amplification syndromes in the general population, where these disorders are less prevalent. An indication that this hypothesis seems reasonable is our finding that on follow-up for a significant minority of cases no mental illness could be detected even though somatization persisted.

9 China's aborted Anti–Spiritual Pollution Campaign began with criticism of a leading cadre's assertion that alienation was legitimate in the Communist state. This enlightened viewpoint was swiftly criticized and recanted. Obviously the idea is still regarded as too threatening by China's leaders. But it is a sign of changing times that articles in the Chinese journal *Medical Philosophy* have appeared discussing social pathology, and research is being published in the PRC on social stressors and social problems.

EPILOGUE

1 In the People's Republic intervention for some psychosocial problems seems to be effectively conducted by street and neighborhood committees and by work units and communes (non-compliance with public health programs, crime, protection and rehabilitation of the physically and mentally handicapped, care for childless, aged, and so forth). But there are other problems, including those illustrated in the preceding chapters, that are not well handled by these institutions. Psychosocial interventions, furthermore, are often haphazard and undertaken on a very part-time basis by individuals with little or no specific training. More troublesome still, the very agencies of the state that work closely with police and party to extend propaganda, surveillance, and social control to society's smallest units, are the ones responsible for activities that require confidentiality, protection of individual rights, and an independent, critical assessment of local conditions. For these reasons, these institutions are not the appropriate ones to identify and respond to the kinds of human misery reviewed in these pages. Rather a strong case can be assembled for developing the helping professions as a parallel, at least partially autonomous, social structure that is less bureaucratized, less central to the apparatuses of state power, and thereby not part of local systems of social control. These professions could help mitigate the tendency toward oppression and abuse of centralized power that communist societies exhibit, while making available a more independent, expert source of community interventions.

Professionals should be accountable to local communities, but should stand outside of the state system of political and police control. They should be accountable as well to their professions. Though there is always the danger that in professionalizing the response to social problems the solutions offered will be overly technical and narrow; this danger is offset by the opportunity professionalization offers to identify and intervene on behalf of problems that, in totalitarian societies especially, are otherwise off-limits to criticism and change.

2 I purposefully do not delimit the boundaries of local systems (the micro or local context of relationships of power). For analytic purposes, the family, social network, or workplace may be the appropriate setting for analysis. On other occasions a particular institution may be more appropriate, or even an entire community. The boundary can be adjusted depending on the question under study and on-the-ground realities of the case at hand.

3 S. F. Moore (1978:48–53, 54–59) argues that local contexts of social negotiation may be more
   or less autonomous of determinative macrosocial influence. She insists that frequently such
   contexts are semi-autonomous, meaning that human agency (individual judgement and action)
   plays a substantial role in influencing local contexts through processes of negotiation that
   she defines as "regularizing" and "adjusting" social interaction. Our data support this perspective by providing case examples oscillating between a major influence of individual experience on social problems and the determination of those problems by societal forces.

Glossary

anxiety	*jiaolüzheng*	焦慮症
anxiety disorders	*jiaolüxing zhangai*	焦慮性障碍
chronic pain syndrome	*manxing tengtung zonghezheng*	慢性疼痛綜合症
depressive affect	*yiyouxing qingxu*	抑郁性情緒
heart-to-heart talk	*tanxin*	談心
hypochondriasis	*yibingzheng*	疑病症
hysteria	*yibing*	癔病
major depressive disorder	*zhongxing yiyuxing zhangai*	重性抑郁性障碍
melancholia or depression	*youyuzheng, yiyuzheng*	憂郁症, 抑郁症
neurasthenia	*shenjing shuairuo*	神經衰弱
neurosis	*shenjing guannengzheng*	神經官能症
neurotic depression	*shenjingzhengxing yiyu*	神經症性抑郁
somatization	*qutihua*	軀體化
study	*xuexi*	學習

Bibliography

Akiskal, H. S., and W. T. McKinney. 1973. Depressive disorders: Toward a unified hypothesis. *Science* 182:20–28.

Albrecht, G., and J. A. Levy. 1984. A sociological perspective of physical disability. *In* J. Ruffini, ed., *Advances in Medical Social Science,* 2:45-106. Boston: Gordon and Breach.

Alexander, L. 1982. Illness maintenance and the new American sick role. *In* N. Chrisman and T. Maretzki, eds., *Clinically Applied Anthropology,* pp. 351–68. Dordrecht: D. Reidel.

American Psychiatric Association. 1952. *Diagnostic & Statistical Manual,* Edition 1. Washington, D.C.: American Psychiatric Association.

———. 1968. *Diagnostic & Statistical Manual,* Edition 2. Washington, D.C.: American Psychiatric Assocation.

———. 1980. *Diagnostic & Statistical Manual,* Edition 3. Washington, D.C.: American Psychiatric Association.

Amerisingham, L. R. 1980. Movement among healers in Sri Lanka. *Culture, Medicine and Psychiatry* 4:71–92.

Angst, J. 1973. Masked depression viewed from the cross-cultural viewpoint. *In* P. Kielholz, ed., *Masked Depression,* pp. 269–74. Bern: Hans Huber.

Armstrong, D. 1983. *Political Anatomy of the Body.* Cambridge: Cambridge University Press.

Arney, W. R., and B. J. Bergen. 1984. *Medicine and the Management of Living.* Chicago: University of Chicago Press.

Averill, J. R. 1980. Emotion and anxiety: Sociocultural, biological and psychological determinants. *In* A. O. Rorty, ed., *Explaining Emotion,* pp. 37–72. Berkeley: University of California Press.

Balint, M. 1957. *The Doctor, His Patient and the Illness.* New York: International Universities Press.

Ballet, G. 1908. *Neurasthenia.* London: Henry Kimpton.

Bandura, A. 1977. *Social Learning Theory.* Englewood Cliffs, N. J.: Prentice-Hall.

Barme, G., and B. Lee, eds. 1979. *The Wounded: New Stories of the Cultural Revolution, 1977–78.* Hong Kong: Joint Publishing Company.

Barsky, A., and G. Klerman. 1983. Overview: Hypochondriasis, bodily complaints and somatic styles. *American Journal of Psychiatry* 140:273–83.

Bazzoui, W. 1970. Affective disorders in Iraq. *British Journal of Psychiatry* 117:195–203.

Beard, G. M. 1881. *American Nervousness.* New York: G. P. Putnam.

————. 1880. *A Practical Treatise on Nervous Exhaustion (Neurasthenia)*. New York: William Wood.

Beck, A. T. 1971. Cognition, affect and psychopathology. *Archives of General Psychiatry* 24:495–500.

————. 1976. *Cognitive Therapy and the Emotional Disorders*. New York: International Universities Press.

————et al. 1979. *Cognitive Therapy of Depression*. New York: Guilford Press.

Beeman, W. 1985. Dimensions of dysphoria. *In* A. Kleinman and B. J. Good, eds., *Culture and Depression*, pp. 216–43. Berkeley: University of California Press.

Beer, G. 1984. The language of discovery. *Times Literary Supplement,* no. 4257, 2 November 1984, pp. 1253–56.

Beiser, M. 1985. A study of depression among traditional Africans, urban North Americans, and Southeast Asian Refugees. *In* A. Kleinman and B. J. Good, eds., *Culture and Depression*, pp. 272–98. Berkeley: University of California Press.

Berkowitz, M. 1981. Social policy and the disabled. *In Social Security and Disability: Issues in Policy Research*. Geneva: International Social Security Association.

Binitie, A. 1975. A factor-analytical study of depression across African and European cultures. *British Journal of Psychiatry* 127:559–63.

Blacking, J., ed. 1977. *The Anthropology of the Body*. New York: Academic Press.

Bloom, A. 1981. *The Linguistic Shaping of Thought*. Hillsdale, N.J.: Earlbaum.

Brown, G., and T. Harris. 1978. *The Social Origins of Depression*. New York: Free Press.

Bullock, M. 1980. *An American Transplant: The Rockefeller Foundation and Peking Union Medical College*. Berkeley: University of California Press.

Burton, R. 1977 [1621]. *The Anatomy of Melancholy*. New York: Vintage.

Buytendijk, F. J. J. 1961. *Pain*. London: Hutchinson.

————. 1974. *Prolegomena to an Anthropological Physiology*. Pittsburgh: Duquesne University Press.

Bynum, W. F. 1983. Psychiatry in its historical context. *In* M. Shepherd and O. L. Zangwill, eds., *Handbook of Psychiatry, 1: General Psychopathology*, pp. 11–38. Cambridge: Cambridge University Press.

Carr, J. 1978. Ethnobehaviorism and the culture-bound syndromes: The case of amok. *Culture, Medicine and Psychiatry* 2:269–93.

Carr, J., and P. Vitaliano. 1985. Theoretical implications of converging research on depression and culture-bound syndromes. *In* A. Kleinman and B. J. Good, eds., *Culture and Depression*, pp. 244–66. Berkeley: University of California Press.

Cacioppa, J., and R. Petty, eds. 1983. *Social Psychophysiology*. New York: Guilford.

Carroll, B. et al. 1981. A specific laboratory test for the diagnosis of melancholia. *Archives of General Psychiatry* 38:15–22.

Carson, T. P., and H. E. Adams. 1981. Affective disorders: behavioral perspectives. *In* S. Turner et al., eds., *Handbook of Clinical Behavioral Therapy*. New York: Wiley.

Chang, Y. H. et al. 1975. Frigophobia. *Bulletin of the Chinese Society of Neurology and Psychiatry*. (Taipei) 1(2):13.

Chao, Yuanfang. 1886. [ca. 610 A.D.]. *Zhubing yuan hou zonglun* (Treatise on the Courses and Symptoms of Diseases). Hubei: Hubei guanshuju zhongkanben.

Chatel, J., and R. Peele. 1971. The concept of neurasthenia. *International Journal of Psychiatry* 9:36–49.

Chen, Jo-hsi. 1978. *The Execution of Mayor Yin and Other Stories from the Great Proletarian Cultural Revolution.* Bloomington: Indiana University Press.

Ch'eng Chih-fan and Chang Ch'i-shan. 1962. Some early records of nervous and mental disease in traditional Chinese medicine. *Chinese Medical Journal* 81:55–59.

Cheung, F. et al. 1981. Somatization among Chinese depressives in general practice. *International Journal of Psychiatry in Medicine* 10:361–74.

Cheung, F., and B. Lao. 1982. Situational variations of help-seeking behavior among Chinese patients. *Comprehensive Psychiatry* 23:252–62.

Cihai (Sea of Words). 1969 [1938]. Taipei: Zhonghua shuju (reprint of the original Shanghai edition).

Cihai Xinpian (Sea of Words, new edition). 1965. Hong Kong: Zhonghua shuju

Chin, R., and A. L. S. Chin. 1969. *Psychological Research in Communist China, 1949–1966.* Cambridge: MIT Press.

China Medical Journal. 1923. Current medical literature: Neurasthenia. *China Medical Journal* 37:522–23.

Chinese-English Terminology of Traditional Chinese Medicine (Han-Ying shuang jie: Chang yong zhong mingci shuyu). 1983. Changsha: Hunan Science and Technology Press.

Chrzanowski, G. 1971. An obsolete diagnosis. *International Journal of Psychiatry* 9:54–56.

Climent, C. et al. 1980. Mental health in primary health care. *WHO Chronicle* 34:231–36.

Collyer, J. 1979. Psychosomatic illness in a solo family practice. *Psychosomatics* 20:762–67.

Comaroff, J. 1985. *Body of Power, Spirit of Resistance.* Chicago: University of Chicago Press.

Congressional Budget Office. 1982. *Diability Compensation: Current Issues and Options for Change.* Washington, D.C.: USGPO for Congressional Budget Office, the Congress of the United States.

Coyne, J. 1976. Toward an interactional description of depression. *Psychiatry* 39:28–40.

Csordas, T. 1984. The rhetoric of transformation in ritual healing. *Culture, Medicine and Psychiatry* 7:333–76.

Davis-Freedman, D. 1983. *Long Lives.* Cambridge: Harvard University Press.

Demers, R. et al. 1980. An exploration of the depth and dimensions of illness behavior. *Journal of Family Practice* 11:1085–92.

Depue, R. A., ed. 1979. *The Psychobiology of the Depressive Disorders.* New York: Academic Press.

DeVries, M. et al. 1983. *The Use and Abuse of Medicine.* New York: Praeger.

Drinka, G. F. 1984. *The Birth of Neurosis: Myth, Malady and the Victorians.* New York: Simon and Shuster.

Douglas, M. 1966. *Purity and Danger.* Harmondsworth: Penguin.

———. 1973. *Natural Symbols.* Harmondsworth: Penguin.

Dudgeon, J. 1871. Report on Peking. *Medical Reports, Imperial Maritime Customs*. Shanghai: Imperial Maritime Customs. 11(6):73–82.

Durkheim, E. 1952 [1930]. *Suicide*. London: Routledge and Kegan Paul.

Ebigbo, P. O. 1982. Development of a culture specific (Nigeria) screening scale of somatic complaints indicating psychiatric distress. *Culture, Medicine and Psychiatry* 6:29–43.

Editorial. 1966. The need for intensive research on treatment and prevention of neurasthenia. *Chinese Journal of Neurology and Psychiatry* 10(2).

Eisenberg, L. 1977. Disease and illness: Distinctions between professional and popular ideas of sickness. *Culture, Medicine and Psychiatry* 1:9–24.

Ekman, P. 1980. Biological and cultural contributions to body and facial movement in the expression of emotions. *In* A. O. Rorty, ed., *Explaining Emotions*, pp. 73–102. Berkeley: University of California Press.

El-Islam, M. F. 1975. Culture-bound neurosis in Qatari women. *Social Psychiatry* 10:25.

Engel, G. L. 1977. The need for a new medical model: A challenge for biomedicine. *Science* 196:129–36.

Errington, F. K. 1984. *Manners and Meaning in West Sumatra: The Social Context of Consciousness*. New Haven: Yale University Press.

Feinstein, J. 1984. *Becoming William Jones*. Ithaca: Cornell University Press.

Feuer, L. S. 1959. *Basic Writings on Politics and Philosophy: Karl Marx and Friedrich Engels*. Garden City, N. Y.: Anchor Books.

Figlio, K. 1982. How does illness mediate social relations? *In* P. Wright and A. Treacher, eds., *The Problem of Medical Knowledge*. Edinburgh: University of Edinburgh Press.

Finkler, K. 1985. Symptomatic differences between the sexes in rural Mexico. *Culture, Medicine and Psychiatry* 9(1):27–58.

Fischer-Homberger, E. 1983. Neurosis; Hypochondriasis. *In* M. Shepherd and O. L. Zangwill, eds., *Handbook of Psychiatry. 1: General Psychopathology*, pp. 40–43, 46–58. Cambridge: Cambridge University Press.

Ford, C. V. 1982. *The Somatizing Disorders: Illness as a Way of Life*. New York: Elsevier Biomedical.

Fordyce, W. 1976. *Behavior Methods for Chronic Pain and Illness*. St. Louis: Mosby.

Foucault, M. 1973. *The Birth of the Clinic: An Archaeology of Medical Perception*. New York: Pantheon.

Foundations of Psychiatry. 1981. Vol. 1 in *Comprehensive Psychiatry (Jingshenyixue congshu diyijuan: Jingshenyixue jichu)*. Edited by the Departments of Psychiatry of the Sichuan, Hunan, Beijing Medical Colleges and the Shanghai and Nanjing Preventive Medicine Institutes. Changsha: Hunan Science and Technology Press.

Fox, R., and P. Swazey. 1984. Medical morality is not bioethics—medical ethics in China and the United States. *Perspectives in Biology and Medicine* 27(3):336–60.

Frank, J. 1974 [1961]. *Persuasion and Healing*. New York: Schocken.

Frolic, M. 1979. *Mao's People*. Cambridge: Harvard University Press.

Geertz, C. 1983. *Local Knowledge*. New York: Basic Books.

———. 1984. Anti anti-relativism. *American Anthropologist* 86(2):263–78.

Gehlen, A. 1980 [1957]. *Man in the Age of Technology*. New York: Columbia University Press.

Gluzman, S. 1982. Fear of freedom: Psychological decompensation or existential phenomenon? *American Journal of Psychiatry*. 139:57–61.

Goldberg, D. 1979. Detection and assessment of emotional disorders in a primary care setting. *International Journal of Mental Health*. 8:30–48.

Good, B. J. 1977. The heart of what's the matter: The semantics of illness in Iran. *Culture, Medicine and Psychiatry* 1:25–28.

————, and M. J. D. Good. 1981. The meaning of symptoms. *In* L. Eisenberg and A. Kleinman, eds., *The Relevance of Social Science for Medicine*. Dordrecht: D. Reidel.

————, M. J. D. Good, and R. Moradi. 1985. The interpretation of Iranian depressive illness and dysphoric affect. *In* A. Kleinman and B. J. Good, eds., *Culture and Depression*, pp. 369–428. Berkeley: University of California Press.

————, and A. Kleinman. 1985. Culture and anxiety. *In* A. H. Tuma and J. P. Maser, eds., *Anxiety and the Anxiety Disorders*. Hillsdale, N.J.: Lawrence Earlbaum.

Goodman, N. 1984. Notes on the well-made world. *Partisan Review* 51(2):276–89.

Graves, R. 1957 [1929]. *Goodbye to All That*. Garden City, N.Y.: Doubleday.

Groddeck, G. 1977 [1925]. *The Meaning of Illness: Selected Psychoanalytic Writings*. New York: International Universities Press.

Hahn, R., and A. Kleinman. 1983. Belief as pathogen, belief as medicine. *Medical Anthropology Quarterly* 14(4):3, 16–19.

Hankin, J., and J. S. Oktay. 1979. Mental disorder and primary care. *In* NIMH Series D, no. 7. DHEW Publication no. ADM 78–661. Washington, D.C.: USGPO.

Harwood, A., ed. 1981. *Ethnicity and Medical Care*. Cambridge: Harvard University Press.

Haynes, R. B., D. W. Taylor, and D. L. Sackett, eds. 1979. *Compliance in Health Care*. Baltimore: Johns Hopkins University Press.

Heelas, P., and A. Lock. 1981. *Indigenous Psychologies: The Anthropology of the Self*. New York: Academic Press.

Helman, C. 1984. Disease and pseudo-disease. *In* R. Hahn and A. Gaines, eds., *Physicians of Western Medicine: Anthropological Approaches*, pp. 293–332. Dordrecht: D. Reidel.

————. 1985. Psyche, soma and society: The social construction of psychosomatic disease. *Culture, Medicine and Psychiatry;* 9:1–26.

Henderson, G. E., and M. S. Cohen. 1984. *The Chinese Hospital: A Socialist Work Unit*. New Haven: Yale University Press.

Hockschild, A. 1983. *The Managed Heart*. Berkeley: University of California Press.

Hoeper, E. W. et al. 1979. Estimated prevalence of RDC mental disorder in primary care. *International Journal of Mental Health* 8:6–15.

Hofer, M. A. 1984. Relationships as regulators: A psychobiologic perspective on bereavment. *Psychosomatic Medicine* 46(3):183–97.

Hsu, F. L. K. 1971. Psychosocial homeostasis and *Jen:* Conceptual tools for advancing psychological anthropology. *American Anthropologist* 73:23–44.

Izard, C. 1979. Cross-cultural perspective on emotion and emotion communications. *In* H. Triandis and W. Lonner, eds., *Handbook of Cross-Cultural Psychology, 3: Basic Processes*, pp. 185–22. Boston: Allyn and Bacon.

Jackson, S. 1969. Galen: On mental disorders. *Journal of the History of the Behavioral Sciences* 5:365–84.

————. 1978. Melancholia and the waning of the humoral theory. *Journal of the History of Medicine and Allied Sciences* 33:367–76.

————. 1980. Two sufferers' perspectives on melancholia: 1690's to 1790's. *In* E. R. Wallace and L. C. Pressly, eds., *Essays in the History of Psychiatry*, pp. 58–71. Columbia: University of South Carolina Press.

————. 1985. Acedia: The sin and its relationship to sorrow and melancholia. *In* A. Kleinman and B. J. Good, eds., *Culture and Depression*, pp. 43–62. Berkeley: University of California Press.

James, W. 1981 [1890]. *The Principles of Psychology*, 2. Cambridge: Harvard University Press.

Kasahara, Y. 1974. Fear of eye-to-eye confrontation among neurotic patients in Japan. *In* T. S. Lebra and W. P. Lebra, eds., *Japanese Culture and Behavior*. Honolulu: University of Hawaii Press.

Katon, W. et al. 1982. Depression and somatization: A review, parts 1 and 2. *American Journal of Medicine* 72:127–35, 241–47.

———— et al. 1984a. The prevalence of somatization in primary care. *Comprehensive Psychiatry* 25(2):208–15.

————. 1984b. A prospective DSM-III study of 100 consecutive somatizing patients. *Comprehensive Psychiatry* 25(3):305–14.

Keefe, F. J. 1982. Behavioral assessment and treatment of chronic pain. *Journal of Counseling and Clinical Psychology* 50(6):896–911.

————et al. 1982. Behavioral assessment of chronic pain. *In* F. J. Keefe and J. A. Blumenthal, eds., *Assessment Strategies in Behavioral Medicine*. New York: Grune and Stratton.

Keyes, C. 1985. The interpretive basis of depression. *In* A. Kleinman and B. J. Good, eds., *Culture and Depression*, pp. 153–74. Berkeley: University of California Press.

Kirmayer, L. 1984. Culture, affect and somatization, parts 1 and 2. *Transcultural Psychiatric Research Review* 21(3):159–88, (4):237–62.

Kleinman, A. et al., eds. 1975. *Medicine in Chinese Cultures*. Washington, D.C.: USGPO for Fogarty International Center, NIH.

Kleinman, A. 1977. Depression, somatization and the new cross-cultural psychiatry. *Social Science and Medicine* 11:3–10.

————. 1980. Patients and Healers in the Context of Culture. Berkeley: University of California Press.

————. 1982. Neurasthenia and depression: A study of somatization and culture in China. *Culture, Medicine and Psychiatry* 6 (2):117–90.

————. 1984. *Qutihua* (Somatization). *Guowai yixue, Jingshenbingxue fence*. (Journal of Foreign Medicine, Psychiatry Section, also called the Referential Journal of Foreign Psychiatry) 11(2):65–68.

————. In press. Illness meanings and somatization. *In* S. McHugh, ed. Proceedings of the Second International Conference on Illness Behavior. N.Y.: Plenum

————, and B. J. Good, eds. 1985. *Culture and Depression*. Berkeley: University of California Press.

————, and J. Kleinman. 1985. Somatization: Interconnections among culture, depressive experience and the meanings of pain. *In* A. Kleinman and B. J. Good, eds., *Culture and Depression*, pp. 429–90. Berkeley: University of California Press.

————, and T. Y. Lin, eds. 1982. *Normal and Abnormal Behavior in Chinese Culture*. Dordrecht: D. Reidel.

————, and D. Mechanic. 1979. Some observations of mental illness and its treatment in China. *Journal of Nervous and Mental Disease* 167:267–74.

Klerman, G. 1981. The pathophysiology of depression. Menninger Prize Award Lecture, American College of Physicians Manuscript.

Kotaba, J. 1983. *Chronic Pain: Its Social Dimensions*. Beverly Hills: Sage.

Kuang, P. K. et al. 1960. Evaluation of speedy comprehensive group treatment of 87 ambulatory neurasthenic patients. *Chinese Journal of Neurology and Psychiatry* 1:12–18.

Kupfer, D., and F. Foster. 1972. Interval between onset of sleep and rapid eye movement sleep as an indicator of depression. *Lancet* 2:684.

Lamson, H. D. 1935. *Social Pathology in China*. Shanghai: The Commercial Press.

Lasch, C. 1977. *Haven in a Heartless World: The Family Beseiged*. New York: Basic Books.

Lebra, T. S. 1976. *Japanese Patterns of Behavior*. Honolulu: University of Hawaii Press.

————. 1983. Shame and guilt: A psychocultural view of the Japanese self. *Ethos* 11(2):192–209.

Lee, R. P. L. 1982. Sex roles, social status and psychiatric symptoms in urban Hong Kong. *In* A. Kleinman and T. Y. Lin, eds., *Normal and Abnormal Behavior in Chinese Culture,* pp. 273–90. Dordrecht: D. Reidel.

Leff, J. 1981. The language of emotion. *In Psychiatry around the Globe*. New York: Marcel Dekker.

Lesser, I. M. 1981. A review of the alexithymia concept. *Psychosomatic Medicine* 43:531–44.

Leventhal, H. et al. 1982. Self-regulation and the mechanisms for symptom arousal. *In* D. Mechanic, ed., *Symptoms, Illness Behavior and Help-Seeking*, pp. 55–86. New York: Prodist.

Lewis, I. M. 1971. *Ecstatic Religion*. Harmondsworth: Penguin.

Lewinsohn, P. 1974. Clinical and theoretical aspects of depression. *In* K. Calhoun et al., eds., *Innovative Treatment Methods in Psychopathology*. New York: Wiley.

Lewontin, R. C. et al. 1984. *Not in Our Genes: Biology, Ideology and Human Nature*. New York: Pantheon.

Liang, H., and J. Shapiro. 1983. *Son of the Revolution*. New York: Knopf.

Lin, C. P. et al. 1958. The speedy treatment of neurasthenia. *Chinese Journal of Neurology and Psychiatry* 5:351–56.

Lin, E. H. B. et al. 1985. Somatization among Asian refugees in primary care. *American Journal of Public Health*. 75(9):1080–84.

Lin, K. M. 1982. Traditional Chinese medical beliefs and their relevance for mental illness and psychiatry. *In* A. Kleinman and T. Y. Lin, eds., *Normal and Abnormal Behavior in Chinese Culture*. Dordrecht: D. Reidel.

————. 1983. Neuroleptic dosage for Asians. *American Journal of Psychiatry* 140 (4):490–92.

————, and A. Kleinman. 1981. Recent development of psychiatric epidemiology in China. *Culture, Medicine and Psychiatry* 5:135–43.

———— et al. 1982. Overview of mental disorders in Chinese cultures. *In* A. Kleinman and T. Y. Lin, eds., *Normal and Abnormal Behavior in Chinese Culture*. Dordrecht: D. Reidel.

Lin, T. Y. 1953. A study of the incidence of mental disorders in Chinese and other cultures. *Psychiatry* 16:313–36.

———. in press. Shaping of Chinese psychiatry in the context of politics and public health. *In* T. Y. Lin and L. Eisenberg, eds., *Mental Health Care for One Billion People*. Vancouver: University of British Columbia Press.

——— et al. 1969. Mental disorders in Taiwan 15 years later. *In* W. Caudill and T. Y. Lin, eds., *Mental Health in Asia and the Pacific*, pp. 66–91. Honolulu: East-West Center Press.

———, and L. Eisenberg, eds. In press. *Mental Health Care for One Billion People*. Vancouver: University of British Columbia Press.

Ling Ming-yu. 1984. Letter to the author of 25 April.

Link, P. 1983. *Stubborn Weeds: Popular and Controversial Chinese Literature after the Cultural Revolution*. Bloomington: Indiana University Press.

Lock, M. 1980. *East Asian Medicine in Urban Japan*. Berkeley: University of California Press.

———. 1982. Models and practice in medicine: Menopause as syndrome or life transition? *Culture, Medicine and Psychiatry* 6:261–80.

———. n.d. Protests of a good wife and wise mother: Somatization and medicalization in modern Japan. Manuscript.

Lutz, C. 1985. Depression and the translation of emotional worlds. *In* A. Kleinman and B. J. Good, eds., *Culture and Depression*, pp. 63–100. Berkeley: University of California Press.

Lyman, R. S. 1941. Presentations of some physiological systems of integration: Experimental psychology and overlap of sociology and psychiatry. Columbia, S. C.: Third Institute on Postgraduate Psychiatric Education, 18–19 April. Manuscript.

——— et al. 1939. *Social and Psychological Studies in Neuropsychiatry in China*. Peking: Henri Vetch.

McCartney, J. L. 1926. Neuropsychiatry in China. *China Medical Journal* 40:617–26.

McGuire, M. B. 1983. Words of Power: Personal empowerment and healing. *Culture, Medicine and Psychiatry* 7:221–40.

MacIntyre, A. 1981. *After Virtue*. Notre Dame: University of Notre Dame Press.

Manson, S. et al. 1985. The depressive experience in American Indian communities. *In* A. Kleinman and B. J. Good, eds., *Culture and Depression*, pp. 331–68. Berkeley: University of California Press.

Marsella, A. 1979. Depressive experience and disorder across cultures. *In* H. Triandis and J. Draguns, eds., *Handbook of Cross-Cultural Psychology*, 6, pp. 237–90. Boston: Allyn and Bacon.

——— et al. 1985. Cross-cultural studies of depressive disorders. *In* A. Kleinman and B. J. Good, eds., *Culture and Depression*. Berkeley: University of California Press.

Matthew, R. J. et al. 1981. Physical symptoms of depression. *British Journal of Psychiatry* 139:293–96.

Mechanic, D. 1972. Social psychological factors affecting the presentation of bodily complaints. *New England Journal of Medicine* 286:1132–39.

———. 1980. The experience and reporting of common physical complaints. *Journal of Health and Social Behavior* 21:146–55.

———. 1983. Adolescent health and illness behavior. *Journal of Human Stress* 9:4–13.

———. 1984. Introspection and illness behavior. Paper presented at the First International Conference on Clinical and Social Aspects of Illness Behavior, The Royal Adelaide Hospital, August 1984.

———, and A. Kleinman. 1979. Ambulatory medical care in China. *American Journal of Public Health* 70(1):62–66.

Metzger, T. 1982. Selfhood and authority in NeoConfucian China. *In* A. Kleinman and T. Y. Lin, eds., *Normal and Abnormal Behavior in Chinese Culture*, pp. 7–28. Dordrecht, Holland: D. Reidel.

Mezzich, J. E. and Raab, E. S. 1980. Depressive symptomatology across the Americas. *Archives of General Psychiatry* 37:818–23.

Minuchin, S. et al. 1978. *Psychosomatic Families*. Cambridge: Harvard University Press.

Moore, B. 1970. *Reflections on the Causes of Human Misery*. Boston: Beacon Press.

———. 1978. *Injustice: The Social Basis of Obedience and Revolt*. London: Macmillan.

———. 1984. *Privacy: Studies in Social and Cultural History*. Armonk, N.Y.: M. E. Sharpe.

Moore, S. F. 1978. *Law as Process: An Anthropological Approach*. Boston: Routledge and Kegan. Paul.

Mora, G. 1971. Antecedent to neurosis. *International Journal of Psychiatry* 9:54–56.

Muller, F. C., ed. 1893. *Handbuch der Neurasthenie*. Leipzig: F. C. W. Vogel.

Munro, D. J. 1977. *The Concept of Man in Contemporary China*. Ann Arbor: University of Michigan Press.

Murphy, H. B. M. et al. 1967. Cross-cultural inquiry into symptomatology of depression. *International Journal of Psychiatry* 3:6–15.

Myers, F. 1979. Emotions and the self. *Ethos* 7:343–70.

Nandy, A. 1983. *The Intimate Enemy: Loss and Recovery of Self under Colonialism*. Delhi: Oxford University Press.

Nathanson, C. A. 1977. Self, illness and medical care. *Social Science and Medicine* 11:13–25.

Nichter, M. 1981. Negotiation of the illness experience. *Culture, Medicine and Psychiatry* 5:5–24.

———. 1982. Idioms of distress: Alternatives in the expression of psychosocial distress. *Culture, Medicine and Psychiatry* 5:379–408.

Oakeshott, M. 1978 [1935]. *Experience and its Modes*. Cambridge: Cambridge University Press.

Obeyesekere, G. 1985. Depression, Buddhism and the work of culture in Sri Lanka. *In* A. Kleinman and B. J. Good, eds., *Culture and Depression*, pp. 134–52. Berkeley: University of California Press.

Orley, J., and J. Wing. 1975. Psychiatric disorders in two African villages. *Archives of General Psychiatry* 36:513–20.

Osgood, C. E. et al. 1975. *Cross Cultural Universals of Affective Meaning*. Urbana: University of Illinois Press.

Osterweis, M. et al. 1984. *Bereavement: Reactions, Consequences and Care*. Washington, D.C.: National Academy Press.

Parker, K. R. 1981. Field dependence and the differentiation of affective states. *British Journal of Psychiatry* 130:52–58.

Parrish, W., and M. K. Whyte. 1978. *Village and Family in Contemporary China*. Chicago: University of Chicago Press.

Parsons, C. 1984. Idioms of distress: Kinship and sickness in Tonga. *Culture, Medicine and Psychiatry* 8:71–94.

Parsons, T. 1951. *The Social System*. Glencoe, Ill.: The Free Press.

Pavlov, I. P. 1962. *Essays in Psychology and Psychiatry*. New York: The Citadel Press.

Pennebaker, J. 1982. The Psychology of Physical Symptoms. New York: Springer-Verlag.

Pennebaker, J., and J. Skelton. 1978. Psychological parameters of physical symptoms. *Personality and Social Psychology Bulletin* 4:525–30.

Pickering, G. 1974. *Creative Malady*. London: George Allen and Unwin.

Pilowsky, I. 1969. Abnormal illness behavior. *British Journal of Medical Psychology* 42:347–51.

———. 1978. A general classification of abnormal illness behavior. *British Journal of Medical Psychology* 51:131–37.

Plessner, H. 1970. *Laughing and Crying: A Study of the Limits of Human Behavior*. Evanston: Northwestern University Press.

Plough, A. 1981. Medical technology and the crisis of experience. *Social Science and Medicine* 15F:89–101.

Porkert, M. 1974. *The Theoretical Basis of Chinese Medicine*. Cambridge: Harvard University Press.

Potter, S. H. 1983. The position of peasants in modern China's social order. *Modern China* 9(4):465–99.

Psychopathologie Africaine. 1981. Special Issue: Psychiatrie et Culture. (Sections on Depression in Africa). *Psychopathologie Africaine* 13(1,2,3).

Qiu Renzong. 1982. Philosophy of medicine in China (1930–1980). *Metamedicine* 3:35–73.

Racy, J. 1980. Somatization in Saudi women. *British Journal of Psychiatry* 137:212–16.

Rao, A. V. 1973. Depressive illness and guilt in Indian culture. *Indian Journal of Psychiatry* 15:231–36.

Regier, D. et al. 1978. The de facto U.S. mental health service system. *Archives of General Psychiatry* 35:685–93.

Reynolds, D. 1976. *Morita Psychotherapy*. Berkeley: University of California Press.

Rieff, P. 1966. *The Triumph of the Therapeutic*. New York: Harper and Row.

Riesman, P. 1983. On the irrelevance of child rearing practices for the formation of personality. *Culture, Medicine and Psychiatry* 7(2):103–130.

Rin, H. 1982. *Linchuang jingshen yixue* (Clinical Psychiatry) Taipei: Maochang.

Roberts, A., and L. Reinhardt. 1980. The behavioral management of chronic pain. *Pain* 8:151–62.

Romanyshyn, R. D. 1982. *Psychological Life*. Austin: University of Texas Press.

Rosaldo, M. 1980. *Knowledge and Passion: Ilongot Notions of Self and Social Life*. Cambridge: Cambridge University Press.

Rosen, G. 1947. What is social medicine? *Bulletin of the History of Medicine* 21(5):676.

Rosen, G. et al. 1982. Somatization in family practice. *Journal of Family Practice* 14(3):493–502.

Rosenberg, C. E. 1962. The place of George M. Beard in nineteenth century psychiatry. *Bulletin of the History of Medicine* 36:245–59.

Sartorius, N. et al. 1983. *Depressive Disorders in Different Cultures*. Geneva: WHO.

Sartre, J. P. 1948. *The Emotions: Outline of a Theory*. New York: Philosophical Library.

Schieffelin, E. L. 1985. The cultural analysis of depressive affect: An example from New Guinea. *In* A. Kleinman and B. J. Good, eds., *Culture and Depression*, pp. 101–33. Berkeley: University of California Press.

Seligman, M. E. P. 1975. *Helplessness: On Depression, Development and Death*. San Francisco: Freeman.

Sethi, B. B. et al. 1973. Depression in India. *Journal of Social Psychology* 91:3–13.

Shanghai First Medical College and Zhongshan Medical College, eds. 1980. *Internal Medicine (Neikexue)*. Vol. 2. Beijing: People's Health Publishers (Jenmin Weisheng Chubanshe).

Shweder, R. A. 1985. Menstrual pollution, soul loss and the comparative study of emotions. *In* A. Kleinman and B. J. Good, eds., *Culture and Depression*, pp. 182–215. Berkeley: University of California Press.

———, and E. Bourne. 1982. Does the concept of the person vary cross culturally? *In* A. Marsella and G. White, eds., *Cultural Conceptions of Mental Health and Therapy*. Dordrecht: D. Reidel.

Sicherman, B. 1977. The uses of diagnosis: Doctors, patients and neurasthenics. *Journal of the History of Medicine and Allied Sciences* 32(1):33–54.

Simon, B. 1978. *Mind and Madness in Ancient Greece*. Ithaca: Cornell University Press.

Song Mingtong. 1936. *Shengjing shuairuozheng* (Neurasthenia). *Tong Ji yixue jikan* 6:87–91.

Starkman, M. N. et al. 1981. Depressed mood and other psychiatric manifestations of Cushing's syndrome. *Psychosomatic Medicine* 43:3–18.

Starobinski, J. 1983. Melancholia. *In* M. Shepherd and O. L. Zangwill, eds., *Handbook of Psychiatry. 1: General Psychopathology*, pp. 42–44. Cambridge: Cambridge University Press.

Stein, H. 1982. The annual cycle and the cultural nexus of health behavior. *Culture, Medicine and Psychiatry* 6:81–100.

Sternback, R. A. 1974. *Pain Patients, Traits and Treatments*. New York: Academic Press.

Stewart, D., and T. Sullivan. 1982. Illness behavior and the sick role in chronic disease. *Social Science and Medicine* 16:1397–1404.

Stone, D. A. 1979a. Physicians as gatekeepers: Illness certification as a rationing device. *Public Policy* 27(2):227–54.

———. 1979b. Diagnosis and the dole: The function of illness in American distributive politics. *Journal of Health Politics, Policy and the Law* 4(3):507–21.

Suomi, S. et al. 1978. Effects of imipramine treatment of separation-induced social disorders in rhesus monkeys. *Archives of General Psychiatry* 35:321–25.

Suzuki, T. n.d. The concept of neurasthenia in Japan. Forthcoming in *Culture, Medicine and Psychiatry* (Special issue on neurasthenia in Asia).

Targun, S. et al. 1982. Neuroendocrine interrelationships in major depressive disorder. *American Journal of Psychiatry*. 139:282–86.

Taussig, M. T. 1980a. *The Devil and Commodity Fetishism in South America*. Chapel Hill: University of North Carolina Press.

———. 1980b. Reification and the consciousness of the patient. *Social Science and Medicine* 14B:3–13.

Teja, J. S. et al. 1971. Depression across cultures. *British Journal of Psychiatry* 119:253–60.

Terrill, R. 1980. *A Biography of Mao*. New York: Harper and Row.

Tessler, R., and D. Mechanic. 1978. Psychological distress and perceived health status. *Journal of Health and Social Behavior*. 19:254–62.

Thurston, A. F. 1984–85. Victims of China's Cultural Revolution: The invisible wounds, part 1. *Pacific Affairs* 57(4):599–620.

———. 1985. Victims of China's Cultural Revolution, part 2. *Pacific Affairs* 58(1):5–27.

Tseng, W. S. 1974. The development of psychiatric concepts in traditional Chinese medicine. *Archives of General Psychiatry* 29:569–75.

Tu Wei-ming 1982. A religophilosophical perspective on pain. *In* H. W. Kosterlitz and L. Y. Terenius, eds., *Pain and Society* (Dahlen Konferenzen 1980). pp. 63–78. Weinheim: Verlag Chemie Gmbh.

Turner, B. 1985. *The Body and Society*. Oxford: Basil Blackwell.

Turner, J. A., and C. R. Chapman. 1982. Psychological interventions for chronic pain: A critical review, parts 1 and 2. *Pain* 12:1–21, 23–46.

Turner, V. 1967. *The Forest of Symbols*. Ithaca: Cornell University Press.

Van Deusen, E. H. 1869. Observation on neurasthenia. *American Journal of Insanity* 25:445–61.

Wang, Y. L. et al. 1984. The risk of occupational lead exposure. *Chinese Medical Journal* 97(9):631–38.

Waziri, R. 1973. Symptomatology of depressive illness in Afghanistan. *American Journal of Psychiatry* 130:213–17.

Wegman, M. et al., eds. 1973. *Public Health in the People's Republic of China*. New York: Josiah Macy Jr. Foundation.

Wen, J. K., and C. L. Wang. 1981. Shen-k'uei syndrome: A culture-specific sexual neurosis in Taiwan. *In* A. Kleinman and T. Y. Lin, eds., *Normal and Abnormal Behavior in Chinese Culture*. Dordrecht: D. Reidel.

Weissman, M. M., and G. L. Klerman. 1977. Sex differences and the epidemiology of depression. *Archives of General Psychiatry* 34:98–111.

White, G. M. 1982a. The role of cultural explanations in "somatization" and "psychologization." *Social Science and Medicine* 16:1519–30.

————. 1982b. The ethnographic study of cultural knowledge of "mental disorder." *In* A. Marsella and G. White, eds., *Cultural Conceptions of Mental Health and Therapy,* pp. 69–96. Dordrecht: D. Reidel.

Whybrow, P., H. S. Akiskal, and W. T. McKinney. 1984. *Mood Disorders: Toward a New Psychobiology.* New York: Plenum.

Widmer, R. et al. 1980. Depression in family practice. *Journal of Family Practice* 10:45–81.

Wolf, E. 1983. *Europe and the Peoples without History.* Berkeley: University of California Press.

Wong, K. C. 1950. A short history of psychiatry and mental hygiene in China. *Chinese Medical Journal* 68:44–48.

World Health Organization. 1977. *Manual of the International Statistical Classification of Diseases,* Ninth Revision. Geneva: WHO.

Worsley, P. 1984. *The Three Worlds.* Chicago: University of Chicago Press.

Wrong, D. 1976. Oversocialized conceptions of man in modern sociology. *In Skeptical Sociology,* pp. 31–46. New York: Columbia University Press.

Xia Zhenyi and Zhang Mingyuan. 1981. History and present status of modern psychiatry in China. *Chinese Medical Journal* 94:277–82.

Xu Youxin. 1956. *Liang Jin Nan-Beichao ji Sui Tang shidai wo guo jingshenbingxue jianjie.* (Brief introduction to psychiatric illness in China during the Six Dynastics, Sui and T'ang). *Shenjing-jingshenke zazhi* (Chinese Journal of Neurology and Psychiatry) 1(1):14–19.

————. 1982. *Shenjingzhengde miaoshuxing dingyi* (Descriptive definitions for neuroses).*Guowai yixue, Jingshenbingxue Fence* (Journal of Foreign Medicine, Psychiatry Section also called Foreign Referential Journal of Psychiatry) 9(4):193–95.

————. 1984. *Qutihua yiji youguande zhenduan wenti* (Somatization and its problem for diagnosis). *Guowai yixue, Jingshenbingxue fence* (Journal of Foreign Medicine, Psychiatry Section, also called Foreign Referential Journal of Psychiatry) 11(3):129–31.

————. n.d. *Shenjingzheng linchuang yanjiude chubu baogao* (First report on a study of clinical neurosis). Manuscript.

Xu Youxin and Zhong Youbin. 1983. *Jizhong shenjingzheng de zhenduan biaozhun jianyi.* (A proposal for diagnostic criteria for several neuroses). *Zhonghua shenjing-jingshenke zazhi* (Chinese Journal of Neurology and Psychiatry) 10(4):236–38.

Xu Yun. 1983. *Shilun shehui binglixue* (Exploring social pathology). *Yixue yu zhexue* (Medicine and Philosophy) 11:30–33.

Yap, P. M. 1965. Phenomenology of affective disorders in Chinese and other cultures. *In* A. V. S. DeReuck and R. Porter, eds., *Transcultural Psychiatry,* pp. 86–114. Boston: Little Brown.

Yelin, E. et al. 1980. Toward an epidemiology of work disability. *Milbank Memorial Fund Quarterly/Health and Society* 58(3):386–414.

Zhao Biru. 1983. On Freud's theory of psychoanalysis. *Red Flag,* no. 16, 16 August 1983, pp. 38–43, 48.

Zhang Jiebin. 1710. *Qing Yue quan shu* (Qing Yue's Complete Works). Guiji: Guiji Lushi Ranben.

Zheng Yanping and Young Derson. 1983. *Shenghuo shijian, jingshen jinzhang yu shenjingzheng* (The relationship of life event change and stress to neurosis). *Shenjing-jingshenke zazhi* (Chinese Journal of Neurology and Psychiatry, Guangzhou) 9(2):65–68. (An English-language version of this paper will appear in *Culture, Medicine and Psychiatry* in 1986).

————, Xu Leyi, and Shen Qijie n.d. Styles of verbal expression of emotional and physical experiences. Manuscript. (This paper will appear in *Culture, Medicine and Psychiatry* in 1986).

Zhong Youbin. 1983. *Shenjing shuairuo jietile ma?* (Has neurasthenia disappeared?) Guowai yixue, Jingshenbingxue fence (Journal of Foreign Medicine, Psychiatry Section also called Foreign Referential Journal of Psychiatry) 10(2):65–68.

————. 1985. *Ye lun qutihua ji youguande zhenduan wenti* (Another discussion of somatization and its related problems) *Guowai yixue, Jingshenbingxue fence* (Journal of Foreign Medicine, Psychiatry Section also called the Foreign Referential Journal of Psychiatry) 12(1):8–10.

ADDENDUM

Boyd, J., and M. Weissman. 1981. Epidemiology of affective disorders. *Archives of General Psychiatry* 38:1039–46.

Index

Date Due

		DEC 0 4 2002
DEC 1 6 1987		NOV 1 2 2002
NOV 0 7 1990		
OCT 2 2 1990		
DEC 0 5 1990		
Dec 2		
DEC 1 0 1990		
OCT 2 3 1991		
OCT 3 0 1991		
AUG 1 2 1992		
AUG 1 0 1992		
NOV 0 8 1995		
DEC 0 6 1995